May
Die
Roaming

By Oisin Hughes

Third Edition

You can find a series of videos uploaded to accompany this book on YouTube at the following link:

http://www.youtube.com/user/roguebikers

Or alternatively you can search for either "Oisin Hughes" or "Roguebikes" on YouTube.

Similarly, All the pictures and route information by chapter are loaded up for you at the following link:

https://plus.google.com/+OisinHughes/about/p/pub

Or just search for Oisin Hughes on Google +

If you've any questions on the route or if you need some advice check out the FAQ section in the back of the book. You can also drop me an email at Oisin.m.hughes@gmail.com

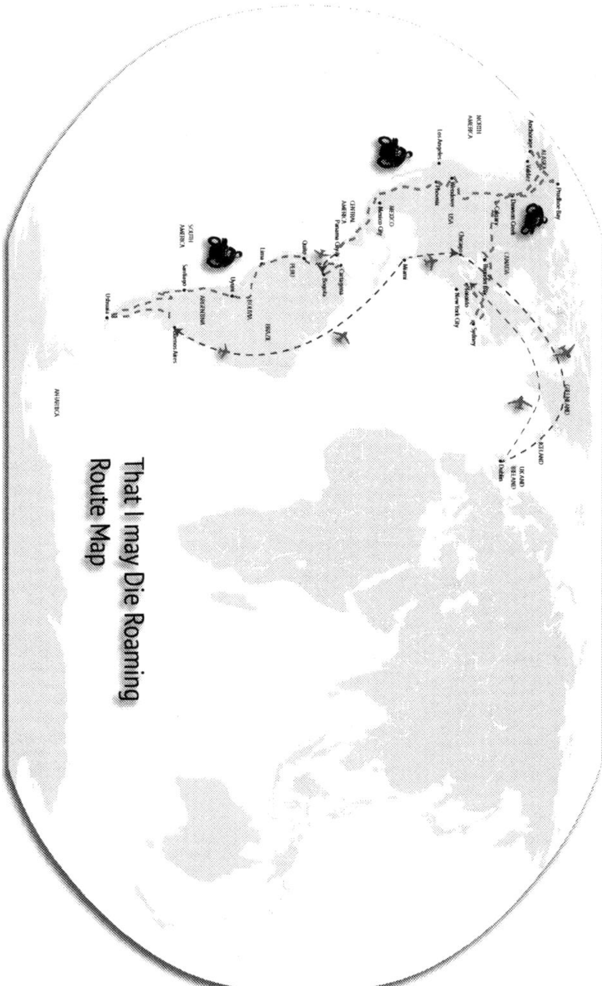
That I may Die Roaming
Route Map

Why a third edition?

This book started as a blog which I maintained while I rode the Pan American Highway in 2008. The blog attracted a large amount of followers and I got repeated feed back that I should write a book. I thought, "Fair enough, I'll give it a shot."

Twelve months later while in Colombia, I contracted Dysentery. Seeing I was held up, I decided to use the spare time to write the first edition of "That I may Die Roaming" and publish it as a free e-book. The e-book was well received and went on to be downloaded over 100,000 times. As time went on, I continued to get large amounts of email asking me to convert it to a paper back. I did, and the paperback went on to become "That I may Die Roaming", the second edition. The problem however with the second edition was that it was never properly edited or proofread. As I mentioned above, it was written while suffering with dysentery and at the time I wasn't in the least bit worried about grammar, expletives or spelling mistakes. I merely converted the original e-book to paperback.

I also published a series of documentary videos to YouTube to augment the books and help the whole project knit together better.
Finally, I updated the book with an FAQ section for anyone out there who is considering a trip like this.

I hope you like it.

Prologue

Hi there, my name is Oisin and I'm from Ireland. Unless your from Ireland, your probably asking yourself "How the hell do you pronounce Oisin?" For the purist's its pronounced "Ush-een" or "O-Sheen" is close enough. Now, where was I? Oh yeah writing a book.

Anyway, In July 2008, I undertook riding a motorbike 34,000 miles through North, Central and South America.

The route I intended to take started in Toronto Canada, riding initially east to Nova Scotia before riding thousands of miles across Canada eventually arriving in Anchorage Alaska. I planned to continue north to Prudhoe Bay Alaska, the most northerly town accessible by road in North America. From there I would ride south for months finally stopping at Ushuaia near Cape Horn, the most southerly point of South America. The final leg of the journey was a 3200 km ride north to Buenos Aires in Argentina, where I'd fly both myself and my bike back home to Ireland.

In total, I planned to go through 15 countries, namely Canada, USA, Mexico, Guatemala, El Salvador, Honduras, Nicaragua, Costa Rica, Panama, Colombia, Ecuador, Peru, Bolivia, Chile and Argentina. I had an adventure filled with thrills, spills and some unbelievable situations. In my wildest dreams, I could never have imagined all the stuff that would happen to me. This book is my account of the journey.

I went on this trip to put some excitement in my life. Every kid I knew growing up, wanted to be Luke Skywalker or Han Solo. In my head, going on this trip represented my chance to go and "Blow up the Death Star" and shag Princess Leia if the opportunity arose. When I started, I knew the outcome was far from certain but that the days ahead would be filled with adventure. I hope after reading this book, maybe you'll think about "setting your sail" and having an adventure all of your own.

Thanks for reading, and May the Force be with you.

Not Dead Yet Introduction

In November 2009 while traveling through Central America, I found myself looking down a road at a bridge full of heavily armed soldiers. The bridge traversed the Rio Coco, a river which marks the border between the two Central American countries of Honduras and Nicaragua.

I was in Honduras desperately hoping to cross into Nicaragua, but as the day wore on it was looking increasingly unlikely. I had no immigration entry stamps in my passport for Honduras and had thus entered and traveled in the country unlawfully and judging by the pitch of the shouting coming from Honduran customs, my motorbike was here illegally too. It was time to face reality, I was in deep shit. The "dumb smiling Irish paddy" routine would not avail me this time.

There were gangs of people standing around shouting at me for one reason or another. No one spoke English and I was armed only with the Spanish phrases you'd expect to hear in a Speedy Gonzales cartoon.

Politically, Honduras seemed close to melting down. The recently ousted President Zelaya was due back in the country at any time. It was only a couple of weeks since a coup had removed him from office and the atmosphere in the country felt like things could get nasty at any moment. I could not wait to get the hell out of there. Without the proper paperwork, it looked like there was going to be no way through. The only option was to go back to the border with El Salvador near Perquin and try to explain to the immigration center that they forgot to stamp me in. All this would have to be accomplished with a smaller grasp of Spanish held by the average mongoose. It was going to be a nightmare to get this mess sorted out. I asked myself "How did I end up in this situation? How do I always, always, always end up in these fucking situations?"

Chapter 1
Ireland

I remember it like it was yesterday. It was a cold and wet Friday in September 2005. I was out shopping in the pissing rain and was enticed off the rainy street by a DVD stand with a "Buy 3 DVD's for 30 Euro" banner. I picked up two movies I really liked and because I couldn't see another movie that caught my fancy, I grabbed a DVD called the Long way Round. It was a documentary series with Ewan McGregor and Charlie Boorman detailing their trip around the world on two BMW motorcycles from London to New York, heading east. I had seen commercials for the series but wasn't remotely interested in motorbikes or in two lads heading off to foreign shores. That said, it was as appealing as anything else on the stand and Ewan McGregor had been in Star Wars. Good enough for me.

The relentlessly crappy Irish weather continued and with Liverpool losing to Stoke on the Saturday the weekend was turning into a complete washout. I picked up the Long way round DVD and stared at the cover photo of Ewan and Charlie with their motorbikes thinking to myself "I'll give this a bash" and threw on the DVD. To my complete surprise I watched it straight through, episode after episode, finishing up the following morning at around 2am. I was hooked. I wanted to do something like this, no I simply had to! There were however a couple of minor obstacles to overcome, I didn't own a motorcycle, nor was I even able to ride one.

At the time I was married. Things weren't going well primarily down to the fact that I was a bad husband, about as emotionally available as a tin of processed peas. I was spending far too much time in work.

As the winter wore on, my enthusiasm to do my own trip started to wane, with ongoing marital problems and being up to my tonsils in work, I had to put any thoughts of "high adventure" to the back of my mind. In November of the same year, one of my best mates, Dave, asked me along to the annual motorcycle show in the RDS arena in Dublin. As I was walking around the displays looking at all the bikes I came across a stand for Globebusters, a motorcycle tour company based in England specialized in huge overland adventure trips. After exchanging a couple of pleasantries, I

My first ever bike show in the RDS, Dublin
That's a BMW 650, with the 1200GSA next to it.

walked away with one of their brochures.
On the back page of the brochure was the Pan-American motorcycle trip stretching from Prudhoe Bay, the most northerly town in Alaska the whole way down to Ushuaia in Terra del Fuego near Cape Horn in South America. I thought to myself, "This looks absolutely amazing!" I took

the brochure and plonked it on my office desk to remind me on the bad days, that there was an alternative to what I was doing.

That Christmas, my marriage ended.

Australia

After a few months of wallowing in self-pity, I made a decision to go on a road trip to Australia for a month to help me clear my head. I came up with the idea on a Tuesday and flew out Thursday of the same week. I hired a 4X4 and spent the month driving around Australia to try to work some of the post-marital breakup blues out of my head. On the journey, I learned a couple of things about myself. Firstly, I was fine being by myself for long periods of time. Furthermore, I really liked long journeys where you didn't really have a place to get to. There was nothing wrong with driving until you got bored then finding a place to stay, going out for something to eat and having a beer and going to bed with no real notion of where you were going to end up the following day. It was as good a way to spend a holiday as any other I'd been on before.

In Australia, I set myself the goal of never driving over the same piece of tarmac twice. That way, the road would always change for me. Every day would be a mini adventure because I didn't have to retrace my steps on my way home. I carved a loop out on the map in Australia and knocked out about 14,000 km while I was there.

Buying a bike When I came back to Ireland, I made up my mind that I was going to have to buy a bike if I was ever going to consider taking on the Pan-American Highway. My thinking was that I might start with a small trip; I needed to figure out if motorcycling was something I'd like. If I just upped and went, I could end up hating it. I had my doubts, motorcycling was dangerous, certainly more dangerous than a car. When you combine that with the fact that you're out in the elements and in Ireland all it ever seems to do is piss rain, I had enough reason to believe that the whole thing could turn out to be pure misery.

I went to see my friend Jason who has always been a keen biker. He had a couple of copies of Motorcycle News that had heaps of bikes for sale in the back pages. I opened the first classified page and there it was, a BMW bumblebee 1150 GSA for sale. It was love at first sight. It was the same model bike that Ewan and Charlie had used for the Long way round. It came with panniers, crash bars, heated hand-grips and some other goodies and the whole lot was on sale for 11,500 Euro. The bike had less than 10,000 km on the clock so was practically new. The chap who was selling it lived about four miles from Jason's house so off we went in the car to have a gawk at the beast. I'll never make a poker player, I saw the bike and said, "I'll take it!" and wrote him a cheque for the full amount he was looking for. My penalty for such impulsiveness was listening to Jason for the next six months giving me the "Can't believe you didn't even try to haggle!" routine. My first big problem was I couldn't drive the bike. I asked Jason to drive it home for me and when we got to my place, I had my first impromptu bike lesson.

I was terrified when I jumped up on it. The BMW 1150 weighs over 250 kg and has enough low end torque to throw you off the back of the bike in a heart beat. If your stationary and the bike starts to go to the left or right and gets past about twenty degrees from vertical you'll never be able to hold it up and the whole thing will crash to the ground. Picking that weight up off the ground is as tough as crapping a pineapple. Every time I tried to move forward on the bike the engine would cut out as I tried to master the sweet spot on the clutch. Every jump forward resulted in my shins getting clubbed by the metal crash bars, a sore bastard I don't mind telling you. I knew that I tended to jump into things, the niggling feeling that this was going to be another in a long line of bad ideas was starting to grow in my mind.

In keeping with a Hughes family tradition, i.e. full duck or no dinner, I signed up for two full days of intensive rider training with a private motorcycle school. The course was run in March and the weather was absolutely woeful. At various times it was snowing, sleeting, pissing rain and all the while the wind howled as we plodded our way through the mental Dublin City traffic. There was however a positive outcome apart from learning to ride the bike. I've always felt that because I learned to ride in the rain and snow I'm a much better rider in bad weather than most. Most people start the other way, they learn in the good weather and only tend to go out on their bikes when the weather is good, I never knew any different so having started the hard way I never looked back.

I was still struggling to get the hang of the clutch but the instructor had a great analogy to help me get the hang of it."Listen horse, you need to think of the clutch like it's your birds left titty. Would you be grabbing it in and out like that? Eh? Would ya? No, I don't think so. She wouldn't be long about punching your lights out. Nice and smooth! Got it?"

As for the accelerator he said to "Treat it like a budgies neck! Nice and smooth. You don't want to break the poor little budgies neck now do ya? Got it?" I think it was the titty that did it for me, never being one to snatch and grab, at least not since I was in the cot.

When I told him that I was considering heading off to ride the entire Pan-American Highway on the bike, he simply replied "Me hole!"

So, now I had the bike and I could drive it. It was time to plan a road trip. I talked to my mate Dave about heading down to the Rock of Gibraltar in Spain, a 7000 km round trip. I said I'd chance the run with him even though I didn't have a full license. We started planning in earnest. After a couple of weeks the excitement started to build until one day Dave phoned me. His opening line was "You'll never guess what!" I replied, having read the tone in his voice "Sheila's up the duff." Dave's girlfriend was pregnant. I was delighted for him but knew it meant that the trip to the Rock of Gibraltar was over unless I wanted to go on my own, but with so little experience and no license, it was just too risky.

Some months later, when Dave and I were out for a couple of pints, I asked him "So how come Sheila got pregnant? Did the French letter split?" (A pertinent question, Dave has a lad on him like dyno-rod, the sort of thing you would normally expect to see hanging out of an elephants face) Dave replied, "Nah sure I can never get one to fit" which to his credit, he said with true humility. Then I asked, "So was Sheila not on the pill?" Dave replied, "Nope." Realizing that he'd been bare backing and risking our trip if Sheila got pregnant I said, "So you were just pulling out! Ya plonker ya! You are some bollix, it's not like the tadpoles would have far to swim, you were practically delivering them to the front door with that baseball bat of a lad, you bollix!" So that was it, there was no other opportunity to go on a medium length trip to see if traveling on a motorcycle for six months was something I would enjoy or even be capable of doing. I was left with the dilemma, "If I'm going to go on this trip who am I going to go with?"

The summer of 2008 was when I was targeting to leave, leaving in July would allow me to follow the summer south through the America's. There were no organized tours running that year with Globebusters for the Pan American Highway, and none of my friends could go with me. I kept asking myself, was I capable of going by myself, I doubted it. The sort of things that went through my head centered round needing to try to go with someone who is good at fixing stuff. I'm the sort of guy who, if the house was falling down around me, I'd probably buy a tent for the back garden, I'm just not that good with my hands. Now that's not to say that I don't rub a good boob, I do, but with machinery, I may as well be looking up a bulls arse.

John Mundy

I went in search of kindred spirits on the web. I was convinced there must be a couple of people out there with the same sort of thing in mind, I still had a year to plan it so it was plenty of time to meet some guys or girls who might be into same thing. I got a serious amount of ribbing from the lads about the gay connotations of searching for "like minded bikers" on the web. Lois Pryce, who wrote the wonderful book "Lois on the Loose" steered me to a website called Horizons Unlimited. This site was founded by Grant and Sue Johnson and is a one stop shop for people considering going on big adventures on motorcycles or other modes of transport. I pumped in the words, "Pan-American July 2008, anyone interested?" and waited to see if I'd get any responses.

A chap living near Felixstowe in England called John Mundy replied and said he was up for it. We talked on the phone and seemed to have quite a bit in common. We both said that if we were serious about it we'd have to meet and talk to hammer out what we both wanted to get out of the trip. A couple of weekends later, I flew to England and John picked me up at the airport.

John Mundy

On the phone John seemed a very gentle spoken sort, however when I met him, I nearly fainted. He was about 5ft5in, a serious looking skinhead with tattoos the whole way down his arms. "Oh my lord!" I thought to myself.

It turned out he was an ex British soldier who served in Northern Ireland, not an obvious traveling partner for a southern Irish paddy. Again, I thought to myself, "Oh my...!" My initial thoughts were either this guy has gone online to reel in some "ass" or he's logged onto the equivalent of "dial a sucker to murder and leave in your fridge for six months while you take out his torso to have sex with while watching Coronation Street reruns.com." We got to his house and headed off down the pub for some pints and grub. On the way we walked down a pitch black lane, for a good while I was certain he was going to knife me. I can remember vividly walking down a pitch black lane which seemed to go on forever where I could only see 6 inches in front of my face thinking, "How did you end up in this situation, ya big gobshite?"

As it turned out I needn't have worried, John was a sound skin and we got on like a house on fire. He worked on the Felixstowe docks, drove the same type of bike as me and was very interested. The only problem he had was getting his house sold on time as well as getting leave of absence from his job.While all this was going on Ewan and Charlie decided to do the Long Way Down, another motorcycle trip, this time from John of Groats in Northern Scotland to the Cape of Good Hope in South Africa. All this just helped to intensify my feelings of needing to go. I decided that whatever route I was going to take it had to add up to more miles than the Long way round, and the Long Way Down combined. Why? Just, that's the why! Not a good enough answer? Well, it's a guy thing. Nuff Said.

The Route

We talked a lot about the route. Flying a bike into the states since 9-11 was a nightmare so we decided to fly into Toronto, Canada. This also happened to be where my brother lived, so it would be a lot easier to get lifts out to the airport to collect the bikes and deal with any unforeseen logistical items. From there, the plan was to head west to Nova Scotia and Cape Breton, and then track back west, the whole way across Canada to Anchorage in Alaska. Once in Anchorage we would ride north to Prudhoe Bay, the most northerly town in Alaska and then south for many months, the whole way to Ushuaia in Argentina and finally back up to Buenos Aires. I "back of the enveloped" the trip at over 30,000 miles. The route had some big advantages, namely you didn't need a carnet de passage in any of the countries, and we would only need two languages, English and Spanish.

The "ifs and buts" were driving me crazy so to start firming things up, I made up my mind that I was going to leave on July 12th 2008. I also made up my mind that if John wasn't able to come along and I couldn't get someone to go with me, I would go alone. Although I still desperately hoped that I would find a riding partner, I wasn't going to let it hold me back. John had two kids who were in their twenties and unbelievably, no sooner had he decided to go on the trip, than they popped round to his house to tell him that they were getting married that year. John was torn and he said he was going to come over to Dublin to talk about some things. I knew he was coming over to tell me that he wasn't going to be able to go, he was too decent a guy to tell me over the phone. He knew it had quickly turned into an obsession of both of ours and wanted to tell me face to face that he was letting me down.

At that point, a Welsh guy called Geoff popped on the Horizons website and said he was also up for it, I told him John was on his way over so why not plan to come over the same weekend. Geoff was in his mid fifties and his wife had passed away less than a year previous. It was obvious that he was still on the run from his grief but he was a good person and very friendly. If he wanted to come along "sure why not?", I said.

As expected, John pulled out. Geoff hadn't been in touch for over two months so I resigned myself to going alone. The piece I was unbelievably nervous about was Central America. “How in the name of Jesus am I going to get through those borders on my own?”

About a month before I was due to leave, I got a phone call from Geoff saying he was going. I was a little disappointed because I had rather gotten used to the idea that I would be a solo traveller. However, when I thought about things like the Dalton highway in Alaska and all the dangerous countries that I’d be going through, it would be better to not have to do it alone. As the day approached, the comments from family friends and people in work all revolved around “It’ll be a life changing experience” or “You must be crazy!”

My nerves were at fever pitch. The date was set, and the only thing left to do was ship the bike to Toronto. This part, while expensive was easy. I dropped the bike off with James Cargo in London with all my kit about ten days before I was due to fly out. I had the rough timelines for the trip worked out, I wrote in my diary:“I plan to take 59 days to complete the USA and Canada leg. Fourteen days through Mexico, another fourteen through Central America and the rest in South America finishing hopefully in time for Christmas!" I structured the journey this way because in my head I reckoned I could do North America again when I was fifty-five if I wanted to. The bigger challenge would be Central and South America so it would better to allocate the majority of time there.

I nicknamed the bike "Molly" which I later changed to Sam Gamgee, I was Frodo. What happened to Luke Skywalker? What happened to Han Solo? Well, I decided that I was going to be a mixture of Frodo, Conan, Luke Skywalker, Han Solo, Jason Bourne, James Bond and Frodo, and no I don't think that's too many heroes to combine into one persona. The week before I left, I completed the last mandatory task before undertaking any adventure, I went out on the rip. After about fifteen pints and multiple "You're gonna get raped by FARC rebels, you know that don't ya!" type statements from my mates, the last task before traveling was complete.

With my flight merely hours away, I sat on the couch in my sitting room drinking a cup of tea while looking out the window at the rain doing its best to break the glass. I asked myself "Am I ready?" I kept replaying a quote I'd read in my head, "The only way you'll ever be 100% prepared for a trip like this is to have done it before."

I had completed less than four thousand miles on the bike since I'd bought it and I had zero off-road training. With the Dalton highway in Alaska ahead of me, an 1100 mile round trip gravel fest, I told myself that I would have nearly ten thousand miles done by that stage so I'd be a lot more experienced and "it would be fine."

I'd still almost no Spanish, but reckoned that I could either hook up with some dudes who did when I would have to cross the borders or I'd get some Spanish lessons loaded up onto my I-pod, again I figured I'd be grand. I was fine for money and had heaps of travel equipment. Space on the bike was the only concern and picking the bike up would be a massive problem if it ever fell over.

I had only met Geoff once and that was a worry, what if we didn't get on? I couldn't fix a thing on the bike if it broke down. I never even had to fix a puncture so if it happened I'd just have to deal with it at the time. I spent hours and hours worrying, and all I had to console myself with was the fact that there was no going back now.

My brother and his girlfriend dropped me and my cuddly toy rabbit Mr. Fluffykins to the airport in Dublin. As I boarded the plane, I couldn't help notice the lack of fanfare. When Ewan and Charlie had headed off on their adventure there were support crews, a cake and big bunch of well-wishers and it felt a bit weird for just me and my bag heading off. I flew out on Saturday, July 12th exactly as planned nearly nine months previous, despite the best attempts of an air traffic controllers strike to halt my progress. As we taxied down the runway, I couldn't believe it was about to start.

Toronto

The flight to Toronto was wedged with people and I got stuck in a middle seat spending the next seven hours battling for elbow room with two fairly substantial lassies, although I doubt they talked in glowing terms about the hefty dude stuck in between them on the flight either. It was quite a bit of hassle to clear customs. Note to self: when filling in the customs form, always check "no" when asked "Are you shipping any goods to Canada, which are not on your person?" Invariably you'll find things go a lot smoother.

About ninety minutes after arriving and post a surprisingly gentle rubber glove routine from Gail in Canadian customs, I was out in the arrivals hall getting picked up by my brother Ernan and his father-in-law, Jack. The first question out of their mouths was nothing to do with the trip, rather "What's the story with Ireland and the European Union and the whole Lisbon treaty thing?" Ireland had just rejected the Lisbon treaty and it was getting massive airplay, so much for being treated like a superstar biker setting out on a terrifying expedition. I was starting to notice a trend, as much as I would like to think that what I was doing was the equivalent of Luke Skywalker attacking the death star, I had to be content with the fact, that I was the only one who thought so. On the way back to the house the three of us stopped for some nosebag and after a pound of wings and three frosty bottles of Coors light, it was time to go and meet up with the rest of my extended family. After a lovely evening catching up it, was time to unpack and hit the scratcher.

The plan was to collect the bike from customs that Monday morning, which would be the point at which the journey would really start. I'd arranged to collect Geoff from his hotel on the way to the airport cargo hanger. Hopefully, we'd collect the bikes and be on our way by Monday evening. I kept thinking about the scene in Die Hard 3, where Samuel L. Jackson tells Jeremy Irons to "Stick your well laid plans up your well laid ass." I wondered if we weren't being wildly optimistic to think that we would clear customs in an afternoon.

Shannon, my brothers wife asked me "do you know where the cargo place is?" I said, "Don't worry, I have a GPS!"

After a few hours of being hopelessly lost, we arrived at the customs hall and stood in line to clear the bikes. When we went up with our paperwork, it was obvious that the gents behind the counter had never done anything like temporary motorcycle importation before. After some head scratching they told us to "come back tomorrow" as they needed to take some soil samples from the bike to make sure we weren't bringing in any fungi in the mud on the tires, a complete load of cobblers. There was nothing to do but turn away and come back the next day. They gave us a number to ring to check to see if the bikes were ready, and told us not to come back out to the cargo hangar unless we'd checked with the call line first. They gave us the impression that it might take a couple of days, which really put a downer on things.

In our eagerness to get going we'd gone out to the Cargo area in Enduro-Motorcycle gear hoping to just jump on the bikes and drive off into the wild blue-yonder. With the heat and the fact that the cargo terminal was a solid walk away from the customs area, we were cooking in our own juices as we waited around. Somewhat dispirited, Geoff and I got a taxi to a hotel together, and shared a double room. This was the first of many weird moments on the trip for me. There I was, in a hotel room in Toronto with a guy maybe twenty years older than me, who I barely knew waiting to go and collect our bikes to start a trip. Who knew what would be ahead of us. It was surreal. Sharing a hotel room with a friend is easy, it's quite a bit harder when you barely know the person. As we were nodding off to sleep, Geoff started to snore like a pig with a cold. I lay there staring at the ceiling as I fitted some ear plugs wondering just what the hell I had gotten myself into.

On the road

Early the next morning we rang the number customs had given us and we got the news that the bikes were good to go. Joyously, we set off to uncrate the bikes and go through the paperwork formalities, it wasn't long before we were shooting east in the direction of Nova Scotia.

Leaving Toronto gradually five lane highways became four then three and finally two as we made our way further and further away from the urban sprawl in the direction of Cornwall on the St Lawrence River. The stifling heat combined with wearing too much gear and slow moving traffic made the early going almost unbearable. I was riding along thinking to myself "Is this it? Is this how I'm supposed to feel? This is the trip of lifetime right?" It probably sounds unbelievably selfish to say it, but I was having a horrible time. When we were stopped in traffic, it was easy to imagine what it must be like to be a rotisserie chicken.

It's only when you start traveling in Canada that the sheer scale of the country starts to dawn on you. We drove two hundred and seventy-seven miles on the first day, or rather afternoon but if you were to look at a map of Canada on an A4 sheet, you would barely be able to perceive the distance at all. In Canada you have to stop saying things like "two hundred miles away" or "400 kilometers away" and revert to saying things like such and such a place is "a three day ride" or such and such a place is "18 hours away." To put some numbers on it: Canada is the worlds second largest country behind Russia, over one hundred times the size of Ireland, and more than forty times the size of the United Kingdom with less than half the population. Note to would-be travelers to Canada - there are ten provinces and three territories, just don't call them states. The Canadians don't like that. Anything that hints north of the US border is just like south of the border is generally poorly received.

In Ireland and the UK it's common for motorcyclists to filter between traffic, that means making a second or third lane where there's none marked. It drives the rest of the driving fraternity crazy but makes us bikers feel like studs. It turns out Canadian driver's don't like you filtering on your bike, in fact they hate it enough to roar out the window "Hey A-hole get in fucking line." By the end of the first day I'd already had a couple of these greetings. Thankfully, due to the lack of availability of handguns in Canada I felt I was able to return the greeting with an extended index finger, not the sort of reply I would consider giving in Texas!

Cornwall

The Canadian highways are full of bikers, mostly driving big Honda Gold-wings made to cover the sort of distances one comes across in Canada. Every time we stopped for Gas or a cup of coffee, which was about every hour or so we met loads of people and my first impression was that the Canadians were a friendly bunch.

After a shower that evening, I headed out to find a computer to send an email to my family to say I'd survived the first day. I looked up Cornwall in my Canada rough guide, it didn't mention it. Hmmm, "let me try Google" I thought to myself, where I found that its biggest claim to fame is that its home to one of the biggest distribution centers in Canada. It was the first time the realization dawned on me that while there are really great places in the world, in between them are really average or just altogether boring places.
I guess there wouldn't be such a thing as great places if it wasn't for towns like Cornwall, so I saluted its mediocrity while draining a beer and signaling to the waiter for another round. I lay in the bed that night staring at the ceiling wondering "Is this how I'm supposed to feel? Shouldn't I be

feeling better? Shouldn't I be happier? Why am I still thinking about work? I'm on the trip of a lifetime, why doesn't it feel like it, and how the fuck does Geoff snore that loud without waking himself up?"

Riviere du Loup

The next day we got up early, jumped on the bikes and set off to a town called Riviere du Loup in the province of Quebec. It was my first experience of French Canadians, a strange bunch who wont speak English to you unless you try to speak French to them first. I did my best to remember my secondary school French and managed to get by. I have to admit to the French mob giving me a pain in the ass. I was a tourist in a place spending money, you would think they'd do their best to communicate with you. Don't get me wrong I'm all for learning the culture before you go somewhere and having to adapt, but when you know the guy behind the counter can speak English and he's just trying to teach you a lesson, it all feels a bit shit.

Although I was only two days into the trip one of my bubbles was about to be burst. Before I started the trip, I had images in my head of driving along the road with women in corvettes or Ferraris pulling up beside me and inviting me back to their hotel room for a Shagathon. As I was driving along I tended to be just a bit faster than the average traffic flow. So, as I passed a car I could peek into the car to see whose driving, desperately hoping it might be a nude centerfold with loose morals. Thus far, it was all Canadian men with big hairy hands and some of the plainest women I'd seen since I studied engineering in college. I told myself, "Don't worry big fella, when you get to small town Canada, they'll never have seen anything like ya and you'll be kidnapped to become the sex slave of an all-women cult." (Yes, you are right, I just referred to myself in the first second and third person in that last sentence. That rustling you can hear outside is my secondary school English teacher turning in his grave.)

Geoff and I went out in the town that night and had dinner in a lovely restaurant and had a good chat. He told me about how his wife had died and how he was completely lost without her. They had been together since they were very young and you could see that when she died it left a huge hole in him. After dinner we went out for a couple of beers and talked some more. We stood looking out over a balcony with the St Laurence River in the distance as the whole horizon kept flaring with lightning as a stiff summer breeze blew into our faces. It was the first time I felt like I was having a good time.

Moncton

The next day we rode off for Moncton in New Brunswick, three hundred and eighty miles further down the road towards Nova Scotia. I was starting to feel just a little hard core as I rested up on the bike at one of the gas stations when up rode a guy on a bicycle. His name was Alex and he'd cycled the whole way from Vancouver in Western Canada to there, over six thousand kilometers. I thought to myself "This guy must clank when he walks!" It just goes to show that no matter how crazy you think what you're doing is, there's always someone doing something crazier, buns of steel doesn't even come close to describing this guy.

Moncton was supposed to be a good place with lots to do and see according to some folks we met along the way, so we were quietly looking forward to it. On the way into town we noticed some strip bars and tattoo parlors, while not necessarily a bad thing, it's never a sign that you're rolling into a good area. I pumped "find nearest lodging" into the GPS and it took us to an Econolodge. It looked a bit rough but my ass was so sore I would have slept under a bull for the night if it meant getting off the bike for the day a bit quicker. As we pulled into the car park, three dudes pulled up in a car, got out and checked into the motel room just opposite ours. They left the door open in their room and were drinking beer roaring and shouting sitting on the bed. All four had their tops off and were doing an inordinate amount of scratching. I was beginning to think these lads were on a gay cruise. As I was stripping the bike and bringing the gear into the room, I worried these guys were going to be doing their shopping out of our stuff if we left the room.

Parking our nervous feelings about leaving our stuff in the Motel, we had to go wash some clothes, my kit bag was starting to smell so bad I risked getting hosed down with fungicide by the EPA the next time we stopped. We asked the guy in the motel where the nearest launderette was and off we went. We got to the place and said, "Hi there, what time do you close?" The girl said 9pm, we said grand and started to load up our stuff into the machines. She said, "Eh dufus! Its 8:50pm, you won't get a run through!" We looked at each other and said, "no it isn't, its only 7:50" at which point we both realized we'd crossed a time zone, another new thing you have to deal with when riding across very large countries.

After some grub, Geoff was knackered but I still fancied a couple of pints so I asked the cab driver on the way back to the hotel to take me to a good bar. The cab guy started raving about this place called "Rockin Rodeo" where there was a 4:1 ratio of women to men and that he'd gone there the last few weeks and never failed to score. "It's wall to wall women!" Now the cab driver looked to me like he wouldn't score in a brothel with a pocket full of twenties so I thought the odds must be good, I said, "Take me there Andre!" He dropped me off, I paid a $4 dollar cover to get in, and yep you guessed it, I was the only one in the whole football field sized bar. I nailed a Coors light (watching my figure) so fast that it gave me brain freeze and as I turned for the door saying "fuck this for a game of soldiers" and left. As I walked out, the same taxi driver was starting to drive off with another fare. I let out a roar at him, something traditionally Irish, "Ya lying bastard ya!" Feeling a little dejected, I got a cab back to the motel. The next cab driver raved about this "other bar!" I think these guys were on retainers from the bars to bring dopey hairy arsed tourists in, but seeing I was on holidays I tried the "must visit Irish bar" called the Auld triangle. The bar turned out to be about as Irish as Margaret Thatcher's underpants, so I had one more Coors and headed back to the Motel.

When I got back Geoff was up to "high doe." He went out for a smoke and left the door open with the light on, there was now thousands of mosquitoes and black fly in the room. After two hours of Mosquito slaughter with more fatalities than the battle of the Somme, I went to sleep itchy as hell.

The big tourist attraction in this part of New Brunswick is the Bay of Fundy famous for having the worlds largest tides. Each day over 100 billion tons of sea water comes rolling up the channel which apparently is more than the combined flow of all the fresh water rivers in the world. Take a moment to think about that. Got it? I'm not sure your quite there yet, think of it like this - "the sum of all the rivers in the world flowing right there!"

We left in a hurry the next day after a restless night worrying about a mixture of mosquitoes and baddies robbing our motorcycles, driving three hundred miles to Sydney in Nova Scotia. We had intended to go to Halifax but there was a Harley Davidson convention in Sydney with open air rock concerts and ride outs. It would be much more our style and it would be great to meet a bunch more bikers.

Sydney, Nova Scotia

These conventions draw bikers from all over and the closer we got to Sydney the more bikers we met on the road and our moods were soaring. Every time we'd stop at a garage, we'd end up spending twenty minutes talking to everyone about where we were from, and where we were going - the Nova-Scotians were incredibly friendly. Nova Scotia translates to New Scotland and as you travel towards it and pass out of the province of New Brunswick, you get an instant reminder of where it gets its name from. I'm not kidding, the temperature dropped around twelve degrees and started to piss rain. I'm certain that two hundred years ago when the pioneers were heading this way, a bunch of hairy arsed Scots hit this spot and said, "Fuck me Jimmy, it's just like Scotland" and the rest is history. Having said that, I would move to Nova Scotia in the morning, it was full of wonderful people and felt just like Ireland and Scotland.

The first night in Sydney was great, the Harley convention had five open-air bands playing mostly heavy rock and to add to the experience there was about two thousand Harley heads around the place creating a cracking atmosphere.

The next morning the plan was to do the Cabot trail, which for the great unwashed out there is one of the top ten motorcycle routes in the world. It's a two hundred and seventy kilometer ring around the highlands and ocean views of Cape Breton. We talked to people who had been up on one of the hills that day looking down into the ocean and they were waxing lyrical about whole pods of whales feeding at one of the inlets, we couldn't wait to get going. We set out at around 8am and less than an hour later the heavens opened like Noah was due to take the Arc out for another spin. Within twenty minutes of the rain starting and despite wearing some of the best enduro gear on the market I was soaked right through to the butt crack. In the end, we only did forty miles and rode to a place called Baddeck to spend the night.

That night we met a father and son team doing a motorcycle trip of their own from New York State to Cape Breton. We went out for grub and beers and finished on the veranda drinking whiskeys. This part of the world is full of hunters and one stopped by for a chat. This guy was boasting about having killed twelve moose in his hunting career. Geoff started taking this piss out him saying, "Isn't that just like shooting a big cow?" I asked what he did with the meat to which he replied that he ate it, at which point we all roared laughing. There's nearly seven hundred pounds of meat on a Moose, so even if this guy was having moose steak three times a day for 10 years he still wouldn't have eaten that much Moose. I said to him that as part of preparing for the trip, I had kept reading to be wary of Moose, if you hit one on the bike your finished. In fourteen hundred miles we hadn't even had so much as a sniff of one. I made a joke that it was his fault. We spent the rest of the evening drinking whiskey and killing mosquitoes. Not unexpectedly, the night ended in a sombre mood. Geoff had started to recount stories about his wife, I guess by talking about it, he was working the pain out of his system.

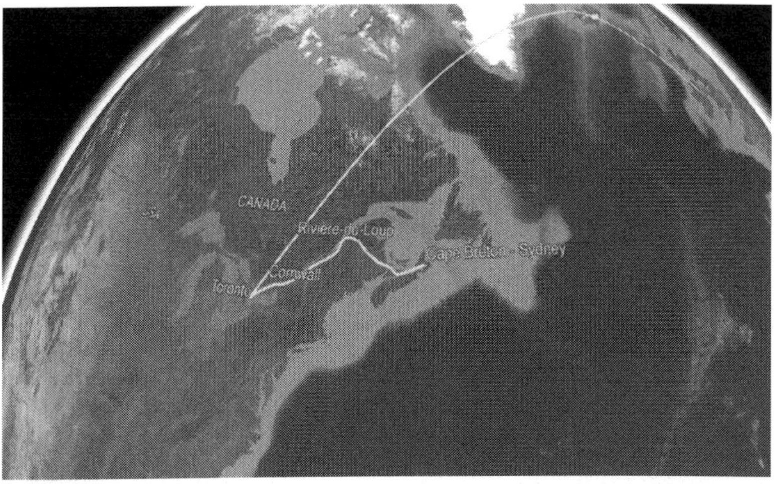

The Cabot Trail

The next morning it was time to give the Cabot trail another go. The weather was perfect. Although at this point I hadn't logged that many miles up on a motorbike, the Cabot trail was the best motorcycle road I'd been on. We took some great advice which was to do it anti-clockwise, that way the sea is always on your right and you don't have to cross traffic to pull over. There were sweeping bends, hairpin turns, mountains, cliffs and incredible views of the ocean all accompanied by brilliant blue skies and warm sunshine. I was driving the bike right at the extremes of my capabilities and a couple of times I had the hammer down way too hard and nearly flew off a cliff.

On the way round as part of letting the sphincter sort itself out after a couple of near misses we pulled up to a whale watching tour and went out and saw a heap of Minke and Bottle-nose whales. After an hour or so of watching the whales we were back on the Cabot trail and I was doing as good an impression of Valentino Rossi as a fat bastard from Clondalkin was able to on an overloaded 1150GSA.

The Cabot trail is so good you can get caught in two minds very easily. Do I just ride it? The road twists and bends so much through the countryside its like a motorcyclists wet dream. On the other hand the views of the landscape and ocean are so good you want to keep getting off the bike every five minutes to take pictures. My advice is to do the Cabot trail twice, and each time, ride it counter clockwise. Do it once for pictures, and then do it again just to appreciate the ebb and flow of the road as it makes its way through Cape Breton and Eastern Canada at its most pristine.

With the sights saw and the senses full it was time to leave Nova Scotia and blaze a trail for New Glasgow starting the long journey west, the next time I'd see the ocean would be in Anchorage, Alaska.

Chapter 2
West to the border with Alaska

Having knocked out the Cabot trail, Geoff and I decided it was time to start the long road west to Alaska. Even taking the most direct route it was over five thousand miles away, a lot further once detours for sightseeing were factored in. We decided that New Glasgow would be a good place to stop for the night, it was about three hours west. We weren't on the road long when the weather turned miserable. The forecast said it was down for the day so we stopped every forty minutes or so for coffee and donuts in the ubiquitous Tim Horton's chain.

We got to New Glasgow that evening soaking wet and checked into a motel. As we were parking up another biker called Ed pulled up driving a BMW 1200GSA, if your driving the same bike as another motorcyclist, your automatically their friend (definitely a thing).

We introduced ourselves, and invited him along for dinner. We got stuck into a round of wings and beers and chatted for a good few hours about bikes and stories from the road.

As the night wore on Geoff started to talk about his wife. I guess because the grief was still so near for him, it occupied a massive part of his consciousness. He struggled to talk about much else really.

It was at that moment that I decided I was going to break off and go my own way in a day or two. The journey was the adventure of a lifetime for me, I didn't want to spend it helping someone I barely knew through their grief. If we'd been best buddies before the trip, it was something I would have gladly done but when you barely know someone, it was too much, for me at least. I knew that I'd go my own way in the next town and ride the rest of Canada by myself. Ed listened to the story and was very sympathetic but it was my fifth of sixth time through it, so I guess I looked bored. When Geoff went to the bog I said something I regret, "You can't get that guy to stop talking about that stuff, it's really head wrecking!" No doubt Ed just thought I was an insensitive plonker.

The next day, the three of us, as part of back peddling across Canada decided to ride back for Riviere du Loup, we had a great night there first time round, so it made sense to just stay there again. The roads in Canada are unbelievably straight, so straight they would drive you to drink. You end up counting every mile and end up just sitting there bored out of your mind. Every now and then you might slip into a trance where you don't notice the miles passing, but it doesn't last long and then you're back in the helmet; just you and your thoughts and your very sore ass. At times I'd have conversations with myself, "Hmmm, what do I usually think about when I'm trying to pass the time? I can't think of anything!"

Along the way I noticed Geoff and Ed were burning me off the back, which is where the lead bikes keep up a very hefty pace, one just above where you're comfortable riding at. I was at the back wondering, "Since when did I become the un-cool guy? When did I become the guy who gets burned off the back?" Ed had obviously thought that I was a dick-head having talked behind Geoff's back, he was right. I found myself thousands of miles from home, rallying down a Canadian highway absolutely miserable, wondering just how the fuck all this bullshit had happened.

We covered over five hundred miles in total arriving and staying in the same guest house we had the first time round. We'd travelled 2200 road miles in only a couple of days, not to mention flying to Toronto from Ireland and I was knack-ered. The next morning I met Geoff for breakfast and said to him that I was going to go a different route around the Great Lakes and was he ok with that. I think he knew it was coming and I think he was happier that way anyway. Once we cleared the air it was amazing, we were back getting along like a house on fire. Ed by this stage had already left so we agreed that we would go as far as Montreal together at which point he was going to burn south towards the USA. His plan was to circle the Great Lakes from the South; mine was to continue to cross Canada. We made a remark about meeting up on the other side of the lakes, but never did.

When it came time to part ways it was very sad, we had stopped for lunch and talked some more about his wife and I really did understand how he felt and was very sorry for him. As we drove up towards Montreal we got to the turn off, Geoff blazed to the left and I went to the right. I held my finger on the horn and then held my left fist high in the air as we both went our separate ways. I was on my own now and I couldn't stop from welling up, and having a good old cry in the helmet.

Arnprior, Ontario

I kept riding, feeling like an asshole after everything that had happened. I felt like the only way to fix the way I felt was to keep riding and riding until the feelings went away. I pulled into the town of Arnprior in Ontario Canada, just west of Ottawa. The town sits on the Ottawa River and is very easy on the eye. I walked down to the riverfront and sat on a bench to soak up the summers evening. Tens of people were casting their fishing rods into the river as the sun was setting just behind the town on the far bank of the river. I was feeling a bit lonely and thought to myself, "Your going need to come out of your shell more or your going have a shit time, you need to start meeting people."

If you've ever travelled by yourself I'm sure you'll agree that at times things can be weird. If you're a guy and you just go up and start talking to a guy, the guy will think, "This dude must be gay." If you go up talking to a girl, "This loser just wants a shag." People in the western world can tend to think that there must be a reason why this "fucker" is talking to me. The last thing we would ever admit to ourselves is that people might be just looking for company. Everyone I talked to said that once you got west of Toronto and passed the Great Lakes there was nothing but flat farm land for thousands of miles. In a way, I was quite looking forward to it, in my mind's eye I reckoned that I might be able to get "in touch with myself" and really work some stuff over in my head, realistically I'd no clue what to expect.

My next port of call was Sault Ste. Marie, a town on the border between Canada and the USA, about 450 miles further west along the Trans-Canada Highway.

I couldn't get over how large Ontario is. At three times the size of Germany or about the size of Texas and Montana combined, it is immense. While I had just ridden 450 miles further west and had clocked up over 3000 miles total, I had barely tickled Canada's armpit.

Sault Ste. Marie was formed as a result of connecting two parts of the Great Lakes, Lake Huron and Lake Superior and its locks are busier that the Suez and the Panama Canal combined. I don't remember much about the road there, it wasn't very scenic, that's not to say that the countryside wasn't nice, it just wasn't very memorable. The land was mostly flat with crop forests of ever green pines running right up to the road intermingled with farms. I went down to the locks to take a look and spent a lovely evening walking along the boardwalk finishing off the evening with the movie Hancock. I'd developed a little routine when I pulled into a town. In the evening I'd take off the enduro gear, head in for a shower and then go for a spin on the bike with just a leather jacket, jeans and a pair of sun glasses. I'd ride around the respective town looking for something to do, but mostly just to look cool. I reckoned that some of these Canadian women wouldn't be able to resist it. Wrong!

The further west you go in Canada, the less and less populated the country becomes, as a result I had to contend with being on my own a lot. I hadn't met anyone apart from shop keepers and gas station attendants in two days. I guess crossing Canada on a motorcycle isn't something that too many people do and I was beginning to wonder why I had decided to do it. Oh yeah, I wanted to do more miles than the Long way Round and the Long Way Down combined, that particular molten bronze droplet of an idea was beginning to lose its shine.

I was driving over four hundred miles a day, its sounds a lot, and it is, but there's so little to do in this part of the world, its best to just push on. Manitoba, the neighboring province of Ontario while twice the size of Britain, only has a population of 1.2 million people, the place is utterly empty. I would love to be able to say that there were some fun spots to pull over and have a good time but the only thing to keep you amused are the clouds in the sky. I had completed about 10% of the total journey eleven days after leaving Ireland, at this rate I'd be finished sixty days ahead of schedule. I consoled myself by saying, "Dude, spend your time in the happening places."

Thunder Bay

The next day I was looping north around Lake Superior on my way to Thunder Bay. This was the first time since Nova Scotia that there was a decent bit of scenery. That's not to say that there is no scenery in Manitoba, just none visible on the Trans-Canada Highway. Lake Superior itself is huge, bigger than Ireland by over ten thousand square kilometers, so for the whole day I had a lake on my left side and forest on my right. It's hard to believe the lake is fresh water, it looks just like the sea with waves lapping up onto gravel beaches. I stopped every hour or so pulling over and walking by the lake having a chat with anyone who looked in the least bit friendly. Yakking away to the locals in any given area you tend to pick up little tidbits of information. For example; believe it or not, they get waves of up to thirty feet on Lake Superior during storms and it's fed by over two hundred rivers. Also, some of the Great Lakes are officially dead with all the pollution, Lake Superior is still hanging in there though.

When I was about an hour from Thunder Bay I pulled over to the side of the road to take a few pictures. The sun was low in the sky on the right with the lake stretching out in front of me flickering in the evening sunshine. On my left, still a few miles distant a thunderstorm was starting to go into high gear. I thought to myself, "I wonder if my ass was struck with lightning would it be as sore as it feels now?" I don't know if it's how Thunder Bay got its name but I can tell you the whole time I was there the sky was thundering away like crazy. The reason the town exists is to transport grain from the prairies out onto the Great Lakes where it's ferried off to various ports.

I got up the next morning absolutely knackered and couldn't bear the thought of riding, but I said to myself, "C'mon push on to the next town and stop there." I was a bit down in the dumps and was feeling very lonely. I'd lost my phone and was wondering if I should replace it. I was starting to get pissed off that I wasn't getting any text messages from home. It was like the whole world had forgotten about me and was getting on with their lives. The phone in a way became a reminder of people not getting in contact with me, so I made a decision to do the rest of the trip without one. When I look back on it, it was a stupid idea, if anything bad happened I would have been rightly fucked. My thinking on it was, "What would phoning someone do anyway, it would only get them worried." I was really on my own now.

I pulled in at a town called Dryden, which was built around a large paper mill. I hadn't been able to get near the internet for a couple of days so once I booked into a motel I headed out to look for the local library, internet cafe's are noticeably absent in central Canada. I guess there's an assumption that everyone has a computer so why would you bother. As I went looking for the library a guy pulled up on a bike beside me and said, "Hey how are you doing? What are you doing here?" I told him and next thing I knew I was back at his place swinging out of a couple of beers. He was a keen biker and I got lots of "off road" tips from him, which would come in handy in Alaska which was getting closer every day. The suspicious person in everyone always thinks that someone just walking up to you must have an agenda, and I have to admit thinking, "Maybe this guy is a serial killer or gay and he's gonna take me back to his place and stab me up the ass with his pork sword!" I needn't have worried, he was a great bloke. Over a couple of beers I told him all about the trip so far, and that I thought it would have been better, that I thought I'd meet more people and that it wasn't really working out as a dream trip, and to top it all not a whole pile of interesting things had happened so far. He really understood and told me not to worry, There'll be bikers galore once you get to the Pan American highway. I headed back to the motel after about eight bottles of various types of beer, the evening was just the tonic I needed to get my spirits up.

Relatively rested after a short run the day before, I headed for Brandon, a town west of Winnipeg. On the way I passed through the geographical centre of Canada, I was officially half way across. That I was only half way seemed hard to believe when I thought about the distance I'd covered, some 4300 miles completed, almost the distance from Dublin Ireland, to Mumbai in India.

My ass was officially turning into a different life form, every time I sat on the saddle it felt like I was sitting down bare ass in a field of thistles. With the heat, my motorbike boots smelt so bad I reckoned they might force an early migration of the Caribou herd. Mosquitos and black fly had by this point taken a penchant for my extremities and on average I had about twenty bite marks on the go at any one time. I even had a couple on my bum and nether regions, that particular mosquito was taking his life in his hands, I don't mind telling you.

The Prairies

I had hit mega prairie land, namely the province of Saskatchewan, the Canadian equivalent of Montana in the United States. This was big sky country. The whole "flat land and big sky" thing is an amazing thing to drive through. You can see right to the horizon in all directions. The roads are completely and utterly straight with no bends for hundreds of kilometers. After a few hours the novelty of the landscape starts to wear off and the tedium of the road starts to grow. You just sit on the bike. The road is straight, your speed is constant, the horizon is perfectly flat and the blue sky extends the whole way to the horizon. The fields by the side of the road are sown with same crop so nothing changes. The only things on the road are trucks and the occasional car.

Everything seems constant. You are aware of every mile and every minute you're riding. There is nothing you can do to take your mind off the vast unchanging landscape, and it takes days to cross. I felt it was like driving through purgatory, only the velocity and noise of the wind changed. The farmers in the area all joke that because the land is so flat,"If your dog ran away, he could run for three days and you'd still be able to see him in the distance."

It was here I had my first "nearly killed" moment. There were two big eighteen wheelers blocking the highway doing about 50mph, they were talking to each other as they were driving up the road and no one could get by.This went on and on for 40 miles or more and yours truly not being known for his patience, especially while getting the shit kicked out of him by both the wind and the turbulence from the juggernauts was quickly losing the rag. I decided to bomb up a very skinny hard shoulder to the right at close to 100mph and flew by the lads in the trucks, giving it a bit of "yee hawww!" in the process. Later, a couple who saw me passing the trucks on the road, came up to me at a filling station where I had stopped for lunch and said that the trucker swerved for me as I was passing on the inside. They had called the police. I had to spend an hour or so talking to the cops who had arrived before I knew it. Most of the time was just spent talking to them about where I was off to I didn't really want to bring up the fact that I used the hard shoulder as my own private race track. We chatted for a good while and to be honest I was glad of the company. It seemed to me that these guys were glad of the company too, I doubt too much goes on to keep the police busy in these parts.

I got into Wolseley that night too late to get any grub and there was absolutely nothing to do, not really surprising as the town is just an agricultural hub. I hit the hay starving and my stomach started talking to me as it often does, "Aren't you forgetting something fat boy? Where's the fucking nose bag!" Too hungry to even have a hand shandy, I just drifted off to sleep.

The next day I was back on the road in a familiar routine; rise, ride for about an hour and then stop for breakfast, then ride for another hour and then stop for gas and so it would continue stopping every hour or so in an attempt to break up the monotony of the flat unchanging land.

The further into the province of Saskatchewan I went, the

more I saw prairie storms, a thing to be feared. They can get violent enough to send you running for your mammy. In the distance you can see black clouds and as you approach the storm, day becomes night. As you get into the middle of it you, start to notice an off-yellow sulphur color in the clouds, its then you know you're in deep shit. The temperature drops about ten degrees and you go from roasting to freezing in just a couple of minutes. The rain starts to come

down in sheets with drops so large your visibility drops to about fifteen feet. Fork lightning fires all round you and the thunder is so loud it drowns out the sound of the engine on the bike. You start to remember all the stories about how a car is the safest place to be during lightning and then start to think, "Hmm, I don't recall hearing anything about motorbikes in storms." On these vast planes there are very few places to shelter so there's nothing you can do but put the hammer down and try to run like a blue bastard straight through it.

Every second you're in a storm on a motorcycle your shitting bricks, feeling like a nervous dog at Halloween when the fireworks are going off. Often when I would stop for gas, the locals seemed to take relish in filling me full of fear with statements like, "There's a storm warning son." I was driving along saying to myself, "Just my luck, the day the hairy arse dub shows up, a twister the size of Galway bay will drop straight on me." Living in Ireland or the UK, realistically we never see a real storm, at least not like they have them in North America, and "You ain't seen nothing till you've seen a prairie storm." The mad thing is that once you drive out the other side of it, it's like it never happened. You're back under clear skies with roasting temperatures uttering some choice phrases like, "What the heck just happened?"

The influence of the Native American communities who originally inhabited these lands starts to jump to the fore as you continue west, towns named Moose Jaw, Medicine Hat and Swift Current all conjured up images for me of what this country must have been like before the wagons started to roll west. The towns may have had cool sounding names but as with most towns in North America, they were mostly grid towns with no centre square and for the most part impossible to tell apart.

The colors of the crops either side of the road thankfully started to break up the monotony. It was still July so most were in bloom and there was a sea of yellow rapeseed and blue flax planted as far as the eye could see. One farmer who I met in a garage told me that there was now an area the size of Germany planted with flax in Canada that used to be planted with wheat and corn. With Oil prices shooting up and food prices dropping the farmers were turning to non food crops. I wondered what would the implications of it would be, surely you can't take that much food out of circulation without causing a famine somewhere. Riding through this sort of terrain you go through the full range of emotions. The day always starts well, you knock out the first two hundred clicks in two or three hours and stop for a coffee. Then the second leg is always tougher. Your brain starts to go crazy looking at a road which never bends and just keeps going straight for an eternity. On top of that, as the miles pass your boxer shorts start to ride higher and higher till they're literally sawing you in two halves. With another four to five hours in the saddle, you start to feel like your ass needs to be put in a sling. The wind never seems to let up, ripping your head one way and then the other. When you're passed by a huge truck, the turbulence punches you so hard you almost take it personal.

Train tracks run in parallel to large sections of the highway and often you ride beside massive trains which snake for miles through the vast flat countryside. They all stop at massive grain silo's which stand like sentries along the train track visible for miles. The people you meet along the way are normally farmers. Most are friendly up to a point but keep their distance, not surprising really when you consider they're talking to a bearded loony from Ireland, "So you've over here doing what?"

The prairies were very tough, not in the dangerous or physical sense but mentally challenging, maybe akin to the doldrums for sailors. Straight roads for thousands of kilometers, long distances, storms, howling winds, maniacal truckers and boring one horse towns, I was bored to tears. However, every now and then the wind stopped blowing, everything was calm and there were no trucks or cars on the road. I would ride along surrounded by a sea of yellow and light blue flowers under a cloudless blue sky, with the fragrance of the fields coming in through the helmet. For a fleeting moment I imagined this must be what heaven is like.

I made myself a promise on the trip that I would where possible avoid big cities unless I was getting the bike repaired and in keeping with that promise in mind I burned straight through Calgary and headed for Canmore, a town in the Alberta Rockies.

The Rockies, Alberta

I can't tell you how good it felt to see mountains again. After nearly two weeks of flat unchanging landscape to have the horizon dominated by massive snow capped peaks had me smiling like a Cheshire cat.

I headed out that night for one of the biggest pizza's I've ever had and washed it down with a couple of celebratory beers. I was sure that now I was in the Great North West that I'd meet a lot more people on motorbikes or at least tourists who might be kindred spirits.

The road turned north for the first time in nearly two weeks as I drove the Icefields Parkway between Banff and Jasper, one of the most famous roads in Canada. No matter who you talked to, they recommended it and it didn't disappoint. For over two hundred kilometers this road ambles its way through the feet of giant snow capped mountains. The mountains, three times the size of Ireland's largest mountain were so impressive I doubted if anything would ever top the sites that lay before me, I rode completely silent and lapped it all up, it was unbelievable. Glaciers feed the rivers and lakes in the area turning all the water a beautiful turquoise blue, as if the scenery didn't stand out enough already. Every time I'd see a mountain or a scenic view I found myself saying, "Yep that's it nothing will ever top that" then just around the bend would be something even more spectacular.

The Rockies chain stretches south the whole way to the Andes in South America, I liked the idea that this mountain range would be like an old friend by the time I was done. The day ended in Hinton, a small town based around the lumber industry north east of Jasper. The part of my head where one stores images of scenery was completely full for me. After what I'd seen I had a strange feeling that nothing could ever top it. This area is renowned as one of the most beautiful areas in the world I was worried it might be all downhill from here. At moments like these I told myself, "Its an adventure ya big bollix, it's about driving from Prudhoe Bay to Ushuaia and going coast to coast at the widest point in the Americas so stop your whinging and fill the tank up with petrol, it's time to get going again."

I decided the following day would only be a short run of about five hours or so taking me from Hinton to a town called Grande Prairie. The day started out crap due to it pissing rain and for the first time on the trip it was really cold. It was hard to believe that in July, things could be this cool, but the chill rolls off the snow on the peaks Rockies and it may as well have been November. I was absolutely freezing and after only thirty minutes I had to pull in and put on my arctic gear which involved stripping naked by the side of the road and putting on an inner body skin, and an outer layer which is both water proof and wind proof and over that donning the enduro suit. I also put on a balaclava to turn off the chill factor on my face which was quickly turning the color of a beetroot.

I'd expected this weather on the Dalton highway in Alaska or down towards the south of Argentina, not in Alberta Canada. The problem with a bike is that once you get cold it's almost impossible to get warm. It's not like there's a heater you can turn on and after about forty minutes rain, wind and cold I was thoroughly miserable. I pulled into a small town off highway 40, on the road to Grande Prairie. I sat down in a diner dripping wet while shivering with the cold and ordered two huge mugs of steaming hot coffee with some hot sandwiches, desperate to heat up. The woman behind the counter took pity on me and was quick to refill my rapidly emptying mugs of coffee.

Frenchy

Just then, the whole room darkened when the biggest man I've ever seen walked into the room, comfortably six feet eight inches and built like a brick shit house. He nodded to the woman behind the counter who said to him, "We're real busy Frenchy, you can sit down with that guy over there (that's me) if he doesn't mind." "Not at all", I replied. I was sitting in a booth where you'd normally sit four people. There was me with my motorbike gear on one side with Frenchy sat down opposite me taking pretty much the entire booth opposite. He stretched out his legs and I quickly moved mine out of the way apologizing, as you do. (Especially when a white version of Shaquille o' Neil sits down opposite you) The dimensions of Frenchy were something to behold. His shoulders were gigantic and had a set of hands which looked like a bunch of bananas. His rib cage was like a barrel and I thought he looked like the Incredible Hulk. Anyway you get the picture, he was a massive dude, I reckoned he had about fifty-five years on the clock, but that was a guess.

"Usual Frenchy?" said the woman behind the counter to which he gently nodded twice. With that, I put my hand out to shake his and said, "Hi! I'm Oisin." He shook my hand.

It looked like a little girls hand in his and his skin had the texture of tree bark. One shake had me wanting to grab a tube of moisturizer to treat my delicate skin. He didn't say anything, I guess he'd figured out I already knew his name. Somewhat awestruck I said to him, "Dude, if you don't mind me saying so, you are the biggest bastard I've ever seen!" He didn't say anything. Thinking the bastard remark might have offended him I quickly back peddled saying, "No offense on the bastard thing, it's just a turn of phrase in Ireland, that's where I'm from." I was dying on the vine.

He still didn't say anything but at least he didn't look offended. Just then Doris showed up with the coffee saying, "How are you today Frenchy?" to which he just replied, "Doing good Doris" to which she smiled and walked off, leaving me with the behemoth. I started to try to make conversation with him and I'm not bad at this sort of thing normally, shy and retiring are not attributes which feature anywhere on my resume but this guy was a piece of work. I was also anxious that Doris bring him his breakfast just in case he started to butter me and eat me. The rest of the conversation went on: Oisin: "So I'm over doing this big motorbike trip, y'know shipped the bike in from Ireland to Toronto, went to nova Scotia and then over to here. I'm heading for Alaska" Frenchy: "Uh huh" Oisin: "Yep and from there I'm going to Argentina, will end up riding 30,000 miles total" Frenchy: (Silence) Oisin: "Cold out today huh?" Frenchy: "Guess so" I think what he really meant was, you wouldn't know cold from a cabbage ya big Irish dumb ass. (It gets to -40F here in the winter) Oisin: "So are you from here, like Canada? I mean or...." (was desperate that he'd latch onto that "or") Frenchy: "I'm from here" Oisin: "So Alberta..? or this town... or " (Was pushing my luck with the "or's") Frenchy: "here" Jaysus, this was tough going. "Talkative old bollix aren't ya!" I wanted to say to him if I wasn't in absolute fear of my life that he'd either eat me or punch me in the head for yakking so much Doris arrived thankfully with the grub for Frenchy which was really a trough of food poured onto a serving plate where one might expect to find the carcass of a roasted pig at a banquet. Oisin:"Holy fuck!!, that's some amount of nose bag!" (It was a nervous knee jerk remark) Frenchy:"Nose bag?" Oisin: "Yeah like a horse's nose bag, know what I mean?" as I made a motion like a horse emptying nose bag into itself and through in a neeaahhhh for good measure. Frenchy smiled and said, "You're a bit crazy, y'know that!" Seeing my opening and not that I needed any invitation, I just kept blabbing on and Frenchy sat their listening, at least I think he was listening. He asked me why I was doing the trip, I told him, to which he just said, "Hmm, ok."

I asked him did he ever do any traveling, to which he just replied no.

Now that we were getting along just dandy, although it wasn't so much a conversation as a monologue, looking at the size of his hands I just blurted out, "Dude with fingers like that who needs a dick! Although you'd want to get the oul Oil of Olay on the go before any girls would let ya near them!" Frenchy roared laughing. A laugh that was so deep it was almost like he'd been holding onto it for years. After he'd finished laughing he took up his cup of coffee which looked like a play cup in his hand and said, "Irish man, your ok in my book." Oisin: "Glad to hear it, I thought you were gonna fucking eat me there for a while" (more laughing) Frenchy sat there eating the rest of his breakfast shoveling fist sized pieces of scrambled eggs and ham into his mouth seldom looking up from the plate. Frenchy: "Looks like you got pretty wet huh?" Oisin: "Right through to the crack" after a delay of about three seconds Frenchy roared laughing again, there was no way anyone was going to tell him to quieten down. We talked about all sorts of stuff, I was desperate for a reason not to go back on the road because of the rain and cold. We talked about willow herb, a plant which dominates the side of the roads here; I told him we have it in Ireland too and that it was left there by the last ice age. I asked him was he married, he wasn't wearing a wedding ring but that wouldn't have mattered, it would have required a kilo of gold to round one of his fingers. When I did finish the question he just looked forlornly out the window into the vast expanse of forest, "Nope" he replied after a time, I didn't pry any further. He went on to tell me he'd worked in lumbar all his life and that he loved the mountains and could never leave them. I remarked that he didn't need a saw for the trees all he'd need to do was lean against them, to which he smiled charitably. We walked out together to the car park and I showed him the bike. I asked him to jump aboard and try it out; he did and made the bike (one of the biggest model motorbikes anywhere) look like a scooter. I told him about the blog I was doing and that if he was ever online to check it out. He replied, "I don't have much call for computers, wouldn't have a clue about the internet, too old to learn now." We shook hands and said goodbye. I watched him get into his truck testing the suspension as he sat in and started her up, "Watch out for bears" he said as he smiled and drove off. I stood there for a while thinking, "Oh my god I forgot about the fucking bears!"

Frenchy in my memory was the biggest dude in the whole world but also one of the most gentle. I was quickly discovering one of the key downsides of the trip was that you only ever met people once and then you move on, most likely never to see them again. In some peoples cases, that's great, but Frenchy I still think about. I reminded myself of one of the things I'd read, "It's not the places you visit, it's the people you meet."

When you travel alone you have no one to give you a second opinion and I made the mistake of cutting further north from Grande Prairie which as the name suggested brought me straight back out onto the Alberta prairies. When I realized what I'd done I didn't have the heart to double back on myself so I pulled into a motel, had a bath and headed out for some grub. I invested in a small portable laptop which was great for keeping in touch with people, and watching a non illegal amount of porn. After only three hours in the saddle which you'd expect to knock out in Canada with one swing of your John Thomas, I was off to sleep with the prospect of a better day to come tomorrow.

Fort Nelson, BC

The next two towns I planned to stop in conjured up for me what life must have been like in Canada in the early part of the nineteenth century, namely Fort St John, and Fort Nelson. Fort St John dates back to 1794, and Fort Nelson to 1805. I could imagine wooden forts and lads with beaver skin hats all trading furs and whiskey, and Daniel day Lewis shouting "I will find you. I will find you!" The next morning

I got up in bad form again, mostly as a result of being lonely and jumped on the bike and left. I was starting to doubt the reasons why I'd come on the trip. I realized that the attraction of the Long Way Wound TV series for me wasn't the bikes or the trip they took, what I really liked was the camaraderie that the guys had. Fat lot of good that did me out in the middle of British Colombia on my Sweeney Todd. It had taken me 6000 miles to figure it out, but there was no turning back now. That day I was driving along and I passed a lay-by where two bikers who were both driving BMW's were parked up. I drove over to say hello, in a weird sort of way you almost expect people to greet you with open arms. "Yay, you're a biker too, and you drive a BMW, and you're on a big adventure. Lets be buddies!" These two chaps were about as friendly as a bull with a sore hole so after a few minutes I was back heading north again.

I hadn't seen any moose or bears or any form of wild life really so I was really struggling to keep my focus on "This is the trip of lifetime!"

That night I couldn't sleep. At 4:17am I was still awake and wrote the following into my journal: I'm in a town called Fort Nelson right now in British Colombia and am going to make a break for Whitehorse, which is over 1000 km away. The reason for the long burst is because the only town between here and there is Watson Lake and staying there is the moral equivalent of having to stay the night in a nursing home.

Fort Nelson is not a place you would ever visit, it's a town you drive through to get somewhere else and its sole existence is based around lumber. The whole town is stained by debris from the forests, a by product of pulling trees out of the woods. It was however supposed to be way better than Watson Lake the next town I'd encounter along the Alcan highway so I decided to make my way to Whitehorse sooner than stay in another crappy town for the night. I guess I should have expected very little of what was essentially a frontier town but when you've ridden such a long way to get somewhere, a part of you expects it to be better.

I was watching the news that night and there was a report about a guy who killed another guy on a greyhound bus in Manitoba, Canada. The guy killed him with a Rambo knife and then cut off his head. The eyewitness was interviewed at the scene by the news reporters and said the dude who was decapitated was asleep and the dude with the knife had just got on the bus. Can you believe it? One minute you're asleep and the next some dude is walking down the bus isle carrying your head? The eye witness said that the killer blamed the bus driver for making him drop the guys head and had then continued to follow them with the knife when they ran away. Anyway so now you know why I was awake, but as if the thing wasn't bad enough, the news guys followed the incident with a story about some kitten that got its head caught in a drain. So as if there wasn't enough to be worrying about with bears, moose on the road, maniacal truckers, getting a puncture, Dublin winning the Leinster football final, now I had "not getting your head hacked off by some lunatic" to add to the list and just to add insult to injury, having it dropped on a greyhound bus floor after its been hacked from your torso, which let's face it, is dirtier than a coal miners arse.

The goal the next day was to get to Whitehorse before nightfall, a journey of over six hundred miles all of which would be done on the famous Alcan Highway. The Alcan highway is famous for the duration it took to build mostly. During WWII after the attack on Pearl Harbor, the US feared a Japanese invasion in Alaska so they needed a road to connect the lower 48 to Alaska. The road stretches 1700 miles and was built in only nine months. Starting at about 5:45am I set off on what turned out to be an assault on the senses. After only an hours riding I had seen Bears, Wild Deer and Goats, I was well chuffed.

I stopped for a coffee in a campsite which also sold gasoline. I had a wonderful chat with the owner and this older American couple who were up driving the Alcan Highway to celebrate their retirement. This is a good point to mention that with soaring gas prices, all of North America was in crisis. Families who would have normally taken RV's up to this region were staying at home and it was regular enough to drive for an hour at a time and hardly meet a truck or a car on the road. It added to dreamy feel of the whole thing, that you were alone and all this incredible scenery was just for you.

I passed through a place called Charlie Lake, one of the places where Ewan and Charlie had stopped and filmed a scene for the Long way round. They had remarked that they had only fifteen days left to go in the program and I loved the look of the place. I hadn't planned to pass it, I just saw the sign and pulled off the road. It felt magic to be in one of the places that had inspired me to do the trip and to have arrived there by complete chance. The sun was shining and at the end of a small wooden pier there was a boat parked up. The lake was a mill pond of beautiful blue water and the gentlest of breezes was blowing into my face as I soaked up the moment.

Further along the road I met three guys who were motorcycling up to Fairbanks from Washington State and we rode together for a good few hours. I'm not a skilled enough writer to describe how awe-inspiring the scenery we drove through was, hopefully some of the pictures included with the book will help. Whether it was a mixture of having some company, the great weather and some of the most beautiful countryside anywhere in the world, I'm not sure, but all of sudden I realized I was having the time of my life. Isaac, Roger, Bruce and myself had some great chats about what all bikers tend to chat about, for example what was the best pound for pound motorcycle in the world, given I knew nothing about motorcycles bar how to drive one and that the BMW 1150 was my favorite only because it was the only one I'd ever owned, I offered little to the debate.

Later on we ran into a herd of buffalo on the road. When you're in a car thats a good thing but when you're on a motorbike it's definitely not. These animals are massive and temperamental. The buffalo are not owned by anyone and certainly aren't tame, and much as they've always done, they are allowed to roam free. All I could think of was the movie Dances with Wolves. I definitely had some "Tatanka" ahead and was really worried one of the bulls would charge me on the bike, thankfully they didn't and I lived to fight another day. I had been worried by stories which I'd heard about loose buffalo "hooking" you, a process whereby a buffalo takes one of its horns and drives it straight into you.

It was like someone turned on the wildlife switch, at various points I saw three black Bears all out near the road, a herd of Caribou, Chipmunks, mountain Goats, Deer, and of course the Buffalo, I was loving every minute of it.

I kind of developed a theory on traveling that your mood maps the way it does at home except your peaks and troughs are higher and deeper. So for example if you're a moody bollix at home it's likely that you'll be the same when you travel, except that if you're in a good mood it'll be better and if you're in a bad mood it'll be worse because you don't have any of the support structures you have at home that might get you to snap out of it.

It could also be very tough on you physically. Motorbike 101 for those of you that don't drive them, the contact area of a motorbike tyre, unlike a car, isn't flat, its semi circular. It's by leaning the bike right and left on the highways that you turn it, i.e. moving the contact area of the tyre on the road to the shorter circumference areas causes the bike to turn (yawn), I can hear you but I'm going somewhere I promise.

This is where the fun starts.

Imagine your driving down a two lane highway with oncoming traffic in the other lane. On your side of the road is a hard shoulder but it's made of gravel, great if you're in a car with four wheels, really dodgy if you're on a motorbike with only two wheels contacting the surface. If you hit gravel straight on its no problem on a bike, however if you hit it while your turning there is a really good chance the bike will slip straight off the road. So the key point is that you really don't want the bike going onto the gravel on a bend where you've a much smaller amount of tyre contacting the road and the bike is leaning to one side. As your driving straight ahead there's a forty mile an hour wind coming from the left side, which is doing its best to push you off the road or at least closer to the pesky aforementioned gravel.

Now, throw in that it's gusting up to about sixty-five miles an hour and you can probably guess things are starting to get a bit awkward. How you cope with it is to lean your body into the wind and keep the bike straight, i.e. compensating for the wind. If you didn't it would push you straight off the road. With the gusts you can find yourself sweeping up to three to five feet across the road, so you adopt a position on the road close to the divide at the centre to allow you to drift a little if an unexpectedly large gust comes up. With the pot beginning to simmer, throw in the rain and truck drivers coming at you from the same direction as the wind is coming from. In pissing rain an eighteen wheeler can throw up more than ten gallons of water per second and when they pass they shower you with a waterfall of turbulence bad enough to make your kidneys wobble.

Finally, watch out for moose, deer, bears, pot holes and every other manner of obstruction that you're likely to find out in the cuds and do it all through a visor on a helmet speckled with rain droplets and grime. Like I said earlier, I was having the time of my life.

Whitehorse, YT

I arrived in Whitehorse that evening checking the cheeks of my ass with my hand to make sure that they were still there, I felt like I was sitting bare ass on a bed of nails for the last couple of hours of the ride. I booked into a motel and went out for a bite to eat. Whitehorse, the capital city of the Yukon territory, has a population of just 24,000 souls and is the largest city in the Yukon. The total population of the Yukon at the time of writing was only 33,000 people, in an area the size of Spain in Europe. My initial experience of the town wasn't great, there seemed to be quite a few drunken angry Native Americans hanging around. I knew I'd be stopping there on the way back so this was just a place to get a door between me and the night.

I lay in bed that night thinking that everything I'd done up to this point was just bullshit, what if every day was like to-day, how good a life would that be! I'd now travelled without a break every day for twenty-one days and was getting a bit worn out but I knew I was close to Anchorage where I'd get the bike serviced and have a bit of down time.

I drove off for Tok in Alaska and the roads were empty. I drove through one section albeit in the morning time for two hours without seeing even a single car. The knock on of high gas prices was that over 50% of the gas stations I saw on the road were closed down due to no business. The usual supply of massive RV's from Canada and the USA had dried up due to the massive costs incurred from running the beasts, most averaging less than eight miles to the gallon. It was like driving around in a dream, the scenery was breath-taking and I was driving completely alone on the road. If I pulled over to take pictures, no cars passed, there was no one around, the only sound I could hear was the sound of high flying birds or the breeze blowing but nothing else, eerie didn't come close to describing it.

It's weird seeing some of the most naturally beautiful sights in the world and being completely alone doing it. It was like getting a ticket to see the biggest band in the world and being the only guy there. In a whole days traveling where I stopped many times I met a total of five people, a Dutch couple, a German couple and another German guy, there were seemingly no North Americans on the road.

Before long I was at the border and ready to cross into Alaska. I'd successfully crossed the second biggest country in the world, I treated myself to a diet coke and a snickers.

Chapter 3
North to the top of the world

I got to Tok Alaska having crossed the border into the United States from Canada. The town has a population of a little over a thousand people and mainly offers gas, food and a place to stay for travelers at the crossroads of the Alcan and Glenn highways. I stayed the night in the Golden Bear motel, a family owned place. After a shower I went for dinner in the restaurant, and in true Alaskan tradition there was one choice of meal for dinner, you either wanted it or didn't. I loved it. The owner walked in and sat at one of the other tables and we saluted each other and after a while he swung over and we chatted for a few hours about all sorts of things. I asked him what the weather was like in the winter, to which he dryly answered "Cold!" Apparently, it has dropped on occasion to sixty degrees below freezing. He described what it's like and how everything has a blue appearance, even the air. The family made me feel very welcome and I headed off to the scratcher that night feeling wonderful.

Anchorage, Alaska

I arrived in Anchorage the next day with 23 days and 7,678 miles on the clock and started to find out about getting the bike serviced. At this point I was still in a work frame of mind, "Let's go, c'mon man got to make up the miles" so was looking for a pit stop to get the bike prepared for the Dalton highway rather than a place to hang out for a couple of days. It takes time to learn to how to relax I think. About a week into the trip I started to get less worried about the time and after two weeks I had completely forgotten about it. As the third week had progressed I started to forget what day it was but I think a month had passed before I stopped thinking about schedules or distances and really started to just enjoy the ride and forget about the destination.

I didn't care for Anchorage, it's a good city but it's not why people go to Alaska. It's a town like every other town in the states so after spending three days there getting the bike fixed up I was more than ready to get going again. There was one highlight that sticks in the memory that happened on a bus tour of the town. A girl tour guide told the bus that there were twice as many men living in Alaska as women which she qualified with "While the odds are very good for us women, unfortunately the goods very are odd!"

It's impossible to overstate how empty Alaska is, but I'll give it a shot. Size wise, its seven times bigger than Britain and if you were to superimpose Alaska on the lower 48 states, Alaska would extend coast to coast. The total population however is just 700,000 and a third of those live in the city of Anchorage, and if it wasn't for the fact that 25% of all the oil produced in the USA is drilled in Alaska, that population would be much smaller.

The next big barrier ahead of me was the Dalton highway, a road which runs from Fairbanks up to Prudhoe Bay at the Arctic Ocean. I had run into lots of people who got me very worried about taking on the highway without any off road experience. I kept telling myself to only take on board information from folks who had actually driven the road telling myself the rest was probably just hearsay. Some of the stories I'd heard included advice to make sure my throat was covered because the eighteen wheelers will throw up huge amounts of razor sharp shards of gravel, "A guy got a lump right into the throat last year and it killed him" one guy had told me, I was starting to become shit scared.

The Alaskan highways with the ongoing oil price problems continued to be like ghost highways, and I was starting to fall in love with the fact that the roads were so empty. I had driven so many miles on empty roads that it was uncomfortable being back in a city in some respects, in my journal I'd called it "solitude on tap!"

Fairbanks, Alaska

It doesn't get dark in Alaska in the summer, at least not as we know it in Ireland. The sun was setting around 11pm but it was still bright out and stayed a dusk color for the whole night. At the peak of summer in Anchorage they get twenty-two hours of daylight, that's with the sun up but the other two hours it's still bright, it's just that the sun isn't in the sky. It was there I learned why the Arctic Circle got its name. Its the line of latitude where you get complete darkness and complete brightness for a whole day on the various solstices.

With the bike serviced and sporting a set of brand new knobby tires, I made the three hundred and seventy mile trek from Anchorage to Fairbanks, a trail which takes you through the Denali national park.

There were many massive mountains with snow capped peaks, lovely rivers and wonderful bendy roads, it was heaven. The further you head north the colder it gets and the icy wind chills you to the marrow. I had over 20 pounds of gear on me at one point, here is the list: Helmet, Balaclava, a buff (yoke that goes round your neck for keeping your neck warm and making you look cool), an enduro jacket, enduro set of pants, motorbike boots, motorbike gloves, wind/water proof under layer jacket, wind/water proof under layer pants, two T-shirts, two pairs of socks, a thong (just kidding) a pair of football shorts, ear plugs, glasses and breathable under layers which act as a second skin. Even with all that I was brass monkeys. I guess the bottom line is that once you get wet and throw in the wind from riding through the countryside at 60mph, not to mention the fact that you're only a stones throw from the Arctic Circle, you're bound to have a chilly willy not to mention a face redder than a baboons arse.

The Dalton highway was wrecking my head, planning to ride it without having the skills on a motorbike to take on the road felt like another in a long line of dumb decisions. I surveyed the route in my motel in Fairbanks and sat with my mouth wide open. Wait till you here the three towns you have to pass to get there, I was sure it was an omen. Livengood, Coldfoot and finally the peach, Deadhorse! I'm not kidding. "Fuck me" I thought to myself, if that isn't a bad sign, the horse (me) may finally meet his waterloo, I'd bitten off way more than I could chew. I sat working out how I was going to approach the trip. It was about 80 miles to Livengood, a town about the size of a toenail. You can get petrol there, however it'll have an octane rating lower than whale shit. Then it's up to the sprawling metropolis of Coldfoot (Population 10 people) which was about a hundred and eighty miles further up the road testing the two hundred mile limit of the BMW fuel tank, I'd be riding mostly in third gear and wouldn't have great fuel economy. Apparently is the most northerly truck stop in the world. There is a place to stay in Coldfoot but it costs $285 dollars a night and from reports it's the equivalent of staying in an orangutans arm pit, "Warm but don't expect anything else" was how I'd heard it described.

Then the hard part would kick in. From Coldfoot it's about two hundred and seventy miles to Deadhorse, twenty miles beyond the capability of the bike so I would need to get a Jerry-can and carry spare petrol on the back of the already overloaded bike. I thought to myself, "If I slide on the bike and catch some sparks on the gravel the bears are in for some char grilled Oisin steaks" although if the octane of the gas was any lower it may not even light, at least I wouldn't be crispy!

Once you get to Deadhorse which by the way is over two hundred miles north of the Arctic circle you can't get to the sea, the oil companies own the land and you have to pay $30 for a bus tour where you can get out and go for a swim in water that's about 2deg C, not very romantic at all. If that wasn't bad enough, a "hotel" room equivalent to the size of a priests confessional can cost up to $200 without any of the fringe benefits. Now for the nice part, it was to rain all day and despite trying to find someone who was heading my direction on various motorcycling websites I was doing it solo. When I'd done the trip planning, based on what people were saying on the various websites there were going to be so many people going up this way on bikes around this time of the year that it would be a veritable traffic jam. The truth however, as with many things in life is that when it comes to game time, nuff said. As I sat in the motel with the map in front of me and thought about the journey, I was completely shitting bricks. I hadn't been this scared since I asked Lorna Donoghue out for a dance at the rock disco when I was fourteen, she said no. As I lay in the bed trying to get my mind into the right frame to take on the task I said to myself, "So Lorna baby, this one's for you and just FYI, I'm a great break dancer."

The Dalton Highway, Alaska

The day had finally come, today was the day I was taking on the Dalton highway, over five hundred and fifty miles of some of the worst driving conditions between here and what used to be the planet Pluto. I had burned so much nervous energy thinking about this part of the trip that I was a nervous wreck. I left my motel at 6am with more layers on me than a Spanish onion and rode out of the town of Fairbanks in the pouring rain. The road as far as Livengood was fine apart from the freezing cold and pissing rain, the first eighty miles were over and everything was going fine. For a moment I allowed myself to think, "Maybe this isn't going to be as bad as everyone was making out." Two kilometers up the road I came to a sign saying, "Dalton highway." It may as well have read "Abandon hope all yee who enter here" and fifty yards up from the sign the tarmac stopped and the road became gravel, I gritted my teeth and muttered something like "Ah fuck it anyway!", and plowed on.

It wasn't long before I noticed a constant companion on the road, namely the Alaskan oil pipeline which runs the entire way from Deadhorse in Prudhoe Bay to Valdez in Southern Alaska, a distance of over 800 miles. Apparently, to get permission to build the pipeline the oil companies had to commit that when the oil runs out, they'll deinstall the entire pipeline and the 12 pumping stations and return the landscape to exactly as it was before they got there. The early part of the road was easy enough going, I kept the speed at about fifty miles an hour and stayed on the most used track through the muck and gravel. Before too long I'd knocked out nearly a hundred miles. Things were going well although my hands were so cold that they'd gone beyond numb and were now just stinging like I'd grabbed a handful of nettles.

The road soon after deteriorated from gravel to pure "muck and shit!" I was looking up a really steep hill in the pissing rain with the makings of a decent size stream cascading down towards me when, as I started to go up the hill, the back wheel just spun in place struggling to get any traction. At the same time the front wheel of the bike was sweeping everywhere, moving around like a hard boiled sweet in the mouth of a granny with no teeth. As I started to go up the hill the bike kept on inching further to the left until I was fully on the opposite side of the road, in the middle of where the other lane would be if it was a road and not just a dirt track. As if on cue, a truck started to come over the crest of the hill. He saw me and knew there was no way he could stop before he hit me so he started giving it loads on the air horn, meanwhile at the bottom of the hill I was revving the fuck out of the bike to try to get it moving in the direction I wanted, namely out of his fucking way. I was stuck on the upward slope of a hill on a KY Jelly like surface with almost no control, I was panicking. A thought came into my head "Just give her the hammer, if in doubt accelerate!" I gave it the hammer and thankfully the bike eventually started to bite. I was out of danger, at least from the impact of a truck, my heart was beating so fast I thought I was going to keel over at any second.

After I'd checked my underpants for lumps I got back on the road and tried my best not to count down the miles. When driving a bike in the muck and shit there's some golden rules. The most important is that the engine is always biting i.e. keep the rev's high which keeps the traction high. If your idling or cruising with the clutch engaged the bike has no traction and if you try to brake on the sludge, you'll probably just come off. The other one to avoid is gurgling, i.e. when you're going too slowly for the gear you're in, you always need to keep the bike hauling ass with high rev's, that will give you the best chance of getting through whatever you come across.

The counter intuitive element to the whole thing is that your only way out of trouble is with high revs, in other words more throttle. If you get into trouble your instinct says, "FUCKING BRAKE!" but you have to do the opposite. If you brake you'll just slide straight off in the gravel and muck so you have to kick down a gear and always keep the bike above 4000rpm, breaking only with the engine and never the brakes. Also, the faster your moving the more chance you give the bike to cut through the gunge on the road with just sheer momentum, its only if you go slowly that you struggle. Can you imagine telling someone back home how you crashed your bike and ended up in hospital "Yeah, I was going too slowly!"

I made it to the first milestone of the Dalton, a cafe and gas stop on the far side of the bridge over the Yukon River. This was the first sign of life that I'd seen since I left Livengood. Alaska really was living up to its billing as the last wild frontier on earth. It was still before 9am so I fancied my chances of making it the whole way to Deadhorse in one day. While I was at breakfast trying to drink a coffee through teeth rattling like a set of maracas I said to myself, "Why am I going up here in the first place, maybe I'll stop at the Arctic Circle and turn back." I ordered a roasting hot breakfast and heaps more coffee and talked away with the waitress.

This was probably the tenth restaurant or Cafe that I'd gone to in Alaska. The women who work in these places are about thirty pounds heavier than the equivalent waitress in the lower forty-eight states. I reckoned that a women up here has to display different qualities, "Stick with me sugar, there's great heat in me for those long winter nights!" I mentioned to the waitress that I was wavering on whether to go to Deadhorse or not and she said, "Look you've made it this far, it doesn't get any worse, and from here to Coldfoot (which was about 190 miles) there's lots of paved sections, so you'll be fine."

My resolve stiffened and with a full tank of fuel and a full pot of hot coffee in my system I headed off for Coldfoot. I kept the engine at 4000rpm and bar a good few scares on corners where I had come in too hot and ended up overrunning completely onto the other side of the road, things were going fine. A thing to note is that on the Dalton Highway, you just pick the best line on the road, it doesn't matter if it's on the wrong side of the road. I got to Coldfoot in one piece and was starting to feel like a bit of a hero, "Dalton slayer is what they'll call me" I thought to myself. I filled up with gas and filled both Jerry cans so I'd make the final leg to Deadhorse.

Keeping things simple by just keeping the rev's high and the speed at around 50mph things were going great the only problem was I was so cold and wet, I was hallucinating. Signs on the road from a distance off started to look like bears and moose, I was going a bit nuts. I got into the Brooks Mountain Range and it was like being on a different planet. They still had snow on them and looked very rugged and harsh, like the way you'd expect mountains to look near the Arctic Circle I suppose. Parking up to take some pictures with no one around for hundreds of miles in some of the most severe terrain anywhere in the world, I was starting to feel like how the first explorers of this land must have felt. One of the highlights of the entire trip was taking the Atigun pass, which rises to 4800ft as it meanders through the frozen Brooks range. Once you come down out of the mountains the world starts to flatten out as you pass closer to the Arctic tundra.

The only thing you bump into along the way is oncoming trucks which tend to cover you with a shower of mud, shite, gravel and water. This road is one of the routes featured on the TV series, Ice Road Truckers which has done a lot to advertise it as an adventure holiday location.

Things were going well, from a "miles on the clock" perspective. I passed the Arctic Circle, stopping to take some pictures and be bitten by 40 million mosquitos. In the Arctic Tundra during the summer months its estimated that there are a metric ton of mosquitos per square km. Think about that for a few seconds. Think about how small and light a mosquito is. Now think about an area 1000 meters long and 1000 meters wide and now fill it with 1000KG or 2200LBS of mosquitos. Now empty the whole place so its just you and the mosquitos. Now drop the tweeds for a number 1, and imagine your John Thomas becomes the only piece of bare skin in that square kilometer. I'll take the high road from here.

I continued on and passed the point where no more trees grow into a flat never ending grey world where it was impossible to tell the sky from the land. Every twenty minutes I had to stop to heat my hands on the piston heads of the bike, beyond the Arctic Circle I was introduced to a whole new definition of cold. I was just seventy miles from Prudhoe Bay when the road turned into Swiss cheese. Spreader trucks had put a fresh three inches thick coat of wet gravel on large parts of the road making the journey impossible. I was on the road for over twelve hours at this point and my teeth were chattering uncontrollably, I couldn't feel a thing with my hands and the cold had even got to my John Thomas. When I would try to drive forward the front wheel was washing out completely and the potholes were so bad it was like driving over the rhythm section of a band.

Prudhoe Bay, Alaska

I pulled over to the side of the road completely and utterly fucked. I couldn't go back, I didn't have enough juice to make it, nor the stamina. I couldn't go forward at that moment because I just couldn't control the bike. I stood there in the pissing rain completely covered head to toe with mud, myself and the bike unrecognizable. I had to get off and take a leak. When I went, it felt like I was pissing barbed wire, the end of my lad was like something someone had glued on. It was like a dead persons hand was holding my lad. In the arctic tundra there is no shelter, no trees, nothing to stop in under out of the rain. It really made me appreciate how hardy an animal a Caribou is out there grazing the whole time. In my mind's eye I said, "Dude you're Luke Skywalker. No, you're his older better looking brother, the one with the beard. "C'mon its only seventy miles, you can do this, when you get into Prudhoe there'll be a parade for you, you'll be washed down by fifty-five naked women who'll all refer to you as the Dalton slayer. Britney spears will get on the phone and she'll say dude on your way down why not pop over to see me, you can give me a lick of the cango." I filled my mind with hundreds of motivational thoughts to pump myself up and for the next ninety minutes I battled through the worst conditions I've ever come across making it to Deadhorse fifteen hours after I started in Fairbanks.

When I got there the hotel was booked out so I had to stay in place called Camp 1, one of the places where they house oil workers. For $179 dollars I got a room in a prefab which had three other beds and no toilet or hot water, all that was communal. When I went in to the wash area I was faced with two naked dudes in the shower, one of whom had the hairiest arse I've ever seen, it was like he was wearing a pair of fur shorts. Desperate not so see the front section, I went over to the sinks to brush my teeth where I looked in the mirror, smiled and said to myself, "I did it, I rule the world."

I peeled off and got in for a hot shower. The feeling of piping hot water running all over my frozen body felt as good as shagging Princess Leia.

I went to the camp cook guy and asked him could I have something to eat. He said, "Dude were done" to which I replied "Dude just give me a plate of hot food, anything I don't care, just once it's hot." He returned with a plate of pasta and two pieces of ham which looked like they were pulled straight off a boar and I sat in the corner eating like I was about to go into hibernation. There was no parade, no welcoming committee, no fifteen hotties in the shower, not even alcohol (banned in that area). I just went to bed at 9:20pm with a smile from ear to ear. I had to do it all again in reverse the next morning. The road back down to Fairbanks the next day was much easier and dryer and with the experience gained from the previous day it took only ten hours to get back, fully five hours quicker.

Having talked to many people who completed the Dalton highway it's a coin toss, if you get good weather its very doable, if you don't, "Its gonna be rough going!"

The Dalton highway did extract a heavy toll though, my back pannier hopped off somewhere on the road, no doubt jarred off by the potholes, I didn't even notice until I got to Fairbanks and I certainly wasn't going back five hundred miles to get it. It was laden with much needed stuff but I knew I'd be able to replace the stuff in Fairbanks so I wasn't too upset. By the time I got to Fairbanks, after eleven hundred miles of dirt roads through some of the toughest terrain in the world, I was too tired to care about what I'd lost. The next morning the extent of what I'd lost set in - about a hundred hours of video along with the camcorder and chargers - I was sick as a dog.

The motel in Fairbanks had two guys from Alabama working behind the counter. They saw me coming in off the road destroyed with mud, and asked "Where the hell you bin boy?" I told them and also told them where I'd been so far on the trip and where I was going, to which they replied, "Mayannnn that is baaad ayass, ya'll must be one hardcore sonofa bitch!" I went to my room beaming. Make no mistake, there is no greater compliment for a biker than to be called hardcore. I headed off to sleep and slept like a hedgehog in the winter.

Valdez, Alaska

Before I started to head south for Argentina I decided to take three days in Valdez, Alaska, famous for many things but mostly for the Exxon Valdez oil spill. I met a Scandinavian guy who was over there training the military on survival tactics and he told me that Valdez was the most incredible place that he'd ever been, never one to doubt a Scandinavian, I decided to go. I also reasoned that it was entirely likely that I'd never again see Alaska, so I should soak it up while I was there. It was a detour of over three hundred miles but nothing is close in this part of the world so I just puckered up and got on with it. After the previous two days on the Dalton highway my ass felt like I'd been on the wrong end of some prison love in Sam Quentin, so there wasn't much joy in the helmet, I needed a bit of time off the road.

When I was about a hundred miles from Valdez the road steadily started to climb until you reach a place called the Thompson pass, which is a route through the Chugach Mountains to Valdez. The cloud formations were a wonderful spectacle, every now and then they would part to let the sunshine through and reveal a massive snow capped peak and just as quickly, it would vanish only to be replaced by another on a different section of the road.

Valdez is a small fishing village on the coast and is surrounded by mountains and blue glacial water. It doesn't matter which window you look out of in Valdez, if you've a clear unobstructed view you are looking directly at mountains. I went for a walk around the town stopping to eat in a Thai restaurant, owned by a woman who came there on holidays ten years earlier and never left.

The next day I took a whale watching cruise with a heap of European tourists, and at various times we saw Killer whales, Minke whales, Sea Otters, Puffins and seals all on a waterway surrounded by gigantic snow capped peaks.

At breakfast the next morning I introduced myself to a guy who was also driving a BMW around Alaska, Helmar from Los Angeles. We went on a tour of the surrounding area on our bikes even took the time to take the bike off road onto a rock precipice and take some pictures. I was standing there taking some pictures with my small Canon point and shoot camera, and over my left should Helmar appeared carrying a camera you'd expect to see in a fashion shoot, while it wasn't quite penis envy, I did feel a bit girly standing there with my palm sized girly point and shoot. Helmar was an American of German extraction and ran his own business. It was a software company which allowed him to spend a lot of time on the road, it sounded like the ideal life to me. We went out for a skinful of beers in a local Irish bar, I found it hard to believe that even in Valdez Alaska you could find an Irish bar. Helmar was the sort of guy who would just to camp out by a river for a couple of days by himself and do a bit of fishing. Unfortunately we were on different routes and different timelines so I only got to spend a day with him. We said goodbye and I left Valdez.

The biker community on the road is quite small so people run into each other quite often and Helmar mentioned that he'd met a guy from Venezuela and a guy from Switzerland and some other Europeans. At the time I said to myself, "Man Alaska is a big place, there is no chance of bumping into them." I made a note in my diary that night, "Heaven is a place called Valdez!" it's that simple Tok, Alaska

The following night I made it to Tok and the place was jammed with travelers, it seemed like a different place than just a week earlier. I met lots of people who were all on different stages of their journeys, two of them, incredibly, Rafael and John who I had just talked about with Helmar the night before, had just finished the Pan American trip going South to North. We talked about Central America, Colombia, the Ruta 40 in Argentina, the places at whose mere mention sent shivers of fear down my back. Rafael had some great advice for me, "Open your mind, open your eyes but even more important, open your heart and you'll have the time of your life!" I was awestruck that the guys talked so nonchalantly about locations that I was scared shitless about. We talked for about an hour in the rain and they allayed all my fears for the trip south, I was beaming when I left them. These guys had completed what I was about to undertake, they were so chilled out it was untrue, "Any more laid back and they'd fall back!"

John, Atilla and Rafael

Dawson City, YT

The next day I swung north to traverse the Top of the world highway on the way to Dawson City in the Yukon, Canada. My first stop was in a tiny gold mining village called Chicken, Alaska. I sat down in a small cafe and had an amazing slice of apple pie. Dawson City was supposed to be a great night out and I headed off all guns firing for the town after twenty minutes yapping to the restaurant owner. On the Taylor highway aka the top of the world highway I realized I had crossed the 10,000 mile mark of the trip, I'd about a third of the distance completed for the entire trip and I still hadn't got out of Canada. It was 33 days since I started.

Dawson city is only accessible by river ferry. I think it must be one of the only inland towns in North America where this is the case and I was surprised that no one had mentioned it. The ferry is small with room for about eight cars and it struggles to maneuver on what is a very large and fast flowing Yukon River. I imagined I was crossing into the planet of the apes. Most of the people I'd met who were incidentally all North American said, "No doubt about it, Dawson City is an absolute must see" and after visiting the place and spending quite a few hours walking around I have to be honest, I don't get it. It was an overpriced cheesy place I thought. It's kept the older type building facades, and the roads don't have tarmac so its feels fairly earthy but at $179 for a cheap hotel I was expecting a bit more. I went to the casino which was mediocre, the centerpiece was a stage and a bunch of slot machines with a large wooden bar. I think the reason the North Americans like it, is because it represents their recent history, as close to a frontier town as you can still get. It wasn't my cup of tea, but everyone to their own as my old gaffer used to say.

As I was walking around I met a German guy who had just spent the last sixteen days kayaking in the Yukon, pulling off the rivers at night to sleep in the woods. He didn't even have a tent, man this guy was hardcore! He told me that he does that every year, coming over from Germany and heading into the Canadian woods for seven weeks, alone. He had me "oohing and aahing" at some great stories about Bears and wildlife. He was like talking to Michael Schumacher. The Germans would put you to shame coming from Ireland. Most can knock out about three languages and don't get me started about the pesky Dutch, more languages than fingers!

I left Dawson City the next morning feeling a little blue. I missed the conditions of the Dalton highway in a perverse sort of way, I loved the excitement of it, the uncertainty of the whole situation helped me forget about my loneliness. I decided I was going to set the GPS to take me to Moose Creek using off-road tracks. I got about fifty miles of dirt road and then was back on the highway. I was now circling south by way of a different loop back to Whitehorse along the Klondike highway. It's straight as a ruler for hundreds of miles and after the off-road escapades early in the morning, it was a cruel torment.

Jim Green

On the road I met a cool gent from Washington State named Jim Green and we rode a couple of hundred clicks together. We were both headed the same general direction so we decided to hook up for a couple of days. Jim had also completed the Dalton highway and said it was very emotional for him as it was something that he'd dreamed about since he was a boy. He was driving a BMW 1200, a newer model than mine and he was like Inspector gadget with all the bits and pieces he had round the bike. He was also armed with a big "fuck off" SLR camera. I was beginning to think that they gave them away free with BMW's in the states.

Jim Green and Myself

Jim was one of the easiest going characters I'd ever come across. While we were parked up having a soda I looked at the back of our bikes, my wheels had gnarly knobbies and he had a worn out looking street tire. I said to him, "Jim did you ride the Dalton on that fucking tire?" He replied, "Yep, theres still plenty of rubber left on that bad boy too." I couldn't believe it. I wouldn't have dreamt about doing it without the best of tires and there's Jimbo cruising along on a slick without a care in the world.

We got to Whitehorse, for me it was the second time round. I couldn't believe the amount Native Americans who were absolutely wasted drunk. Apparently the Native Americans lack an enzyme to break down alcohol so get drunk quicker and stay drunk longer. However the sad thing was, none of them looked happy they all just looked really angry. I think the whole problem could be fixed by sending a bus load of Irish men up to shag the Indian women, that enzyme would be bred in over night. On my first run through Whitehorse a guy offered to suck my John Thomas for $20 as I passed him by on the street, he looked out of his mind on drugs and was in a wheel chair. I tried haggling him down to $15 but he was having none of it (only kidding), I gave him the $20 and declined the BJ.

The motel I stayed in became night of the living dead at around 2am with nothing but druggies and alcoholics all wandering around the car park and streets outside, if there was a sadder place on earth I had yet to see it. The night was topped off when I went to a bar beside the motel for a Coors light to celebrate a long day on the bike and knocking out some massive miles, when a woman who was obviously a close relative of Jabba the Hutt asked me if I was, "Looking for company sugar?" I downed the Coors light in one go and walked out of the bar door, I couldn't help wonder what sort of dudes would take up that offer, I guess in a town when you get BJ's on wheels anything's up for grabs. I'm sure there's a good side to Whitehorse but in two visits I hadn't managed to see it, but hey, at least it's lively!

It was my second time through this part of the world so I was pushing things fairly hard, averaging four hundred miles a day on the Alcan highway. My thinking was that this would allow me to drop to a hundred miles a day in South America for a good length of time. I was having a ball with Jim who was ex army, ex law enforcement and was a world of stories and fun. When two people are traveling on the road I think you tend to meet more people, I think people tend to shy away from people who travel on their own, "He's traveling on his own, that dudes weird!" Every time we stopped on the road we would get talking to bikers or fellow travelers who all seemed really interested in who we were and where we were off to, we were having a ball.

Coal River, YT

We stayed for a night in Coal River in a motel come campsite. About half a mile from the back of the motel there was a river and we decided to take a non gay stroll down to the riverbank. Harassed the whole way by giant mosquitoes, when we got there we were greeted by a river flowing east as the sun set in the West. The dusk air was cold but the sun was warm on our faces as we stood watching the river slowly pass us by. The moment ended quickly when Jim spotted bear tracks close to where we were standing so we both hauled ass back to the motel.

We had great weather for days at a time and met great people on the road everywhere we went. Everyone we met was traveling. When we stopped at a rest stop, people would come up and say, "So where you headed to?" We'd share twenty minutes of stories from the road and then be on our way.

We stopped at the sign forest in Watson Lake and I left my mark, a custom that people from all over the world perform as they leave a sign on one of the masts. The last time they counted there were over 76,000 individual signs and its growing daily.

Both Jim and I just loved to ride the motorcycles and in just three days had knocked out over a thousand miles. The days tended to started foggy which burned off as the sun rose. The sun always turns the scenery on, if you know what I mean. When I passed this way ten days earlier it was lashing rain and I didn't think too much of it. Well, that day the sun was out and it was mesmerizing. I'm also sure the company made it feel a lot better too, every time you stop you have someone to share the experience with.

The roads continued sweeping left and right as they meandered through mountain passes all the time flanked by jade green rivers and forests. Muncho Lake provincial park which the Alcan passes through was particularly good. The roads continued to be almost completely deserted so we had the run of the highways, I was living the dream.

After Fort Nelson the sun started beaming and the temperature soared, for the first time in over two weeks it was time to put away the fleece lining and water proof layers. I was down to just a t-shift and the enduro suit with all the vents open, long live the heat! As the evenings drew on with clear skies the bike would cast long shadows and as the roads circumnavigate large hills my shadow danced to the left, front and right as we made our way. At the time I wrote in my journal that, "I've never felt as good as I do today."

The only real downside of this part of the world is mosquitoes and black fly. Canada and Alaska are overrun with them. They stalk you, if you're walking home, they actually follow you and wait till you leave some bare skin open and then dive straight on it. In these parts of the world they have real mossies, not the caffeine free diet mossie that has made its way into Ireland, for one thing they are about three times the size of the Irish variety and they would suck the sheets up your arse. One fantastic quote I heard was, "The skeeters round here are so big they could stand flat foot and fuck a turkey!" As if that wasn't enough, there is also black fly, which is basically a flying set of teeth which tries to bite you a new bum hole when it lands on you. The final piece of the jigsaw is completed by a little bollix called a noseem, no-see-em, get it? It's the North American equivalent of a midge. So, as soon as you hang a bit of bare skin out the door one of these three amigos is going to try to feast on you. An all out nuclear offensive with DEET is the only thing that keeps them at bay.

As you're driving along on the motorbike, your visor gets hit with a variety of insects, about one every five minutes, normally right at the centre of the visor so you can see it with both eyes. This part is quite a bit worse than a car because at least you're three feet from the windscreen in a car and you can spray the windscreen and wipe them off, with a helmet you're about two inches away so you get to inspect the lower intestines of anything exploding on the visor. A June-bug hit my visor and it was like someone threw a bottle of Colman's mustard at the helmet, "Ewwwww!" I was straight off the bike spitting onto the visor to wipe him off. If you don't get off and clean the visor the only way to get rid of them is to try to turn your head to the right or the left and see if the carcass will blow off the visor in the wind.

We met many hunters, I don't get the hunting thing, but everyone to their own. They would come up and ask you "Hey did you see any caribou?" Yeah like I'm gonna tell you so you can go up and shoot them! It's mad, you've 99% of folks looking out of the windows of their cars like old people waiting for the post man for any sign of a wild animal and then these boys are out shooting them! There's a huge debate in the states about hunting and its relative merits, so no point in taking it any further here.

Rafael

As Jim and I were pulled over on the Icefields parkway a bike pulled up and Rafael from Venezuela jumped off and said hello. This was the same Rafael I'd met in Tok Alaska. It was great, because today was the day when Jim's road and my own would diverge and I hadn't been looking forward to it. It was like fate was paying me back for all the lonely riding in Canada, "Don't worry Ois, here's another biker buddy for ya." The three of us spent the day mucking around on Glaciers, looking at bears and mountain goats and generally having a great laugh. The three of us were pulled over at a glacier car park and given there was Irish, US and Venezuelan registration plates we were attracting a lot of attention. Folks asked if they could take a picture with us, it was one of the first times that I really felt other people thought, what we were doing was cool.

Big Jim Green and Rafael

It came time to say goodbye to Jim, we had rode from Dawson City the whole way down to Lake Louise where he cut off to Washington State. We'd a great four days covering almost 1600 miles together and I knew I was going to miss him. Rafael was a completely different sort of character. He was a tall Latin dude with long black hair who was too cool for school. We immediately hit it off and were straight away having a great time. He was headed for Houston in Texas so our roads would likely be the same for over a thousand miles which suited the two of us down to the ground. I was constantly badgering him with questions about Mexico and Central America, he gave me one piece of advice, "Never look at the news in these countries, if you do you'll be afraid to leave your room!" The first question I asked Rafael was what did he do for a living to which he replied, "I'm a drug dealer."

We spent most of the next day getting some new tires on the bikes in Calgary. I had a full service, the bike had been through a bit of an ordeal by this stage. We didn't go to a BMW dealer to get the work done, and the only thing I can say is that this was a mistake, and I'll leave it at that. While we were waiting on the bikes we went over to a place called Blackfoot BMW to see if they had any bits of kit worth picking up. We met a guy there from Chile while we were hanging around and it turned out he was a veteran overlander who had done the Pan American highway three times. He was the spitting image of a friend of my brothers called Foxy in every way except he spoke with a Spanish accent. This guy was fifty-eight years old and was married to a thirty year old Polish girl who was really hot and about a foot taller than him. I asked him what's his secret and he said, exactly like Speedy Gonzales would have said it, "Eets coz I'm sexy no?!" In his wallet he had a picture of him in the Atacama Desert but the stories he told me made me more nervous than ever about crossing into Mexico.

We rode out of Calgary into a thunder storm as the sun was setting on the Rockies in the distance. We spent that night in a hostel in Canmore.

It was the first time in a while that I had stayed in a hostel and because we arrived late I got one of the top bunks in a room holding six people with three bunk beds. The top bunk was about two foot from the ceiling and had a wooden surround. I hadn't been in a bunk bed since I was about five years old, which was about the last time I was able to fit in one and things hadn't changed. I was too tall for the bed and too wide and with the really low ceiling it was like looking

out of an open casket coffin. I hit the scratcher late to be more tired than normal so I'd sleep but everyone did this so I ended up being first in the scratcher.
For about two hours, on the half hour the rest of the guys in the room would come in, turn on the light, go in and brush their teeth, then go to bed, turn off the light, but the whole time all I was thinking about was the guy that got his head hacked off on the greyhound bus in Manitoba. I guess I'm just not comfortable sleeping in a room with five strangers.

Also the people who go to hostels here aren't the same as in Europe. They aren't inter- railer's or students. Many are hunters, not the sort of folks you'd be striking up a conversation with. I talked with one of them earlier in the night and he was on sick leave for some reason and here was the only place they had a doctor, he didn't elaborate. In my spinning mind this translated to, "Ok this guy is a nutter! No way they have a doctor here in Canmore and not in Calgary." The fact that he had a mustache and a real dodgy comb over didn't do anything to allay my worries. I thought to myself, if I'm gonna get slaughtered in the middle of the night, I don't want it to be by a dude with a tache and a comb over! I could see myself in the serial killer year book. On the left page a full page picture of the serial killer, and on the right a montage of all the people he'd killed, and on the top row, two in from the left was me.

After 12,200 miles it was my last day in Canada. Pablo Escobar, aka Rafael and I pulled into a town near the USA border with Montana called Black Diamond. The town was as dead as a door nail but it was a safe and friendly place. The next day we'd cross into the USA.

Chapter 4
South to the border with Mexico

The trip had been getting better and better and hit a new peak as we crossed into the state of Montana in the USA. It was early in the day and we were headed for the Many Glacier International park to drive the Logan pass. It was a straight forward border crossing and I threw in a joke that I was a Jedi, "You don't need to see my ID, and these aren't the droids you're looking for" the border guard laughed charitably, I think he'd heard it a few times before.

Montana, Glacier National Park

For large parts of the day it absolutely bucketed down but it didn't dampen the scenery. The route through the Logan pass called the Road to the Sun Highway takes you higher than most clouds and the sensation of traveling up, through and above rain clouds is sensational. The road hairpins right and left above massive chasms cut by glaciers and the whole way through you have massive mountains on one side and yawning valleys on other.

We finished the night off in Hungry horse. If I'm honest my only motivation to stay there was because it was one of way points on the Long way round and purely by chance we stayed in the same motel. Rafael thought I was a spacer but the two lads were my inspiration for going, and this was the point at which the guys turned east to head for New York and I would be turning south to go to Ushuaia. For me it was the point at which the whole journey became my own adventure. Everything from this point on was just me. If you think it all sounds a bit silly, you're right. We then popped over to a great cafe where the folks were really friendly and had a great bit of grub and a good laugh with the waitresses. Rafael was winding the girls up that we were gay saying things like "two deserts but only one spoon" which the girls lapped up. It was a perfect end to a great day, certainly the best day of the trip so far, and for me the best since Liverpool beat AC Milan on penalties in the European cup.

The following day as we made our way south through Montana, we met a biker when we were stopped for coffee that had just come up from a massive Harley rally. He was from Australia, average height and sported a beard that would have gotten him a job with ZZ Top in a heartbeat. He was a man's man, he told us that he left the wife back home to go on the trip, he didn't tell her where he was going or how long he'd be gone for, just that he was heading off and he'd be back when he was ready.

When we stopped for breaks, Rafael taught me some Spanish for Central and South America, key phrases like hello, good bye, please don't kidnap me, no I prefer sex with women, please don't spit in my dinner, the usual stuff they teach you in first year Spanish class in Dublin.

Since I got the bike serviced in wanker-works near Calgary

there was a rattle whenever I'd get towards 4000rpm. On a trip like this your completely and utterly dependent on the bike, I had to bite the bullet and drive to a BMW dealer in Helena Montana, a day's ride of a detour all told. On top of that, I lost Rafael that day, he was in a bad mood as a result of some bad news from home about his business and I'm not sure that he didn't just want to be on his own anyway, one way or another I was back on my own and feeling more than a bit blue.

I got to BMW in Helena and a guy called John, armed with a stethoscope came out and started using it to listen to the engine. Within about three minutes he'd found the source of the problem and five minutes later had it fixed. It is great to see guys who really know their game in action. It was amazing how my mood tended to match the bikes condition, if the bike was in great shape I felt great, if there was anything wrong with it at all, I turned into a freak show.

He recommended a 400 mile scenic route from Helena to Yellowstone Park, I'd completed three quarters of it when I stopped in a town called Ennis the following night. I thought it was good karma, as I passed my bike test in Ennis County Clare in Ireland a few months earlier.

If you happen to find yourself alone and want some company in any restaurant or bar anywhere in the lower 48 states just pull out a map and spread it across the table you're sitting at. Draw yourself up a pensive looking face and men of all ages will flock to you. Men are attracted to maps like wasps to jam. When a man is driving a car, obviously he doesn't need a map, nor instructions nor directions for that matter. Like the swallows finding their way to Capistrano every year, a real man will find his way. However, a map in the hands of a third party, well that's another matter. The first thing they'll say to you is, "You need some help buddy?" Next thing they are sitting at the table pouring out the best routes, towns, scenic areas and places where they spent, "Quite a bit of time." It's a wonderful trait.

For the last couple of days the weather had been perfect for riding and the landscape had turned a golden wheat color which stretched off as far as the eye could see in every direction. Montana has a reputation for being flat but it also has huge mountains in the west of the state with great roads that sweep and weave their way through the Rockies. Surrounded by such natural beauty it's impossible to stay in a bad mood and I cured my melancholy by having a fantastic time on the bike. There is nothing like having a bike leaned over as far as you can take it as you corner bends on the ragged edge to get your mood back firing on all cylinders.

Later in the day I was stopped by the cops, I was doing 45mph in a 30mph zone. They were a bit pissed off and made me strip down the bike to get the vehicle registration and do a concealed fire arms check, but in the end let me go with a verbal warning. The day finished on top of a hill looking at the sun setting, not for the first time over the foot hills of the Rockies. The variety in every day sent me to sleep in a daze, it's like there's only so much you can take in and every day your mind is completely filled with memories. Even on bad days, you cover so much ground and see so many things it was getting really hard to remember what day certain things happened.

The Beartooth Highway

The next day I knocked out another four hundred miles and ended up in Red Lodge having completed the Bear tooth highway, renowned as one of the best motorcycle routes in the world. The road runs 69 miles from Cooke City to Red Lodge in Montana over the Bear tooth mountain range. If you got a hundred bikers into a room and asked them to concoct their perfect road, they wouldn't be able to come up with something better than this.

My poor bum had gone through some savage treatment on the motorbike and I'd developed a huge blister on one of my butt cheeks, which burst when I jumped on the saddle too quickly. When it happened first there was the relief as the awkwardness and uncomfortable feeling went, "ahhh, ooooooh!" The original pain was gone but was replaced now with a new pain like someone was washing the area with lemon juice and a Brillo pad.

That morning I saw a bear and her two cubs crossing the road about twenty yards ahead of me on the road, which is about as close as I ever want to be to a bear. I'd seen one crossing the road at full clip a few days earlier with Jim and it was only then I realized why people say you'll never

outrun a bear.

Since I got to Canada I'd been having a recurring nightmare about bears. I drive around a bend in a dark forest and there's a bear standing on the road. I break and stop about ten feet away. The bear stands up on its two hind paws and lets one of those noises that Ben from Grizzly Adams used to make. I try to turn the bike too quickly to haul ass out of there and end up falling over and dropping the bike. I quickly jump to my feet and try to lift the overloaded bike worried that any moment I'll feel the heat of the bear's breath on the back of my neck. I throw the bike back up, jump on, start it up, lash it into first and rally out of the bears reach. When I'm about a hundred yards from the bear I look back and it's standing there, this time with a leash on it and a woman is standing beside the beast. I turn the bike around and drive back to her and sure enough, exactly as you'd expect, its Britney Spears wearing the red leather outfit from the video, "Oops I did it again" absolutely appropriate as it was a recurring nightmare after all.

Yellowstone

Yellowstone park covers an area of 3,000 square miles and is an excellent place to visit. The park is home to rivers, lakes, canyons, mountain ranges and the largest super volcano on the North American Continent. It's also famous for its free roaming buffalo, geysers and thermal features. I had been given a ticket in the park for stepping on a thermal feature. Now don't going thinking that I was trying to climb or walk on Old faithful or anything like that, I wasn't. I had walked off the road to see where some steam was coming from. The park wardens didn't try to coach me and say why it's a bad thing they just issued me a ticket. A bigger pair of condescending pricks I've never met. To be fair, this was a very isolated incident. The US National parks system is an incredible network. You can buy a parks pass for about $80 and it gets you entry into every National park in America and my experience with the wardens in all the places I've been has always been resoundingly positive.

I was picking up some great sayings in the US, for example if your tired. Jim told me one after a long days riding, "I'm beat like a red headed step child!" Another, after a really hard day, "I feel like I was rode hard and put away wet" a phrase used all over Canada and the US. There are many places I could go with that saying, but I'm going to take the high road.

I've left Wyoming and Montana both behind and drove like a fart through a G string through Idaho. Why the rush? Well, after Yellowstone and the Bear tooth highway you start to cut into Idaho which is a mainly agricultural state with less obvious famous places to visit.

Bonneville Salt Flats

I took a right turn at Salt Lake City made my way to the Bonneville Salt Flats on the Utah Nevada border. To get there you have to ride right into the bed of what used to be the Great Salt Lake and with the temperature at 48degC/118degF, I thought my head was going to explode in the helmet. With no mountains and very little in the desert that you would need to build a road around, the road stretches straight as far as the eye can see. Gradually the desert becomes whiter and whiter (that's the salt n'est pas) until if feels like you're on the moon. As I was driving along I started to wonder "Hmm, so is this it?" (i.e. the salt flats) or will there be a sign up here somewhere, as one salt flat looks like the next I guess. After about twenty minutes of deliberating

I said, "Fuck it, I'm pulling off the highway onto the flats." Now a couple of things were going through my noggin at that point: Its 48degC, the oil in the bike is 20/50 which means it's rated for -20 to +50degC; if it got any hotter I'd be in trouble. Would the bike sink? It's a heavy machine, if I went too far out would I be able to get it back onto the road? What if I came off the bike? Out on the flats no one would ever find you and after only a half mile you vanish into the heat shimmer. Is this the actual salt flats or is there another area which is not so soft? This place is like being in a dream. I need a shag.

I drove out about two miles just far enough so that I couldn't see anything in all four directions but white salt, the blue sky and the distant mountains. When you do this sort of stuff you start to feel like Marco polo. I struck up an inner narrative "A lone Jedi treks off into the nothingness, with only his lad for a light saber..." I'll let you fill in the rest. A couple of things that became immediately apparent were theres no sound, nothing, just you, the bike, some distant mountains and blinding whiteness all around. As they say back in Clondalkin, "Deadly buzz!" After only a short duration, either because of the heat or the unchanging surrounding I was starting to get disoriented. At times like that I was thankful that I'm a fat bastard and I just followed the hefty track the bike had made through the salt to find my way back to the road. I was also glad I didn't have a sensible travel mate, to warn me off doing stuff like this, "Be careful, you'll regret it" type stuff. I suppose I was testing myself every day, "Go on ya big scaredy cat, ya big girl's blouse, ya mohair cardigan." If I found myself saying, "Don't do it" because I was a little afraid I constantly said to myself, "Fuck it, I'm doing it, you only live once."

I kept trying to get in the moment. I was obsessed with

it. Loads of people had told me before I left to make sure that I, "Stayed in the moment." I didn't have a clue what it meant, but I'm sure it was important! I spent all my time either forward planning for performing postmortems on things that went wrong in the past, never leaving much time for the now. I thought back to some Billy Connolly DVD's I'd seen, every time he went somewhere cool he'd strip off naked and do a dance, so not to be undone I said I'd give it a go. I did, and it felt great. No sooner had I completed the jig when I noticed in the distance a biker making his way in my direction out on the flats. I noticed him starting to slow down no doubt thinking, "Is that fucker naked?" Then he slowly arced to the right and burned off into the distance. I was rolling around laughing. For my troubles I got absolutely burnt to a crisp, with the intense heat and glare I was glowing like a gas heater. I stayed out there until it got dark, and because I was in a place where the world is utterly flat and very dark, I could see stars right down to the horizon in all directions.

When I got back from the salt flats that night, I was gassing up for the following day when a chap driving an older model BMW pulled up. He was a school teacher named Barry from Wendover, which is where I was staying. We got talking and he took me to one of only two places in the world where you can see the curvature of the earth from land. We drove to the top of this hill and looked out onto the 200 square miles that make up the bottom of what was the Great Salt Lake. It's so flat the lights from the cars driving from Salt Lake City to Reno create a light Arc around the curvature of the earth, too cool.

Barry was also a pilot and brought me down to Wendover Airport where the Enola gay was stored and where they also store the plane prop from the movie Con Air. We were there well after hours, and I'd be lying if I said that I wasn't a bit nervous walking around old WWII plane hangers in the dead of the night. I found it amazing how my natural suspicion was that people don't just come up and talk to you. However, on a trip like this you just have to go with your instinct, if someone comes across as genuine, you have to go with it.

The following day I was supposed to push on towards Lake Tahoe but I stayed another day, the salt flats are too incredible a place to just pass through so I wanted to have another day out there acting the maggot. I went for dinner in a casino in the town, and got talking to Lieutenant Colonel Vader, had to be fate. (If I have to tell you at this stage that Darth Vader was a character in the Star Wars movies, there is every chance that you are an alien from another planet and I'd like to welcome you to planet Earth) We went for dinner and had a great chat about his time in Korea, Vietnam and Desert storm. After dinner the magnet that is the salt flats pulled me back out for more fun. Driving around the salt flats with just a pair of sunglasses in the heat of the desert evening gave me a tremendous feeling of freedom, it really is how motorcycles were meant to be ridden. Out on the flats I got talking to guys who were doing motorcycle speed trials, it was a pure "guys" moment, standing around looking at things going very fast.

Leaving Bonneville I drove towards a place called Wheeler Peak in Great Basin National Park in Nevada. It's a pass that takes you up to about 10,000 feet above sea level with a seemingly endless view of the desert below. The roads up there were in great shape but above 9000 feet the hard top was coated with a very fine layer of gravel which had built up on top of the surface. The back wheel washed out from under me twice and if I didn't have the Dalton highway experience under my belt I'd have come off for certain. When the back wheel starts to wash out, now my instinct kicks in and says, "MORE GAS FAT BOY!"

I was now firmly in the Nevada desert and took B roads for large portions of the day so I could check out two ghost towns. Not a single car passed me for the entire time I was on one B-road, a full eighty-eight miles. I pulled up to a couple of ghost towns and to be honest I was shitting myself.
If your down this direction look up Hamilton, Osceola, and Cheery Creek. The combination of not having seen anyone on the road for so long, and a town full of ghosts was giving me the heebie jeebies. (Yeah, I know that's not what a ghost town is!) I had a 20 second wander around them and I burned out of there like a scalded cat. There wasn't much to see really. I thought it would be like a western town or something like that, but looked more like a knackers yard.

Canyon land, Utah

The temperature continued to rise eventually peaking at 49degC. How hot is that? Well, it had me running to the internet to see how far off a world record it was. Pesky Ethiopia had a day of 134degC, about 56degC. Still it's so hot you've a headache for most of the day, and your goolies feel like they are boiling in your bag.

It was a good few days since I'd talked to anyone and I woke up the following morning feeling home sick, not sure why that day of all days. I was in the town of Panguitch, Utah, which for some reason I kept calling Sandwich. I maintained a journal the whole time I was traveling and I realized I'd passed the 14,000 mile mark. The homesickness was brought on I think because I was getting further away from home and I was getting closer to Mexico, and it was looking increasingly unlikely that I'd meet up with a riding partner to go through the tougher parts of the trip. I didn't speak Spanish and I was starting to fret. As I was checking out, the girl who ran the motel asked me where I was from,

"Where y'all from?" I replied Ireland and then she said in a shitkicker drawl, "Reckon I shoulda known you havin red hair n'all." She came an inch from me breaking my foot off in her ass, calling me a ginger, cheek of her! "Bitch that's strawberry blond!" So in a fairly low mood I headed off to Bryce canyon. I decided to get my spirits up I was going to do as much unpaved roads as possible, as it's hard to feel homesick when your front and back wheels are struggling for traction.The roads I picked were mental. In reality I've nothing like the amount of experience on a motorbike needed to be taking on this sort of terrain, but that day if there was a trail, I went up it, even if it only looked like a donkey once might have went up there for a piss, I went up there on the bike.

At one time I went up trails which had about three inches of fesh-fesh (really fine sand) on them, I didn't come off and really felt that I could handle any type of trail on a motor-bike, which no doubt would be tested in South America.

By that evening my mood was a lot better, in two conversations with other bikers that day, at separate times they both referred to me as hardcore, I felt like I'd won the lotto!

Zion Canyon

The next day the temperature hit 51degC, my only reaction was to take a picture of the thermometer, "No one will ever believe this!" It's a curious thing when you see 51deg on the readout, all you want to do is see it go to 52. While stuck in a traffic jam in a town called Hurricane, with 51deg and a glacial flow of traffic on the way to Zion Canyon, I genuinely thought I was going to spontaneously combust. To cure it, I pulled off the road into a garage, went in and pulled a bottle of water out of the fridge, drank about half it, and poured the remainder down into my boxer shorts, man it felt good! Zion canyon was breathtaking, every now and then I would find myself saying a spontaneous, "Jesus Mary and Joseph!" or its close relation "Holy fuck!" Having lived in Phoenix for a while, I was amazed I'd never heard of it, I thought the place was better than the Grand Canyon, mainly because with Zion, the road travels right into the depths of the canyon. As you drive in the canyon, your head fills with the theme sounds of westerns, The Magnificent Seven, Bonanza, The High Chaparral, you get the gist. Every now and then a silly song would jump in to head too, "Oh the milkman is your friend in the neighborhood, in the neighborhood...." When I start singing the theme sound from Sesame Street I know it's time to get off the bike.

I was inching my way to the North rim of the Grand Canyon. I plumbed the destination into the GPS and selected the shortest distance setting. I started out from a place called Kanab and ten minutes into the journey I was back on the heavy gravel. I don't mind the dirt roads but not ten minutes after a lad is finished his ham and eggs. In total the unpaved portion was about forty miles long, and in the middle of it a mega storm opened up and the road turned to shite. The main worry I had was that I was passing through woods which were supposed to be full of bears and ill tempered squirrels; the North American Grey is known to have a penchant for Irish goolies. I parked up the bike at the Grand Canyon visitor centre and went under a shelter to dry off a bit. I was talking to a guy when a lad overheard my accent and said, "Where are ya from?" I said, "Ireland." "What part?" Dublin I replied (and this is where you know you've just met a paddy) "What part?" Clondalkin! There were three lads all from County Cork and they were on a road trip from Vancouver in Canada to México. They all needed to be back in Ireland for college on the 6th of September, in just 7 days time. We'd a great laugh and took some pictures around the canyon. The lads were traveling back in a jeep Cherokee which they bought in Vancouver for $800, they were having the time of their lives.

Route 66

From there I headed off for the South rim of the canyon, and even though its only ten miles away as the crow flies, it is over two hundred miles to drive. For the entire ride, on one side of the road there was pink desert and on the other side large red cliffs, the ride was awesome. Once done with the canyon I bolted for Flagstaff where I planned to stay that night. Along the way I was chased by storms, getting a bit wet was a welcome reprieve from the relentless heat. I was well ahead of schedule so I decided to knock out about four hundred miles on Route 66, which runs through Flagstaff. It was just like the movie "Cars" with all these old towns now kept alive only by tourists coming in to buy Route 66 memorabilia. The diners sell some of the best pie anywhere, I'd say the average person who completes the whole of Route 66 must end up putting on about twenty pounds with all the good eating en route. In a petrol station I picked up a brass token which said, "Good for 2 screws in dollys!", not bad for $3.69. The whole place was full of European tourists, as one biker remarked to me, "Neva saw so many eye-ties!"

There had been an unseasonal amount of rain in northern Arizona, and large chunks of the road were lined with beautiful yellow flowers which encroached onto the road and as I rode along I was able to hold out my left hand and touch them as I clipped along. The reason for all the mileage apart from doing the whole "it's cool to ride on Route 66" thing was because I woke up like a boar with a sore hole. I hardly got a winks sleep because the motel I stayed at in Flagstaff was right beside the train station. The trains ran all night and the drivers kept blowing their horns on the way past, I was picturing the driver in the engine room, "C'mere Cletus I'm gonna toot da horn an wake up all dem der fellers!"

On top of that they must have been serving oysters in the diner because the couple in the next room were going at it hammer and tongs for about two hours, yep that's right two hours. It started out gently enough but soon it was all "oh yeah, oh yeah, right there honey, right there, yeah, that's it, right there." This was soon followed with some course correction, "No honey, like I showed you, yes, that's it, right there, oh yeah baby right there!" This was just the woman talking. I resisted the temptation to roar in, "Ride her sideways!" To drown them out I turned on the TV and what was on? Basic instinct, more sex, nothing but reminders everywhere and the last time I had a shag you could buy a snickers for 25 cents. I was contemplating "Y'know I'd take an ice pick in the head to shag Sharon Stone, easily worth it." The only cure for me when I'm grumpy is to get on the road. I knocked out the first two hundred miles without even stopping. I pulled in and filled up and did another hundred, then stopped for some scrumptious apple pie and knocked out the final hundred staying in a town called Williams for the night.

Phoenix

I had kept in touch with an Intel colleague, Andy Flanagan who had moved to Phoenix and he invited me to stay with him to get the bike fixed up before heading south of the border. I met Andy about two hours north of Phoenix and we burned down for his place. I planned to give the bike to the BMW dealer and tell him, "Change anything that may or could go wrong between here and Quito in Ecuador, I can't afford to break down in Central America."

Phoenix is always roasting, it was September 1st and every day was still over a 100degF. I spent a great three days with Andy and his family and Andy who's also a keen biker ferried me around all the motorcycle stores so I could restock any of the gear I was missing or that was damaged.

After having had a great rest It was time to get going again. The only wrinkle was that the guys in WankerWorks in Calgary had broke a part of the rear shock where it connects onto the transmission, so it would be a $1200 dollar repair. Had I gone to the BMW dealer they would have covered the damages, but there it was, blue locktite, the BMW garages only used green so I had to fork over the cash.

Before I went further south it was time to go shopping for new underwear. Gone were the cotton boxers. While they looked nice, they were sawing me a mangina as a result of the many atomic wedgies one gets when riding around on a motorbike all day. I replaced them with black Lycra jocks, lovely stuff! They could easily make a brand of lycra underwear for men and call it wedgie free or wedgie proof. In Mexico I didn't think there would be as many launderettes, so all I would have to do at the end of the day is take these bad boys into the shower with me, do a disco on them while showering, squeeze em and hang em up, and the next morning they're dry as a pistachio. The only downside is that they're ultra snug, so you've a male camel toe going on while you're wearing them, y'know, the "division sign" rotated ninety degrees.

I'd been having conversations about crossing into Mexico with people along the way, nearly everyone I talked to thought I was plain crazy. I was beginning to doubt myself as these people lived just next door to Mexico, what made me think I knew more coming from Ireland? Most people who go to México go to a resort or on package holidays so don't ever get to see the underbelly. Apparently the border towns with the US are very violent with frequent robberies, murders and muggings. Needless to say, I wasn't looking forward to it. As I got closer and closer and was stopping in gas stations the tales of woe increased. One chap in particular really put the willies up me when he said “Man they’ll fucking shoot you, they’ll see you coming through and radio ahead and they’ll be fucking waiting, they’ll take you into the desert and kill you, rob your fucking bike and probably rape your ass!”

When I consulted the Irish department of foreign affairs they didn’t fill me with hope either. On their website the following warning was posted: There have been a high number of drug related assassinations in 2008 so far, particularly in the northern border and Pacific states. Seven people were killed and 130 injured when grenades were let off at Independence Day celebrations in Morelia, Michoacán most likely by members of a drugs gang. Foreign visitors and residents have been among the victims in the border region, including the cities of Nuevo Laredo, Tijuana, Ciudad Juárez, Nogales, Reynosa and Maramoros.

I didn’t want to go to Mexico, and I certainly didn’t want to go to Central America, these were areas on the trip that I had to get through to get to Ushuaia. I was petrified. I was pissed off that with so many folks online were saying that they were doing these trips, yet there was no one close by. I started to think that maybe these websites are full of bullshitter's who make up that they are out in the world traveling. I left Phoenix and headed for Tucson, it was my last night in the USA and I'd no idea what tomorrow would bring.

I took some advice on what area to cross and to avoid the bandits I decided to cross in a quieter town called Douglas, just to the east of Nogales. I had no idea what to expect. Realistically, traveling in Canada and the USA is a holiday. Sure you can have days where you have a hard ride but you know that at the end of the day you'll always be able to find a place to stay, and find somewhere to get something to eat. There's certainty when you're traveling there. Once I crossed that border my certainty was gone.

I left Andy Flanagan's place and burst out for Tucson the plan being to get close enough to the Mexican border so I could get to a town called Guaymos about two hundred miles south of the US border in the same day. When I left Tucson I headed south east and I wasn't long into the journey when I realized that I'd completely underestimated how far Douglas was from Tucson, and despite leaving the motel at about 8am, I arrived at the border at midday.

This was "it" I told myself, this is where the shit hits the fan, where the fun stops and the adventure begins. The amount of times I told myself, "Don't worry you'll meet up with people before you have to go through the borders." and yet there I was, going through on my own.

Chapter 5
Mexico

I was absolutely shitting myself as I crossed the border. The downside of arriving at midday was that I was hiking between customs and passport control in an Enduro suit and motorbike boots in 100degF heat, I was sweating like a whore in confession.

I parked up the bike and with no one around to watch it or my stuff, I was certain some of it was going to get swiped. If half of the stuff that I'd heard in the USA was true, any moment now I'd be robbed of my every possession. I went in for processing and to my complete surprise the Mexican border guards were great. They didn't get any Irish passports coming through that border and the guards took a real interest in the journey and had me out of customs and on my way in less than forty minutes. It was however, the first moment that I knew I was rightly fucked. I had no business being south of the border without knowing how to speak Spanish. Most people who go to Mexico go to resorts like Cancun or Acapulco where the locals are used to foreign visitors and most of the folks working in the tourist industry can speak English. In the border towns I was surprised to find out that no one spoke any English, and certainly couldn't comprehend what this big hairy arsed Irishman was saying. The difference between the USA and Mexico when you cross the border couldn't be starker. I thought it might get poorer as you go further south, but once you get across that border, that's it, people don't have a pot to piss in, at least that was the case in Douglas and a couple of the towns I drove through that first day. The route I chose was supposed to be quiet.

Hermosillo

Inadvertently I'd picked one of the most scenic areas to drive through in Northern Mexico, the Ruta Sierra. The scenery was top notch, but all I wanted to do was to get as far away from the border as possible, so if I'm honest I was a bit too nervous to enjoy it. The advice on Mexico I'd been given was that as long as you "Get the hell out of the border areas!" you should be fine. The speed limit on the roads was 80kph, a speed most three legged donkeys could do, so I ended up ignoring the limit and tipping along at about a 100kph.

In the first day, I was stopped three times by customs, the army and finally the police and none of them were for speeding. The customs guy was checking for the motorcycle permit, the army was checking for drugs and while they were talking to me, were busy with two North American girls whose stuff was all over the road, and finally the police were just stopping me to say hello and wondered where I was from and then what football team I supported. He'd noticed the Irish Registration plate and wanted to know was it "Liverpool" or "Manchester United."

Out on the road, I passed at least five people selling what I think was weed, I think they call it Juanita (wan-ita), although I was afraid to ask in case I was taken up the wrong way. The Mexicans appeared to be a devout crowd, all over the roads there were little houses for praying in and shrines where people were killed on the road. On cliff faces, I saw at least half a dozen murals, mainly of the Madonna. My first impressions of Mexico were that the people were very friendly and God fearing and I thought that I was going to like it. I spent that night with a copy of Spanish for Dummies, not being able to speak the "lingidy" left me feeling dumber than pig dribble all day.

I got as far as a city called Hermosillo, better known as the Sun City, the largest city in the state of Sonora. I lay in bed that night and I had to keep pinching myself, "Dude! You've just ridden your motorbike to Mexico!" The trip odometer was up over 16,000 miles and my head was all over the place. Hermosillo was a good town and the first thing I had to get used to was the food. Tacos, Tortillas, rice and beans would no doubt become staples for the next couple of weeks.

That night the heat was brutal. Gone was the air conditioning ubiquitous in the US, replaced with a fan that just rotated hot humid air around the room. I only had to comb my hair to break into a sweat. When you walk out into the air and it's like walking into a warm wet sponge, and this wasn't even supposed to be a humid area. I kept on thinking to myself, what is it that this climate does to the human body that the reaction it fires physiologically is "All the water in my body, get out now!" With all the sweating my motorbike boots smelt like an old used gym bag that you'd left in the boot of the car for a year.

The next day I headed for the coastal town of Guaymos taking the Ruta 15 to the Pacific coast. The last time I'd seen the ocean was in Valdez Alaska and it seemed such a long time ago. That day I did quite a bit of wandering on the bike touring around the mountains, one in particular called Sierra Libre really caught my attention with its name. The scenery was good without being spectacular, but I couldn't help thinking that I'd made a mistake by going to Alaska, Alberta and the US Rockies so early in the trip, would anything be able to compare to it?

I spun over to San Carlos which is the tourist zone of Guaymos and spent a day mucking around by the beach. The hotels owned huge sections of the beach, and you couldn't just walk out onto it, large areas were reserved just for guests. The pier in the town is full of American owned boats and yachts that are sailed down from the US. I'd seen many poor people that day and something felt wrong to be looking out at the sun setting with all these expensive boats in the foreground. I had put the bike up onto the centre stand and was sitting relaxing with the lovely view when a gold pickup full of drunken Mexican youths pulled up and the guys started to walk over. I just played the dumb Irishman card and it all passed off without a hitch. The driver of the pickup was completely wasted. He was drinking cans by the pier and then with the rest of his buddies hopped straight into the truck and drove away. It's tough to listen to drunken people at the best of times, but when they're Mexican and only know two lines of English, which was one more line than I knew in Spanish, it was tough going. Alcohol is sold everywhere along the road. You can stop in a shack by the side of the road and have a Corona or a Pacifico, it seemed that drink driving was no big deal.

Navajoa

I continued on the Ruta 15 for the third day to a town called Navajoa. I was doing very low mileage, an average of less than a hundred and fifty miles a day, it was just too warm and humid to be out and about. The people were brilliant, genuinely friendly although I didn't have a clue what they were saying, I just kept smiling and nodding. It was strange for a guy like me, I've always used humor (or at least tried to!) as a way to get to know people and communicate with them, but no one there had the slightest clue what I was on about. In Navajoa I stopped in a motel which had a pool and that night I lay floating in it looking up into a sky full of stars with the most gorgeous soft warm breeze blowing against my toes and face, "Man, this is the life!" On the downside, I'd two fox sized cockroaches in my bathroom, Mexico is a country of extremes. Navajoa was completely off the English-speaking tourist trail as were most of the cities that far north in Mexico so the plan was to keep moving on. I set off early the next morning, the trees in the car park of the motel were full of birds that made a fantastic racket as the sun was rising and covered my bike with bird shit.

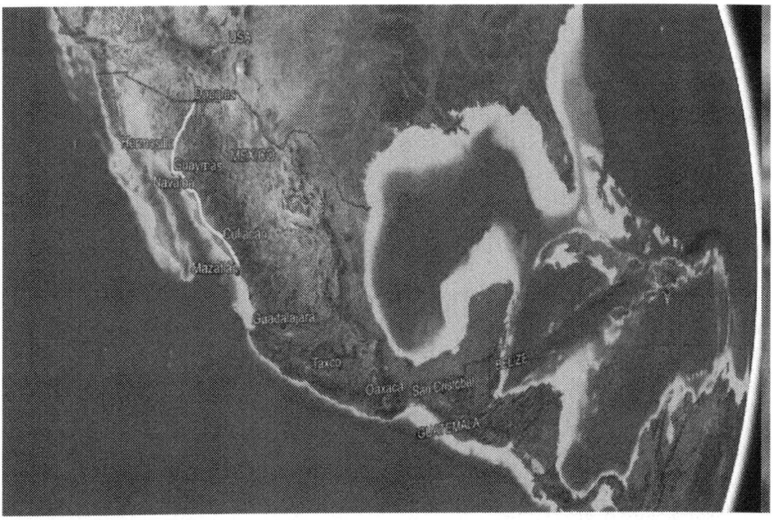

The poverty in the small towns I came across along the way was humbling and the gap between rich and poor seemed vast, there was nothing in the middle, you were either very rich or very poor. I made a point of only going to places to eat and drink which looked "clean and poor" if you know what I mean, I wanted to give the peso's to people who were struggling, but obviously I was keen not to risk blowing out an O-ring in the process.

People get to work by whatever means they could in that part of Mexico, it was common to see six or seven people all piled into the back of an open truck. It seemed so farcical that in the western world we had laws that say you must fasten your seat belts in the back of a car and there everyone bundles in wherever they can find room.

Mexico has two types of roads, the Ruta Cuota, which are toll roads, and the Ruta Libre, which are free. On the Cuota roads, every sixty miles or so I hit a toll road, and these weren't cheap, you would have to pay about five dollars to get through. The fallout of this tolling is that given so many people are poor in Mexico, the Ruta Cuota are completely empty and the Ruta Libre are tremendously congested.

Military check points are very common, and combined with police checkpoints it would make you wonder what's the undercurrent in the society that makes this necessary? I surmised that it was probably drugs. I didn't think I'd ever get used to seeing half a dozen young men with guns, but in fairness to them, they were always very courteous and polite.

Anytime I hit a check point I'd go through the same routine taking my passport out first "No NorteAmericano Señor, Soy Irlanda si?" and smile like I just won the lotto. They would look at the picture and look at the head on me and I would make a face which was supposed to say, "Eets the sun Señor!" Being in Mexico made me feel very far away from home, on top of that I was getting lost at least twice a day (GPS didn't work). The maps I was carrying and the road signs gelled about as well as oil and water. Getting directions unfortunately was in the next chapter of Spanish for dummies. Why not read that first I hear you ask? I was still trying to get through ordering grub, eat first travel later.

Mazatlan

I passed into the state of Sinaloa, which I thought sounded like something from the High Chaparral or the Magnificent Seven and stopped in the city of Culiacan for a bite of grub. In these places wearing a big enduro suit and being about a foot taller than the average Mexican, I stood out like a purple cow. There were only ten customers or so in the restaurant but there was a twenty-piece brass band beating out samba like music. The din was unreal, but it was pure magic. I got a savage feed for about five dollars, not surprising that Mexico is the worlds second most obese country, the first is a couple of hundred miles north. The next town on my itinerary, which by the way I was making up as I went along, Mazatlan, was a tourist destination and so was a bit more built up than I normally like.

The motel I stayed obviously doubled as a knocking shop because in the room was a strippers pole sitting up on a table surrounded by chairs. By the bed there was a dispenser for tissues. It was only when I turned on the TV and saw that it was wall to wall porn that it fully dawned on me. I should have tweaked it when the hotel charged by the hour. I bought twelve hours for $18 dollars, not bad. The chap on the way to the room kept asking me something in Spanish which I didn't understand, looking back, it was probably did I want any women. Mexico has a big population and in the cities its very overcrowded, so if you have a girlfriend it's very unlikely you'll get a free house to have a shag. So the youth, people having affairs, not to mention people who pick up prostitutes all converge on motels to take care of the Dick Dastardly deed. I found this out later on and it explained all the strange looks I received when I asked people were there any motels nearby.

That night I went out to a seafood restaurant and had a massive plate full of freshly caught shrimp washed down with plenty of drink, suffice to say I left the table late. While I was chowing down, a really loud and angry storm hit, it was the monsoon season so the rain was torrential. The whole area was being battered due to several systems in the Gulf of Mexico sending their storm tails that direction. On the way back to the motel I had to drive through 6 inches of rain lying on the road. Standing up on the pegs of the bike going through this sort of stuff is great fun. Most evenings there were storms filled with lightning and flash floods. Far from being a hazard, I genuinely thought this was one of the peak experiences of the trips for me, the stuff that was happening was just so completely unlike anything that happened in Europe or North America. Further along the road as I came over a hill, I had a beautiful tropical wind blowing into my face and out in the distance lightning was flaring in a completely black sky, the view was magical. I went off to hotel for a good night's sleep and just a bit of porn to help drown out the noise from all the amorous couples busy shagging all round me.

As I checked the route for the next day's ride, I realized I had also just crossed the Tropic of Cancer, which gave me a tremendous sense of achievement and had also gone over 17,000 miles - I was over halfway through the trip.

The next day I set off for Manzanillo on the Ruta 200, a Ruta Libre. I took the free roads because the cost of the tolls was brutal. Normal Mexicans who live in the countryside cant afford the toll roads so I decided to join them, well, what a complete and utter fuck story that turned out to be! The Ruta 200 takes you through every small town on the pacific coast and the poverty is overwhelming. The roads disintegrated and at times are no more than gravel and mud tracks peppered with gigantic potholes. When I was coming around a bend in the pissing rain, doing about 30mph the bike skidded out from under me. The bike and I slid along the ground for about twenty yards with my left leg trapped underneath the bike. Three or four Mexican lads jumped out of a truck and picked the bike off me and helped me to my feet, my left ankle felt like I'd broke it.

Hospital

The thing that saved my life apart from the fact that I wasn't going too fast was that in Mexico you drive on the right side of the road, so as I slid I just went off the road and not into oncoming traffic. About ten minutes later the police arrived and started yakking in Spanish, well why wouldn't they it was Mexico after all, but I didn't have a clue what they were saying. One of them spoke a bit of English and told me there was diesel on the road at the bend.

Within about fifteen minutes we were off to the hospital in a town called Tepic in a police car. The bike was driven behind the police car by one of the police officers who appeared to be having a rare oul time. The bike had come off remarkably unscathed. One of mirrors was fucked, the wind shield was scratched to bits, the panniers were scratched along with the tank bag, the ABS no longer worked but other than that it was tip top, the BMW 1150 is a bullet proof machine. We got to the hospital in Tepic under police siren at about 10am and the police brought me to the emergency area, it was absolute chaos. I guess because I was a gringo I was seen quickly. The doctor aided by two nurses told me to strip off in Espanyol by doing the motions. I cringed, remembering that I was wearing the trusty Lycra boxers so when I dropped the enduro trousers the nurses started bursting their shite laughing. I was hobbling, so they got me a wheel chair and wheeled me down to the x-ray area. It turned out there was no break just a serious amount of swelling, thank you my lovely motorbike boots! Armed with painkillers and anti-inflammatory tablets I was sent on my way, the only trouble I had driving was changing gears which hurt like hell. As I'm sitting here, writing several years later my left leg still hurts which should give you an idea of how sore it was at the time.

At 2pm I set off for Puerto Vallarta, a coastal resort in the state of Jalisco on the pacific coast, it was a good ways off but I needed to get some miles up on the bike to get my confidence back. I kept imagining problems with the bike, "Was that a wobble, the steering feels weird, the weight distribution is a mile off." In spite of my paranoia, I got there about 4pm but it felt like an American town in Mexico. I decided I'd drive through it and stay in one of the towns just south of it. This turned out to be a huge mistake. Town after town that I went through were complete and utter shit holes with no hotels or places to stay anywhere to be seen. Don't take me the wrong way, The Mexican people are the best in the world, the food is amazing but the conditions in some of these towns was brutal. Mexico's modern cities rival anything in Europe or America, but parts of the country are in appalling condition.

Manzanillo

For the next three hours riding on the Ruta 200, it wasn't so much a drive as an obstacle course. Pot holes, horses and cows on the road, lunatic driving, torrential rain, dogs trying to take a lump out of your boot as your driving and in places large amounts of sand on the road. In case you don't know, putting sand on the road is like putting a couple of gallons of KY Jelly down if your on a bike, you can't get traction and slide all over the place. At about 7pm I was stopped by the federal police at a checkpoint. At this point I was so tired, fucked off and sore that I couldn't be arsed with my big smiling paddy routine. I reaped having to unpack all my stuff from the pike so these hombres could check through it. I tried to explain why I was having difficulty getting off the bike but it got lost in translation.

When they were done I had ninety minutes of driving still to go to get to Manzanillo all of which would be on the Ruta 200 in the pitch dark. In those hundred miles, I hit rock bottom. The road was full of massive potholes that nearly threw me over the handlebars and with the fading light, it was almost impossible to see them. On top of that, there were many hidden speed ramps. The roads were covered with sand causing me to nearly skid off several times (The ABS wasn't working as a result of the crash), I was nearly driven off the road twice by oncoming trucks, I was soaked to the skin by torrential rain and to top it all off I had to contend with a couple of mudslides covering the road. All of this was going on while my leg was throbbing like someone was playing a trombone in my boot.

With the visor down you are blinded by oncoming traffic as the light reflects through the rain and dirt on the visor, conversely if you keep the visor up the light from the bike attracts thousands of insects so your eyes and face get milled. In the end you reach a compromise position, where the visor is half up and your viewing angle is just above the wind shield about three square inches in size. It took me till 10pm to get to Manzanillo, after one of the worst days I'd ever spent on the road.

I got to a hotel completely knackered. I didn't even bother showering and just hit the scratcher. I kept trying to tell myself as my mood descended into the abyss, "It's not everyone who gets away so light after coming off a bike." I lay in the bed that night and said what every man over the age of thirty says when confronted with a crisis, "I want my mammy!"

The next morning I only had time for a cup of coffee and a bite standing. I had to head off to the BMW dealer in Guadalajara to get the ABS fixed and while I left the bike there to be checked out and fixed up, I headed off to the hospital to get my side x-rayed. Even though it was 24 hours later, I woke up that morning feeling as if someone had helped themselves to one of my kidneys. Everything checked out fine on both fronts, in the hospital I must have come across as a total Benny, trying to explain what happened with just a phrase book and a very poor mime display. A doctor came along who spoke English and he laughed like a hyena when I told him the tale from the previous days, especially about the Lycra shorts.

I left Guadalajara and rode to a town called Morelia, a colonial town with a centre completely preserved in the colonial tradition. The only downside to the town was that it had throngs of beggars, mostly native Americans, it was clear that in the pecking order of society in Mexico, as was the case in Canada and the US, the Indians were at the bottom.

The following day I treated myself by mostly riding the toll roads as they cut a beautiful path through rolling hills and farmlands. The countryside was full of bushes in flower, I thought it was like riding through a painting. It turned out the following weekend was Mexican Independence Day and most of the towns I rode through were gearing up for the festivities. Judging by the preparation that was going on, this was a serious party in Mexico.

I stopped by a roadside cafe, which was a place with an impromptu cooker fired by flames from sticks, with four tables and chairs, where you could either sit or stand. I pulled over and asked for quesadillas, it had been almost a week since I talked to anyone bar the Doctor in Guadalajara so I decided I was going to just talk to this oul one whether she understood me or not.

It went something like this: Me: Buenos tardez Señorita (Good evening) Oul one: Buenos tardez Señor Me: Me no hablez Espanyol señorita (forlorn hope that she might speak English, yeah right. It’s common for poor people who operate roadside restaurants to be bilingual, not!) “You have quesadillas por favor?” At this point I was getting disowned by the writer of Spanish for Dummies. Oul one: Si, then something in Spanish followed which I think meant how many would you like. Me: cinqo por favor (Giz five missus) She then started to cook away at the grub Me: Feckin rain is brutal eh? I started making motions with my hands like it was raining Oul one: Si blah blah blah blah blah blah Rafael Benitez blah blah blah Me: Jaysus I’d love a skin full of Carlsberg in the laurels (local pub), or even a couple of pints of Guinness, although you’d probably need to go to steering wheel (alternate local with decent Guinness) for them, down stairs bar. (Gratuitous hand gestures by the big fella) Oul one: (English translation) Ive no fucking clue what you’re saying you gringo bollix, and if you don’t stop annoying me I’m going to put the juice of a dog into your food

One of the biggest challenges of Mexico lay ahead of me the following day, namely to get to the other side of Mexico City, a teeming urban sprawl with over twenty million inhabitants. I made my way from Morelia to the city outskirts and after coughing up nearly $80 in tolls, I hit the outskirts of the city and with it almost instant logjam. The traffic was insane, I don't think anywhere in the world except maybe India compares to it (I've never been to India but it looks bad on the TV).

The traffic was stopped and made no sign of moving. There was a flood of people, no different than any big city there, the difference being that so many of these people were walking on the road. When the traffic stops, an armada of people walk into the traffic selling every manner of goods. Rafts of window cleaner's descend on the cars and beggars bring their most pitiable face to the fore to scab money from the car and truck drivers who are stuck there for hour after hour. The smog is horrendous, and the fumes coming from trucks and buses that should long ago have been used for spare parts is awful. The only way to deal with it is to turn into a happy nutcase by beeping the horn at everyone, copious use of the finger, break red lights and weave in and out of stalled traffic. If you lined up all the traffic offenses

I made trying to move around Mexico City it would be enough to put me in Sam Quentin for ten years, but it was good fun in a perverted sort of way. I'd hate to have to live through that everyday, but to do it once was an experience. After two hours battling through it and making it only ten miles, I gave up and headed south to break free of it. I made my mind up that this would be the last big city I would go to on the trip except for Santiago in Chile and Buenos Aires in Argentina.

Once you head south out of Mexico City the scenery is excellent, lots of mountains and rolling hills with whole acres covered in beautiful pink and yellow flowers. When it comes to enjoying the scenery in Mexico, the only gripe I would have is that the Mexican tourist board have not bothered to put any lay-bys or scenic area signs on the side of the road. As your riding along you might come across a great looking mountain, river or lake but there's nowhere to pull in and take a picture of it. I guess if you are the government of Mexico your first priority would be better roads, and then work on the lay-bys.

When I arrived into the town of Taxco in Mexico, the trip odometer just clocked over 18,000 miles and per the original plan I'd about 60% of the journey complete. In the process, I had crossed different 10 different time zones and had driven well south of the tropic of cancer. I had done about 3000 miles more than I expected to getting to this point with all the diversions and detours I ended up taking every day, so the final trip distance was likely to be somewhere between thirty and thirty-five thousand miles. It was also the 12th of September, exactly two months since I arrived in Toronto. It is fair to say that the bike had a good workout since then.

Taxco

I decided that I was going to stay in Taxco for five days, mainly to rest up after the crash. My body still felt like shit so I wanted to get myself healthy before taking on Central America. The town is the silver capital of Mexico and they have some really unusual jewelry, inevitably I ended up buying a good bit of stuff and had to stop myself before I ended up looking like Mr T.

This was the first time I'd really stopped on the trip since Valdez and I was keen to soak it up. It was such a culture shock but it's the culture that makes the place what it is I guess, and it was definitely starting to grow on me, although it had taken a while. While I was getting my bearings in the town it felt like every old Volkswagen beetle or van ever made seemed to be in Taxco, there was thousands of them. I stayed in a hotel perched on the side of a mountain and the balcony in my room was perched on the Cliffside looking down on a yawning valley below. I spent the first night in the room reading the Lord of the rings and chilling out. At about 4am I heard an unbelievable scream from the valley below the hotel which sent a huge shiver through my whole body. It turned out there was a pig abattoir down in the valley and the screams from the pigs was eerily like the ring wraiths from the Lord of the Rings. Obviously they use traditional methods for slaughtering, the noise would scare the living shit out of you, specially if you're woken from a sleep at 4am by it, but no one seems to mind.

The noise the whole time I was in Mexico, especially in towns was way above what one would come to expect even in the busiest of European cities. You've got to love mayhem to love Mexico, it's that simple. If you're out in the square having a coffee, at any one time you're competing with election cars screaming out their candidates merits, construction of various stands, mental traffic with more use of the horn than a Kerry Ram and hundreds of street sellers selling every manner of good imaginable. Suffice to say, if its peace and quiet you like, Mexican towns and cities are not for you. There is no doubt it creates an incredible buzz and atmosphere.

I was sitting at the square reading a book when this oul one of about eighty-five sat down beside me. After about ten minutes she cleared her throat and hocked up as big a greener as I've ever seen and gollied it onto the ground beside where we were sitting. She looked at me with a face that said, "What?" I hope there are birds like that around when I'm eighty-five, she was a real find.

The murder rate in Mexico is twice what it is in the USA, and its thirteenth on the world list for AIDS and HIV, so as I was advised very wisely, if in the highly unlikely event that I was to meet a Señorita, "Make sure you double bag!" I gave it a miss, although it wasn't like I had to turn down any offers.

Later that day I met my first English-speaking person since arriving in Mexico. Her name was Alex and she was a trainee doctor from Wales, volunteering near Mexico City in a hospital for the summer. I took one look at her and said to myself "Where were ya in Guadalajara when I needed ya Alex?" She was only twenty years old, a fine thing and over in Mexico alone, it turned out that traveling alone came easy to her, she did the same thing four years previous hiking in Namibia. There is always someone to knock you off your hardcore perch. It was great to have a yap with someone who spoke English and I blabbed my head off for a couple of hours over a couple of tall frosty beers. She told a great story about hiking for sixteen days without changing clothes while in Namibia and at the end of the hike, the whole group burned their clothes. I said to her "Sixteen days without a wash! No wonder the lions didn't come near ya!"

We yapped about Mexico and all the things you see that you don't see in Europe, and stole Leonardo de Caprio's line from the movie Blood Diamonds about Africa "TIA baby, This is Africa" uttered every time you see something completely fucked up, and changed it to "TIM, This is Mexico!" The next day Alex headed away to Mexico City and she was almost running from me. I knew what had happened, the last time I had talked to anyone was Andy Flanagan in Phoenix and I'd given her a pain in her hole. Talking to me was like trying to drink from a fire hydrant as I tried to cram in two months worth of conversation into an evening. It wasn't to be the first time that I scared people off with this particular character trait.

When I asked Rafael "What are the women like in Mexico?" over a beer in Black Diamond, he made a face something like you would make after being asked whether the weather is good in Ireland. Well, let me take Rafael's comments a bit further. The women there are very attractive, but they age like milk. There are many lovely looking young ones but once they hit about forty, well, the wheels start to come off the wagon, ill tidings indeed for a thirty-seven year old Dublin lad traveling with a stork on him that would knock apples out of a tree!

Independence Day in Mexico was one I won't forget in a hurry.

The day started out great with singing and dancing in the square with kids dressed in colonial garb dancing on a stage. The place was packed and the atmosphere was electric.

Later in the afternoon, I had the first of the day's dodgy encounters, namely English gap-year student travelers. If you come across them, don't approach them for they are deadly. I met them just outside the church in the square, two girls and a guy, all from in and around the London area. They were all about twenty, a bigger bunch of "know it all's" you have never met. They asked me what I was doing here, I just used one of Rafael's lines and said I was a drug dealer. I said good luck and wished them well.

As the afternoon wore on everyone went home for a siesta as beer stands and bandstands were set up in the square for that evenings festivities. I knew it would be packed later so I went back to the hotel to drop off my valuables. I had a bit of a kip, a shite and a shower and headed back down to the square packing lightly, just cash and the key for the room in the hotel. I was certain there'd be a heap of baddies down there at some stage so best not to carry a wallet or anything valuable that could be whipped. Another in a long line of mistakes as it turned out. The beer stands were selling corona for about $1.50 a bottle. Everyone was in a great mood and as the band cracked open a few tunes, there was lots of "Viva Mexico!" to be heard all round the square. By about 10pm the mood was getting a little bit more aggressive and there were plenty of dodgy looking hombres knocking around so I said to myself, "Ok after this one call it a night." Note I'd only four bottles total, so I wasn't even the slightest bit drunk.

The Cop shop

I was standing off to the left of the square where two cobble lanes met at right angles, one to go downhill to the circulation road, and one to go up to someplace else. All of a sudden, an Indian girl who was selling cakes was beset upon by two other Indian girls and a guy. My guess was that they have turfs where they allow certain groups to sell stuff, or maybe they didn't like her, I'm just guessing. The guy landed a hefty smack on the girl's face. The girl started crying so I went over to her aid, pushing the guy against the wall and standing between the two girls and the girl they were attacking. I turned to her and said "Vamoose, pronto!", while at the same time motioning to a guy who was standing beside me to come over and help "Señor, por favor!" It wasn't difficult to guess what I meant, but he just turned and walked away into the crowd. I roared after him "Hey Rat features, come back here and give me a fucking hand ya prick." Before I knew it, a sea of people had descended on us. There was cake, drink, nachos and God knows what else flying around, not to mention pushing and shoving coming from every angle. I was in the middle, comfortably a foot taller than everyone else saying to myself "Nice one Ois, nice one." Next thing I knew whistles started going like crazy and what felt like about twenty police officers showed up. "Thank god" I said to myself, except that they started loading me and forty other people into their vans. I was saying to the officer "Hablez Ingles, I was only trying to help, where the fuck are we going?" The door slammed shut on the van and a moment of complete and utter silence followed.

I was sitting on a small bench looking around at about twelve or thirteen other people, who once the van got going, started roaring and shouting. I sat there feeling like a right fucking idiot and in keeping with every other day I'd spent in Mexico, I didn't have a clue what people were saying. I wasn't excessively worried as the police officers weren't too aggressive as they were loading us in, it wasn't a riot if you know what I mean. After only about five hundred yards, we arrived at what turned out to be a police station and we were marched into an area with rows of seats like a church in front of a desk where I guessed we were going to be processed. I sat there thinking to myself, "If one of these lads can't speak English I'm fucked!"

Sure enough, as people were getting led up to the desk it was the turn of one of the girls who did the initial attacking. She started pointing to me and shouting angrily, while talking to the police officer. Then, another girl who I guessed was her sister jumped up and started shouting and making similar gesticulations. "Ah here!" I said to myself and I walked up the counter thinking, "I'm going to say my piece and I couldn't give a rats ass if no one understands me." "Hablez ingles?" I said to the officer to which he replied "No." I looked to the ceiling and said, "Fuuuuuuuuuuuck it anyway!" Undeterred I went into a monologue in English: "Right Señor...I was standing there just having a beer when Pocahontas here ..." (about five police officers started roaring laughing) "and Pocahontas dos(2), and Hiawatha over there started attacking this señorita." "All I did was block them, that's it."

Since the officers were laughing, the sisters went ballistic, all of them were about four foot tall, and it was like getting roared at by a bunch of Lilliputians. "Calm the fuck down!" I roared at them as the noise in the barracks descended into anarchy. The police came out from behind the counter with their hands on their batons and told everyone to sit down and be quiet, or at least that's what I think they said. Everyone was sitting saying nothing in about five seconds flat. I was the only one left standing in the room. Seeing as I was standing, they started to take my details, first looking for ID. "Boooollllllllliiiiiixxxxxxx" I thought to myself, my ID and wallet was in the hotel where I'd intentionally left it in case I got pick pocketed. Not having ID was a big deal, so I started to play the paddy card, "Irlandes Señor!" to which he looked at me as if to say, "So what?" With that, none other than the guy (Rat Features) who walked away from the disturbance in the square walked in and started talking to the police men, pointing at me. Right about then I was really sorry that I'd called him rat features but he walked over to me with the police officer who said, "Amigo, you are free to go" to which I replied "Nice one, nice one, Gracias amigo, Gracias." They asked me what hotel I was staying in and rat features gave me a lift home. He had broken English so we didn't have much of a conversation. My hotel was less than a mile from the police station, but I gleaned enough to understand that all of the folks would be let go in stages over the next hour or so, they were just getting them off the streets. I thanked him and was lying on the bed sipping a bottle of water at 11:30pm thinking to myself, "All that in ninety minutes? Zorro me bollix, he doesn't have a patch on me!"

Mexico celebrates independence over two days, during the second day I kept a very low profile, but to be honest, the above probably reads worse than it was, it never really felt out of control. The stupid side of me wanted to get put in a cell for a while just to say I'd been in one, the non stupid side gave the stupid side a good kick in the goolies and told him to cop on.

Oaxaca

I left Taxco in the rain and headed for Oaxaca one of the more highly recommended towns in all the travel guides. It was supposed to be a great place, full of old Colonial buildings and a Mecca for back packers in this part of the world. It was about two hundred and fifty miles away and the vast majority of the road was Ruta Libre, which just meant absolutely shite roads with large amounts of mental drivers. The journey there was slow going with almost all of the miles running through fog-covered mountains. It took every minute of eight hours to get there. The roads surface was appalling with huge tire shredding potholes and bollix flattening hidden speed ramps.

When I finally got to Oaxaca, I realized that one of my bags was gone. No doubt, it was shaken off due to all the bumps and potholes. What was in it? All my memory cards holding the pictures of the trip so far, my laptop, my journal where I kept all the trip logs, a copy of all my confidential information, Spanish books, maps and a copy of Lord of the Rings which I'd bought in Phoenix. I lost the rag completely, I had lost all the original records of the trip so far apart from what was posted on my blog site and I had no one to blame but myself. It's not like I didn't know the roads were crap there, but because it was raining I rushed packing up my stuff. I lost thousands of pictures of parts of the world, I was unlikely ever to see again, it was a sore blow. Worse was to come.

I stripped off, changed, and said I better go down to the

police station and let them know, maybe someone would hand it in. On the way, I hit heavy traffic and these guys, as is normal when you come to stop in busy traffic came out onto the road cleaning car windows. These weren't the normal squad of down and outs as it turned out. I was stopped, boxed in on all sides by buses and cars. Just then, I felt a blow to the right of my head and on my left out of nowhere a guy was pulling my watch off. I was trying to pull back but in his sponge he had a knife which he waved at me. Startled, I pulled back, in the process getting another punch in the back of the head. He pulled at my left arm and because my left leg was weak, being the one that slid under the bike when I crashed a week earlier, I fell to the ground with the bike on top of me as this guy ran off with the watch. As I lay on the ground as if to complete the misery, my GPS dropped off its mount and landed on my face, right in the schnoz. Thankfully, the bike didn't land on my leg so I was able to pick myself up, by which time the bandits were long gone. It was a strange feeling I went through just then, a calm just before I boiled.

I picked up the bike and put it on its stand. I was surrounded by traffic and was boiling emotionally like a kettle. At that moment the guy who was stopped behind me beeped his horn, as if to say, "Move! You are blocking the road" This was the same dude who saw everything that happened and did nothing to help me. In a complete fit of rage I pitched the GPS unit straight at his front windscreen, smashing it in the process. I walked the bike over to the side of the road out of the traffic, and he pulled in behind me. I saw him on the phone and knew the police would be on the way soon. He never got out of the car, he knew I was in a fit of temper. I sat there for about ten minutes boiling over till the police arrived. The whole process with the police took about ten minutes and I ended up having to pay about $200 for the guy's windscreen. There was never any chance that they would catch these guys, and the watch I didn't care about. Would you believe after standing there talking to them I forgot to tell them about losing the bag on the road.

I headed to the motel and boiled the night away. I think the annoying thing about the whole losing the bag, and getting robbed "thing" was that I'd only myself to blame, but that doesn't make you feel any better about it, it just makes it worse if anything. I spent the night shoulding, "Should have done this, should have done that" As soon as I realized I'd lost the bag I wanted to leave Mexico, I just wanted to go home.

San Cristobal de Las Casas

The only cure I had for a spiraling mood was to get on the road, which I did at 5am the next morning and drove for over four hundred miles over mountain roads through some of the worst driving conditions I've ever seen. Mexico was too much like hard work for me. I decided that I was burning for the border with Guatemala via San Cristobal de las Casas the next day.

San Cristobal is in the Chiapas region of Mexico known to be a revolutionary stronghold. As I crossed into Chiapas, people were waving hello and it seemed to me that it was a particularly friendly place. To get to the town you climb out of a valley and onto a plateau. As I climbed the sun was setting bathing the entire valley below in orange light.

San Cristobal turned out to be a magic spot, despite the fact that the town is ringed with people living in excruciating poverty. I stayed in the Hacienda Don Juan, which was run by a very friendly innkeeper, he was an absolute gentleman. I stayed there two days to get my documentation and my head in order before riding into Guatemala. While I was wandering around the town I went into an English bookshop run by an elderly American woman. I'd only one question to ask, "Do you have a copy of the Lord of the Rings?" "Of course I do" was the reply, I was over the moon.

I met two folks in the town who used to work for the same company as I did. Jennifer and Lorraine were off on a backpacking adventure and that night we headed out for a couple of beers and a bit of nose bag. Both were on the road about two weeks and it was magic to have a natter with folks from home for a couple of hours.

The next day I met two Irish aid workers who were with Trocaire, an Irish aid agency. Mary and Maureen worked in Guatemala on various projects and they did a lot to allay some of the concerns I had about crossing the border.

I was coming to the end of my time in Mexico, and I reflected on the variety that was in every day, good roads, bad roads, check points, lovely scenery, people crammed onto the backs of trucks, grossly overloaded vehicles shedding their load, horrendous poverty, but every day the constant was that the people were wonderful. I passed a poor oul bastard in a wheel chair sitting in the middle of the road collecting coins from passing traffic. He was about ninety years of age. Imagine in your retirement having to look forward to being wheeled out into the middle of the road to beg from passing cars, with the way they drive in Mexico! I tell you a nursing home doesn't look so bad after that! He was smiling his head off, I guess there was nothing on the telly or his wife was giving out, "I've had enough, roll me out onto the road!"

While I was in an internet cafe, I started to instant message a friend back home. I was telling him that I was terrified about crossing into Central America. I had a read part of the Lonely Planet regarding Guatemala and based on what it said you wouldn't go to Guatemala in a million years, a direct quote "In villages lynchings are a near daily occurrence." He told me to just go back up to the states, that I'd gone far enough and that no one would have expected me to make it the whole way anyway. "Well, fuck that for a game of soldiers!" I told myself, "Finish what you've started Oisin."

My form had completely turned, I was back in good spirits. When you see how poor some of the people are in Mexico, and how little possessions they have and yet they are smiling and seem very content you just can't stay in bad form for long. I talked with a friend on the phone about it and we concluded that the reality was that these people had almost no chance of escaping poverty whereas I was only ever a flight away from home, it helped put things in perspective for me.

I left San Cristobal and headed south for Guatemala. I knew for certain it was going to be more difficult than Mexico, more physically dangerous, have worse roads and be much poorer. It officially marked the start of Central America, the bit of the journey I feared the most.

Chapter 6
Central America

I did some research regarding travel advice for Guatemala before I crossed the border and one paragraph which I copied from the British Travel advisory website summed up how I was feeling about it: Guatemala has one of the highest violent crime rates in Latin America with around 40 murders a week in Guatemala City alone and a total of 98 per week in the whole country. Although the majority of serious crime involves gangs or narcotics and does not occur in tourist areas, violent attacks on tourists, including carjackings, assault, armed robbery, murder and rape have increased in the past few years and can happen anywhere. Guns are commonly used, and there is a low arrest and conviction rate for perpetrators. You should take your personal security seriously and be aware of your surroundings at all times. If the above doesn't give you a feeling of how bad things could get, another way to put it is, that there are more murders in Guatemala in a year than there were in over thirty years of the troubles in Northern Ireland. Rafael had warned me not to watch the news or I'd be too scared to go out and I'd also been told that a week earlier a chicken bus had driven off a cliff with all fifty-five passengers killed, the bus driver had been drinking.

The two Irish aid workers I'd met in San Cristobal had also told me that they were a little afraid for me traveling on a motorcycle based on what they had seen on the roads there.

With all this in my mind I got up later than normal. I went and had breakfast and for the first time on the trip I caught myself arsing around the place. I was putting off the crossing into Central America, I was absolutely terrified. Some of the stuff I was doing when I look back on it was surreal.

It felt like all that stuff you do before you start studying for a big exam, buy new pens, and jotters, for what I had no idea, anything to put off the inevitable.

The cafe where I had breakfast was blaring out some awful Jazz music, which was enough to spur me to muster up the courage to leave. I drove the hundred or so miles from San Cristobal to the border and as I approached Guatemala the road deteriorated until it was almost impossible to drive on, no one seemed to be maintaining this last little section of road.The border was a sea of people and in nearly every bank or entrance to an official building there were armed security guards holding pump action shotguns, not the sort of place you would get into an argument with the chap behind the counter.

The problem with crossing these borders on your own is that you have to go through three steps sometimes in three different buildings. First, you have to stamp out of the country your leaving, then stamp into the next country and lastly the most difficult part, you have to temporarily import the motorcycle into the next country. The whole time you're doing this, there is no one to watch your bike and with all your stuff packed on the top of it surrounded with a flood of people, it's impossible not to feel helpless.

The only protection I left on the bike was a set of Rosary beads hanging around the handlebars. The people in Central America are devout and even the worst rapscallion might think twice about robbing from a Catholic Gringo, not that I'm religious but if drinking horse piss would have made it easier to pass through those borders then that's what I would have done. I made it through eventually after much gnashing of teeth and copious amounts of "tsk tsk's" aimed in my direction. I was bluffing the whole way and decided enough was enough, I had to take some Spanish lessons. I couldn't hope to continue to get by playing the lovable "Mick." I headed off in the direction of a town called Quetzaltenango (say that with a couple of pints on you) and for once what I had heard about the driving conditions i.e. that the roads were even more chaotic than Mexico was absolutely true."Yeah yeah" I hear you say? Well, to put some statistics on it, your 16000% more likely to get killed in Mexico and Guatemala on the roads driving a motorcycle than you are driving a car in Britain or Ireland. Now put hat in your pipe and smoke it.

Quetzaltenango

The further I drove, the worse the road safety conditions became. Buses and trucks were over taking on bends often that it seemed to be almost mandatory. I saw three near miss collisions, and every couple of miles there were land-slides which had destroyed the road surface. As you drive along there are no lay-bys, no hard shoulders and no places to pull over and take a picture or have a rest. The result is that the journey can get very frustrating. You pass something you would dearly love to take a picture of but you can't find a place to stop which is even moderately safe so you end up having to keep riding as you mutter some curses about Central American governments under your breath. The ride to Quetzaltenango was a massive eye opener for what lay ahead for the rest of Central America, if you drive expecting other folks to obey the rules of the road you will get killed. The only way to avoid it is to take every corner hugging the very right side of the road, right over at the right line so if some Benny comes round the corner on the wrong side of the road at least you'll have a small bit of space and be able to get up the inside.

The next big problem was the ramps or as they are called in Guatemala, "Reductor's." They are a good idea with all the lunatic drivers on the roads, it's no harm putting them on the road to slow everyone down. The problem for us lily livered westerners is that they are not always signposted and are not always a different color than the road and can pop up almost anywhere. So, you can just be driving along at about 60mph, and whack! Two things happen to you on the bike when you hit a reductor at this speed. First your whole body gets thrown up off the bike as the front wheel hits the ramp leaving you in the air just holding the handle bars. Second, as you're in the air and the back wheel hits the ramp, all 300 kg of motorbike jumps up and smacks you in the balls. For about the next ten minutes you're driving with two lumps in your throat with a forlorn wish that you were five years old again with your jewels still safely nestled just under you nipples. I started the trip with a pair of rocks and finished with a pair of saucers.

Trucks, vans and even motorcycles were completely overloaded with people. The amount of times I saw three people on a motorcycle or people hanging off the back of trucks, buses and vans, or whole families sitting in the back of trucks was too many to count.

On the flip side Guatemala has wonderful countryside, in fact its forests are so vast they are called the Earth's fifth lung. I got a weird sense of irony that a country I only wished to "survive and get through" was so beautiful. I made it to Quetzaltenango and tried to find somewhere to stay. As I was pulled over getting gas, a guy driving a motorbike from the town came over and introduced himself as Juan Antonio. I told him I was looking for somewhere to stay and asked him did he know where the nearest hotels were. Juan brought me to his friends place to stay. Not knowing either of the lads but bowled over by their kindness at the same time, I asked again were there any hotels. The guys were trying to do their best for me but what I wanted was a hotel with a shower in it, somewhere to safely park the bike and see about getting some Spanish lessons, eventually I got the message across.

I stayed in the second best hotel in the town for about $25 a night. The hotel felt like a hotel in Cuba to me, not having ever been in Cuba I'm not sure how I came to that conclusion but was happy not to question myself any further. That part of the Guatemala, on account of the altitude (7500ft above sea level) was very cold and damp, I slept with my arse hanging out from under quilt one of the nights and caught a cold for my troubles. (I know there'll be someone out there saying a cold is a virus and you can't catch it from getting cold and wet, to you I say, "Piss off and stop interrupting the story.) There was no hot water in the hotel so taking a shower in cold water when you've a bad head cold had me sneezing like I'd inhaled a barrel of pepper.

The town has a colonial centre square with many statues and official buildings, and is the second largest city in Guatemala. The town has a population of over 200,000 and the majority of the people living there are descendant from indigenous tribes. No matter where you go there are guns, especially anywhere there's money changing hands, there is always a guy standing with a pump action shotgun. I booked in for Spanish lessons at a local school for five days. In the city they run packages for back packers, for example you get Spanish school for a week and a place to stay with a local family with meals all in for very small money. The lessons for a full week cost less than a $100. My first Spanish lesson was done on a serious hangover, if you haven't tried a margarita, may I wholeheartedly recommend it, just make sure you have plenty of aspirin in your pocket because the next morning, it's like a cement mixer going round in your head. My spanish instructor got a tremendous laugh when I mixed up ano(year) and año, apparently I told her that I planned to travel for half an asshole.

There were many interesting people in the town, for the most part, folks from the United States. I'd met eight folks in total from El Norte, five of whom were missionaries or volunteer workers, two trainee doctors and another person who was off to see the world. All of them were top class! You have to hand it to the missionary workers and volunteers, there are a lot easier places to go to than Guatemala to donate your time and energy to try to help people.

I had lunch with Katie from New York and she was the type of person who would tell you anything. I asked her what was the maddest thing she ever did as we were getting tanked on Margaritas and she said, "I gave a Police officer a blojob so as he wouldn't do me for DUI." I replied "Yeah, that beats mine." She was meeting her boyfriend the next day and they were heading to South America for a couple of months, we wished each other well and went our separate ways.

I talked with one missionary guy who was telling me what the conditions were like out in the countryside and I really admired what he was doing and what he had to put up with in the process. We had a bit of a philosophical discussion around was it "Ok" to feel bad when your football team loses when you are surrounded by people who live in abject poverty. Sure, it puts the thing into perspective, Liverpool only drawing with Southampton making you feel bad, and then all around you are people poorer than church mice, but we both walked away believing that it was still ok to feel bad about our football teams losing. Talking to all these US expats put me in mind of how much America is a land of extremes. Here were all these enlightened individuals all trying to make a difference, when I compared them to some of the rednecks I'd met near the border with Mexico, I just shook my head.

Lake Atitlan

It had rained continuously for three days and I'd seen all Quetzaltenango had to offer so I was starting to long for the road again. Despite only completing two days of Spanish lessons, I headed for Antigua, one of the largest tourist Meccas in the country. I was mulling over a couple of things in my mind, first amongst them was whether to avoid Guatemala City on the way south and second, would it be worth bypassing El Salvador altogether and just go from Guatemala into Honduras. The choices were to take the southern road thus bypassing Guatemala City however, this meant having to go through El Salvador, or take the North Road and get into Honduras thus bypassing El Salvador. The problem with the northerly route was that it wasn't clear whether I could make it to a "safe" town in the daylight hours, and getting stranded out in the Honduran countryside at night was not my idea of fun. These were the thoughts that were dominating my mind as I left Quetzaltenango. Getting out of the town was easier said than done, road signs were about as common as hens teeth so after an hour's driving I ended exactly back right where I started. Yes, you're right, I am a real man and we don't ask for directions. I solved the dilemma by grabbing a taxi, telling him to drive to the exit of the city and that I'd follow and pay when we got there, it worked a treat and it wouldn't be the last time I'd use that way to escape from a big town when I was lost.

The bane of my life in those early days of riding in Guatemala was the chicken buses. I wondered why they were called "chicken buses" but I'm certain it's because they play chicken with oncoming traffic. I saw two crashes that day, it didn't look like anyone was really hurt but negotiating your way through the countryside with these ever present hazards and bad weather was absolute mayhem.

In many places due to deforestation and the rainy season, the hills were collapsing onto the road, leaving a trail of muck and shite all over the place that you have to try to pick your way through. The last time I'd seen roads this bad was on the Dalton highway in Alaska, the difference there was that you were the only one on the road, here the roads were jam packed.

I went to Lake Atitlan, which was tipped to be one of the wonders of the world. It's the deepest lake in Central America and on its banks has three volcanos. Well, if the place does win the nomination and become a natural wonder of the world, the first thing they'll need to do is signpost it. As far as I could make out there were none, at least as you approach it from Quetzaltenango. As I approached Atitlan, there were three or four pull over spots, where you could get out and take a few snaps of the lakes and volcanos from the road however, two of the stop points were being used as police checkpoints and another was a makeshift rubbish dump.

I met a guy there who was so keen on the motorbike trip I was doing, I was worried that he was going to club me over the back of the head and rape me. All that said, Atitlan is the most scenic location in Central America so if you find yourself going to Guatemala, put it on your list.

From there it was on to Antigua, which is renowned as the most picturesque town in Guatemala. I had so many near misses while driving to the town, I felt like a cat counting down from nine and was already at minus three.

Antigua

Antigua was very difficult to find, If I hadn't bumped into two Mormons from Montana I think I would still be looking for it. The Mormons are a great bunch, no matter how shitty and decrepit a town is, you'll find two Mormons there in a perfect set of pressed blue trousers and white shirt with a matching tie. Whatever your feelings are towards Mormons, I've always felt that they are the most courteous people you could ever hope to meet. We had a good laugh and one of the lads when he noticed one of the stickers on my pannier rolled out a "Dude! You went through Blackfoot! That's my home town!"

Antigua is a beautiful cobblestoned colonial town and is a popular stopping over spot for backpackers who want to "Do" Guatemala. Generally anyone who is making their way south or north through Central America ends up staying at least a night there. Antigua is a picture of how Guatemala "could be" if the country could get rid of its corruption. It's a Unesco world heritage site and is about as comfortable and relaxing a place to stay as there is in all of Latin America.

I got myself a hotel anxious to have my first hot shower since Mexico. As with every place I stayed my first question was "Agua Caliente?" (Hot water?) to which the land lord replied, "Si!" Not unexpectedly the water was Baltic, the heat of a warm shower would have to wait till another day. I went out for a couple of pints knowing that I had probably the most mental four or five days of my life coming up with El Salvador, Honduras and Nicaragua standing between me and relative normality of Costa Rica. My passport was starting to look like a coloring book with all the stamps I was collecting at the border posts.

The town is full of young Indian girls selling everything from necklaces to head scarves. They're all about eight or nine years old and are so cute that you just keep putting your hand into your arse pocket to buy stuff. They all have a couple of catch phrases, "Business is Business, I no sell much today, you not buy nothing from me mister, how much you pay for this mister" and so it went every hour of every day for the duration of my stay. I met an Aussie guy called Sam, an Icelandic gent called John and a cockney couple in an Irish bar in Antigua and we all got absolutely hammered drunk, although I was back in bed a little before eleven, I knew I had a big border day coming up.

The next morning started with a dose of the trots, Central American style. I woke up and had one of those "Three seconds to detonation" signals from my rectum, sprinting to the toilet and getting my arse hanging over the porcelain in the nick of time. For about thirty minutes, I was doing a fantastic impression of an upside down busted fire hydrant with intermittent machine gun fire. The whole time this was going on, in the hotel courtyard which all the rooms surrounded, the hotel pet parrot kept saying, "Hola!" "Hola!" As I sat there flexing my stomach muscles so my heart wouldn't plunge out along with the rest of my alimentary canal, I thought to myself "where's a good oul cat when you need one!"

I gingerly packed up, every couple of seconds mournfully glancing at the toilet while trying to make sure there were no more fires in the hole. I left the room and as I opened the door I realized the bog window also faced also out onto the courtyard where there were three or four old women having breakfast. They all gave me a sympathetic look while breathing in sharply through their teeth.

I pulled the bike out onto the street, the clouds had cleared and I saw standing there right at what seemed like the end of the street, a huge volcano, I thought to myself, if that thing ever goes boom this place is never even going to get a warning.

From Antigua to the border with El Salvador was about three hours and I bit the bullet and drove through Guatemala City. It ended up not being too bad, I was only lost for about ninety minutes. I met a bunch of bikers who were from the city who were meeting up for their Sunday afternoon ride, something that happens all over world. When they saw me coming they really laid out the red carpet and made me feel like I was the King of the world. They gave me some directions as there weren't any signs, and I used the GPS to keep my direction south and got through the city without any issues. The whole time I was traveling, I was flexing my arse cheeks together so hard I gave myself a brand new set of wrinkles, thank the lord for Imodium. The road quality had improved once I got to Guatemala City too. I guess the government know that most people come to Guatemala to visit Antigua so they may as well build a decent road. From there it was on to the border town of San Cristobal (A very common name in Central America).

The El Salvador border took a little over three hours to get through. Two young lads had become my self-appointed fixers, although I'm sure it took longer because of them, but they were nice fella's so I was happy enough to give them some money, if only for the company. The bureaucracy was incredible. The humidity while waiting around at the border was enough to drown in, I felt like my boots were filling up with puddles of sweat. I made it out in the end without too much of a fuss and I drove down the road chuffed that I'd made it through my second Central American border unscathed.

El Salvador

I drove under a gathering thunder storm to a nearby town called Santa Ana arriving into the town centre soaked and stinking of a mixture of sweat and lord knows what else and set about trying to find a place to stay.

The town was intimidating in places and I got the feeling that if I rode down the wrong street things could get nasty. All of sudden, a passing private security truck told me to follow them and they escorted me to a hotel. They took me under their wing, no doubt because I looked lost at the traffic lights. Never in my life have I had I an experience which compared to being escorted by five armed guards to a hotel room.

There were no tourists in Santa Ana and I couldn't help but feel that people kept staring at me, I kept checking to see if I had my underpants on over my jeans. I didn't plan to spend any time in the country, it being only a quarter the size of Ireland I planned for just one night. There are those who might say how can you say you've been to a country when you passed through it like a dose of Epsom salts, my answer would be that most of the Central American countries were just obstacles in my mind, something that had to be overcome to get to the good stuff in South America. I was cooked up in my room from about 6pm that night and couldn't believe how quickly it got dark. It was September 25th and it felt like it went from day to night in only a couple of minutes.

The following morning just before dawn I left Santa Ana and headed for the Honduran border. Even though El Salvador is a tiny country, the roads twisted and bent through the mountains so took it took me nearly five hours to get there. Along the way, I pulled over for a swig of water. As I was mid slug a guy walked out of a field with an eight-finger forehead, his shirt was unbuttoned to the waist and in his right hand he was wielding a machete. He said, "Hola!". I was ready to hand him the keys of the bike and all my earthly possessions in the hope he didn't cleave me in two. As it turned out, Machetes are as common in Central America as mobile phones were in Ireland. No matter where you drive you can see people by the side of the road carrying them, its normal, but as I kept telling myself, "Here isn't normal"

Murder remains El Salvador's leading crime problem with an average of ten murders every day. Statistically it has one of the highest per capita murder rates in the world; 59 per 100,000, by comparison the murder rate in New York City is just seven, with numbers like that I was glad to be on my way out of it. For the heck of it I went through San Salvador the capital, traffic wasn't too bad and from there pushed on to the border with Honduras.

Every day you survive in the worlds crazy places you tend to enjoy testing yourself, I was amazed how unafraid I was driving into one of the most violent cities in the world.

Just before I got to the border I stopped for gas, and was immediately beset upon on all sides by six guys all vying to be the one to take me through the border. The roaring and shouting they were doing was deafening. I followed one of them on a motorbike up to the border when another ten or twelve guys all jumped out of nowhere all roaring and shouting, obviously in Spanish. The competition to take the gringos across the border is violently intense. They were unbelievably aggressive and a fight even broke out between two of them. Things were quickly descending into a nightmare, I told them "Fuck off the whole lot of you!" and I drove down the road to see if I could find a less dodgy looking fixer.

Eventually I picked what I thought was the least dodgy looking one and we darted ahead of about three miles of trucks all queuing to get through the border. It was quickly becoming apparent, to me at any rate that the corruption in a country was directly proportional to the bureaucracy you encountered at its borders. When I got to the border post, I had the shock of my life waiting for me. Now it wasn't like that having passed through Mexico and Guatemala and into El Salvador that I was expecting the Ritz but what I came upon was easily the worst place I've ever been, by a country mile.

There were thousands of people all pressing on each other with hours of queues. The whole place stunk of piss and there were emaciated dogs roaming around barking with people throwing rubbish and pouring all sorts of stuff right out onto the street. Everyone there was on the con, the whole thing was a setup to get as much money from people making their way through as possible. From the moment you get there you are harassed, chased, lied to, robbed, bullied and manipulated right to the moment you leave. I had six or seven guys around me telling me that it would cost me $70 to get my bike through fumigation, which I knew I didn't need. All these guys kept roaring and shouting at me and I was standing there just telling them, "No way!"

At this point my passport, bike registration, and license were off being processed by one of the "ass wipes" in the office. He was letting me rot outside with this melee of people around me. Being at one of these borders is enough for you to lose all faith in people. Everyone was in on the conning and exploitation of people who were moving through. The police, the customs officials, even the bank officials were all

taking bribes and all were doing it openly.

The guys who were doing the vehicle importing in the office were wearing jeans, no shirts, literally a bunch of thugs. To pass through you need to pay a variety of charges to the bank, however the banks only take Honduran currency, no credit cards, or Dollars and then send you out to a moneychanger who charges you ridiculous rates. No doubt the moneychanger is the "bastard" in the banks "man on the outside." I completely lost the rag with the place, and thought to myself that I would love one of those guns that Jesse Ventura had in the movie Predator, I could have done a lot of good with it!

Four hours had passed and I was making no progress and was almost despairing when three lights in the darkness showed up, two Swedish bikers who watched my bike for me and believe it or not a gang member who used to live in Miami, who could speak English. If you can imagine a scene where about twenty people were roaring and shouting at me, and there in the middle of the throng I was calmly talking to this gang member in English. (I really wished I'd that machine gun.) This gang lad (Jordan was his name) eventually got me sorted out, you could see that when the other guys saw him with a dose of facial tattoos, showing gang affiliation to MS-13, they weren't going to mess with him.

Honduras

Eventually I got out of there six hours after arriving, hating everyone in Honduras and anything to do with the country. For me the unforgivable part was that the police and the government officials let it happen. If you get into trouble there, you can't even call the police because they are taking bribes from the criminals who are extorting the money from you, so you're completely FUBAR.

I hooked up with the two Swedish bikers and we stayed in a motel in a town called Choluteca in Honduras near the border with Nicaragua. They were great lads and we shared stories from the road over a couple of beers and dinner. The waitress who was serving us was a local girl with dyed blond hair who was about as friendly as a rattlesnake that you had just taken a piss on. It was great to be in a semi civilized situation again and not at that border. I went to bed that night thinking that Honduras was the biggest shit hole that was ever created anywhere, at any time, by anybody + 1.

That night the thunder and lightning almost as if to mirror the days happenings was ferocious.

The Swedes and I left the hotel a little after 6am to get to the Nicaraguan border as early as possible, we were expecting the worst. As we rode for the border the dawn sun burned off the mist which cloaked the hills either side of the road. The road surface was great and it twisted and turned through several mountains, it was a great way to start the day. We got close to the border when we were met by six or seven guys who had a rope and a barrier across the road.

These were not border officials, it was the usual story of thugs trying to extort money, but thankfully there were three of us so they let us pass. As I drove through the makeshift blockade it served to cement the feeling I had in my head that Honduras really was a complete and utter shit hole of the lowest order. We got to the official border and went about stamping out of Honduras. To our complete surprise, it was painless. We walked into an official and she stamped the passports, was very friendly and wished us well, easy as pie. How two border crossings for the same country could be so different was beyond comprehension.

Nicaragua

From there we went onto Nicaraguan immigration, which was also painless, the whole process taking less than an hour. The whole thing immediately set the scene for a very different experience in the country, almost as if the first impression you get tends to set the tone for the rest of the country. I said goodbye to the lads, their road was taking them in a different direction and thanked them for their help the previous day. I hoped we would meet again on the road. The goodbyes didn't seem to hurt so much anymore, maybe I was getting used to them, or maybe it was that I wasn't "leaving it all out there" only for the door to be slammed when you don't get to see people again.

The roads, scenery and people I met along the way to the town of Grenada were amazing with multiple stopping points to see volcanos sitting on the banks of crystal blue lakes. The police stopped me several times, but each time it was just a chat. These were all guys around the age of thirty who were simply wanting to chat to someone to break up the day, and I was happy to oblige. I was having a fantastic time, the best since I'd got to Central America and I rode the two hundred miles to Granada before early afternoon.

Granada

Granada is another in a long line of Colonial Gems in Latin America. I booked myself into a gorgeous hotel, time for a few well-earned comforts after an utterly shit forty-eight hours. The guy behind the counter took a real shine to me, he was one of the most overtly gay guys I've met but in fairness to him, he was great fun. That evening I was sitting in the Cafe Europe sipping some freshly brewed coffee looking out on the town square as several fine women were passing, I just couldn't believe that it was only twenty-four hours since I was in that steaming cesspool at the border with Honduras.

From there I headed out and about in the town and hooked up with a black Nicaraguan from the Caribbean coast. His name was John Oliver (something something) and he was a street poet and artist, which essentially meant that he didn't have a pot to piss in. I said that I'd buy him his dinner and a couple of beers in exchange for the company and a poem about my journey, he was great fun.

This is the poem he wrote:

30,000 miles of road, all the way from Alaska through Mexico and Central America
It is sweet enough cos adventure is fun, Now here I am on the run
Sometimes things seem so far away, That I just can't delay

Sometimes it seems so near, While I drive and drive without no fear
I know I must be there cos now I'm here with the Nicaraguan eastern poet John Oliver having some cold beers,
Still I've got another 15000 miles to go, Just let it flow
So I'll drive and drive through forest, up hills, and down valleys, across bridges Nonstop until I hit Buenos Aires, Argentina in South America

Then I fly home back to Ireland, don't worry loved ones, cos Oisin is going to stand

I thought it was great.

When I got back to the hotel the gay chap who worked in reception was in his civilians, he saw me coming in and we'd the following conversation: Concierge: Oh I luv ur ayre, eets Bonita, so blonde, eets golden! Tu esta Bonita señor Oisin: sorry horse, I don't putt from the rough Concierge: (Confused look) Oisin: I kick with the other foot, Not gay, You know what I mean, I prefer the senoritas Concierge: ah you prefer, but you like men also? Si? Oisin: Nope, just the senoritas I'm afraid, but listen, thanks anyway Concierge: (looked really sad, and a bit hurt) Oisin: listen if it's any consolation, if i was gay, y'know Concierge: (starting to beam) Oisin: Ok where's the JCB, I'm outta here

I was having such a good time I decided to stay a second night. I got up and went out for breakfast and tucked into a delicious round of coffee and pancakes. There's plenty of tours running from the town and I burned an afternoon on a tour of Lake Nicaragua looking at monkeys and small forested islands.

I wandered back to the hotel where I bumped into a couple from the US and Britain, David and Ellie who lived in Costa Rica and were up in Granada on holidays. We had a great chat by the hotel pool and were joined later by a girl called Miriam and her mother, both from Slovakia. Earlier that day, I was sitting by the pool as Miriam stripped off into her Bikini and got into the water. She was red hot. You know that Eastern European / Russian spy / Figure skater type hot? After picking my tongue up off the ground and wiping the foam from my mouth, I introduced myself and we talked for about an hour.

We met for dinner later that evening and Miriam and I ended up kissing, the first girl I had kissed on the trip, it had only taken 19,600 miles. If I'm honest I was desperate for a shag but the gentleman in me didn't want to get involved. The last thing I wanted to do was fall for someone and then have to carry the parting with me for the next 15,000 miles. Lads, I hear ya, If they invent a time machine any time soon, I'm going straight back to that moment. I'll open with "I've passed through time itself to give you my seed!" She'll tell me to piss off, guaranteed.

I bailed out for a walk around the square, whatever chance you have of going to sleep with the light on, with a hard on you've no chance. With the temperature so high during the day the nighttime is really the only part of the day you get to feel cool. I was walking down the cobbled streets when a song popped into my head which made me smile and think of home. "Top to toe in tailbacks, Oh, I got red lights all the way I'm driving home for Christmas!"

I left Granada the next morning feeling very blue. I had met some great people there and as always on a trip like this, you have to say goodbye. It was the most people I had met in one place and saying goodbye to John Oliver, David,

Ellie, Moses, and Miriam made me feel very sad and lonely. I didn't have long to dwell on it as my stress levels began to rise again at the thought of another border crossing that morning, Nicaragua into Costa Rica.

Costa Rica

Costa Rica is the safest and most modern country in Central America and after only two hours at the border I was through pushing on for Lake Arenal, named after the Arenal Volcano, one of the ten most active Volcanoes in the world situated on its banks. I stayed in Tileran, a town near the lake that night, and everywhere I went all I could see was couples. My mind drifted back to Miriam, "Why don't I just go back to Grenada?" I knew it was a bad idea.

My abiding memory of Costa Rica is of a day I spent driving through rain forests near Arenal. The noise of the birds, the smoking volcano and the incessant pissing rain are all etched in equal measure on my mind. The rain drove down all day and when it was combined with the savage humidity, I was either soaking wet from rain, or soaking wet from sweat. The swings in fortune and as a consequence, swings in mood on this trip were almost too hard to deal with. In just five days I went through close on most scared ever in El Salvador, angriest / maddest ever at the Honduras border, a magical time in Granada and that day, feeling down in the dumps and lonely. On the bad days I'd go into Star Wars mode, likening myself to Luke Skywalker heading off to the cloud city to save Han and Lela, not forgetting oul hairy arse himself, Chewbacca.

In the bright lights of the fighter, Oisin loads a heavy case into the belly of the ship. Artoo sits on top of the X-wing, settling down into his cubbyhole. Yoda stands nearby on a

log.
YODA: Oisin! You must complete the off road training.
Oisin: I can't keep the vision out of my head. They're my friends. I've got to help them.
YODA: You must not go!
Oisin: But Han and Leia will die if I don't.
BEN'S VOICE: You don't know that. Oisin looks toward the voice in amazement. Ben has materialized as a real, slightly shimmering image near Yoda. The power of his presence stops Oisin.
BEN: Even Yoda cannot see their fate. Oisin is in great anguish. He struggles with the dilemma, a battle raging in his mind.
BEN: If you choose to face Vader, you will do it alone. I cannot interfere.
Oisin: I understand. (he moves to his X-wing) Artoo, fire up the converters. Artoo whistles a happy reply.
BEN: Oisin, don't give in to hate -- that leads to the dark side. Oisin nods and climbs into his ship.
YODA: Strong is Vader. Mind what you have learned. Save you it can.
Oisin : I will. And I'll return. I promise.
Artoo closes the cockpit. Ben and Yoda stand watching as the roar of the engines and the wind engulf them.
YODA: (sighs) Told you, I did. Reckless is he. Now matters are worse.
BEN: That boy is our last hope.
YODA: Fucking right he is!

The rain cleared and I set off in the direction of San Jose hoping to get to a town called San Isidro following a route from Lake Arenal over the mountains. The roads as you'd expect in a first world country were in great condition as they weaved and twisted through the mountains and tropical forests. The noise from birds and monkeys and lord knows what else as I made my way through the dense tropical foliage was exhilarating, the whole place was teaming with life.

I hit San José, the capital of Costa Rica at about 2pm, and in keeping with every large town that I'd travelled through since crossing the border into Mexico, I got lost. There wasn't a sign to be had for going south in the country but I was getting better at the whole "intrepid explorer" deal because after only an hour I was back on track.

The journey south takes you over a mountain range which hugs Los Quetzales National Park and once I hit a certain altitude the rain came down like I was in a drive through car wash. For four hours, I drove through fog, lashing rain, flooding rivers and landslide residue. I'd started that day feeling really low but I guess your system only lets you feel like that for so long, eventually you hit a turning point, lord knows what triggers it. I started having a great time, it was absolutely brilliant fun, the more inclement the weather, the better my mood. At one point the rain got so heavy I was driving along breaking my arse laughing, there was nothing else you could do.

I think if you're in the right frame of mind you can take on almost anything, if I'd been in a bad mood no doubt I would have been driving along cursing like a sailor in a storm at sea. I'm sure someone said a prayer for me somewhere to snap me out of the doldrums and that's why I was able to get through what otherwise would have been a terrible day. I think the hardship also helps keep you focused and stops your mind wallowing in self pity so in a way it's a good thing.

The plan I had was to hit one of the quieter border crossings into Panama the following day, I guessed it less than two hundred miles to the Panama Canal. I was imagining sitting on the banks of the canal having a tall frosty beer watching all these massive ships go by, saluting the distant figures standing on the decks waving at me and the bike. Panama was going to present its own bunch of problems, the biggest of which being the fact that I'd have to ship the bike to Colombia. I kept thinking to myself, "how the fuck am I going to be able to do this?" I supposed that I'd just head for the airport nearest the city, and then find a Cargo company and just ask them to ship it, and do it all with very poor Spanish. Easy.

The next day I started out before dawn in the direction of the Panama border. I got advice not to take the border on the Pan American highway and instead to detour over the mountains to a much smaller border post near a place called San Vito. The road takes you through gorgeous hills filled with rainforest but as I approached the border and had less than ten miles to go, the road disintegrated into rocks. It wasn't even gravel and I started to wonder had I taken the wrong way, surely this couldn't be it? I kept going never sure I was on the right road and never meeting a soul on the road to ask. Thankfully it turned out fine and the people at the border, not used to foreigners coming across at this entrance were brilliant, I was through in less than thirty minutes. To thank the border guards I went over to the supermarket and bought them seven or eight liters of fruit juice and we sipped and talked for about an hour about all sorts of stuff.

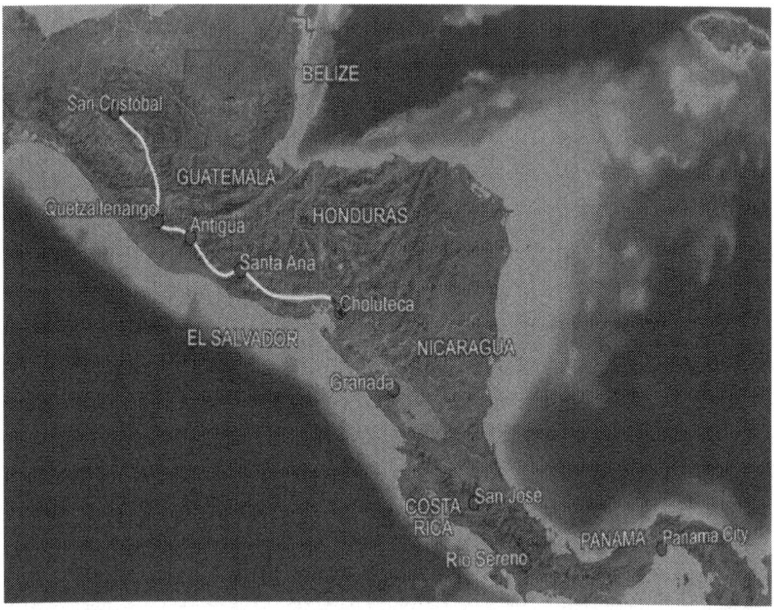

Panama

From there I had to cross mountains which are part of the Amistad International Park in Panama to get back to the Pan American highway. The first thing I noticed about Panama was that the country doesn't so much run north to south as it does east to west. That journey took me through tropical forests that looked like something out of an adventure movie, I loved the fact that every day was so stuffed with so much variety. Seeing things were going so well and God likes to equal things up, for the next two hours the rain pelted down like I was stuck under a bull taking a piss. I had

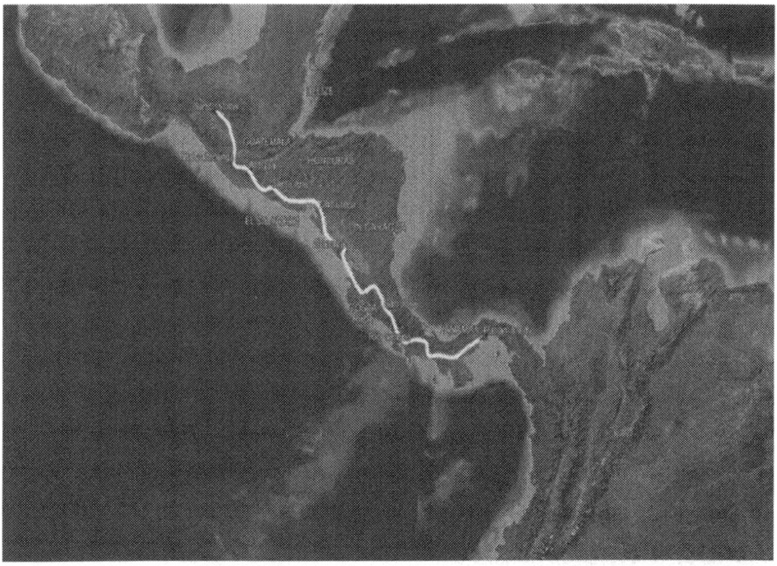

to stand up on the pegs several times to let a pool of water slide down my legs that had built up around my nuts.

Once I got to the Pan American highway, I realized I hadn't fully opened my map and had an extra two hundred and eighty miles of road to go to get to Panama City, which meant I had to knock out over four hundred miles total. The roads in Panama are very modern so I wasn't excessively worried. My main concern was to get to Panama City before it got dark; the city had a reputation of having some serious no go areas. About twenty miles outside Panama City, I got lost and I pulled in to get some gas and get some directions. A trucker pulled over and roared out the window, "What the fuck you doing here amigo!" I said that I was looking for the Holy Grail and did he know where I could find it? It turned out he was heading to Panama City and told me to follow him in. It was a big relief as at this stage it was completely dark and I was going around in circles. I pulled off the freeway into downtown Panama only to pull into an area called the red zone, at least that is what one of the people said it was when I got there. As I was driving along looking for a hotel three people beckoned to me that it wasn't safe there and to get out of the area quickly. As I was stuck at the lights, a woman of about eighty years said to me to, "hurry out of here." I had the most eerie feeling that it was my mother talking to me, so spooky! I did my usual trick, grabbing a taxi and motioning for him to drive to a hotel and that I'd follow. Then with marine efficiency we lashed through the city and found our way to the front of a hotel where he helped me check in. The garage doors to the hotel were opened, my bags were taken to the hotel room and in what felt like five minutes since I talked to the old woman, I was safely tucked up in the hotel room and I lay on the bed thinking, "What the hell just happened?"

I'd officially reached the emotional halfway point of the journey, even though I was up over 20,000 miles at this stage. Everything from this point on would be South America. The first order of business was to find a way to ship the bike to South America, note there's still no way through the Darien gap on a bike or a car, so even though there is a land link you can't get through what is impenetrable forest and swamp. You could get through on a horse by all accounts, but you would be shot by one of several rebel groups or drug lords which control the area.

The next morning I drove the bike to Tocumen airport, armed with only the information that there were two companies out there who shipped bikes reasonably regularly. Now if you think this is a handy thing to do, you'd be mistaken. Imagine you had a motorbike out your back garden and you wanted to ship it to England. Now remove your ability to speak the language and the only tool you have is the schillings in your arse pocket and a rough idea where the companies might be located, it's not easy. I found the place after a while and parked the bike up thoroughly impressed with myself. The bad news was that the first company Panavia had shut down, "Nice one!" I thought to myself. From there I talked to a really helpful security guard who took me to the Girag shipping company, my last and only option. After a while talking to the folks there in very broken Spanish, it turned out that that cost to ship the bike to Quito in Ecuador was $1900 and the flight only left once a week. Alternatively, you could fly to Bogotá in Columbia for $900 dollars with the flights leaving daily, and the bike would be available to pick up that Monday.

Bogotá Colombia was the obvious choice.

Before the bike could be shipped the mirrors had to be removed, battery disconnected and the fuel removed which is where I came unstuck. I'm one of these guys who isn't good with his hands, bit like a donkey making fine china, and I didn't know where to start. Just then, a Japanese lad named Hiro, who spoke very broken English and worse Spanish came over and helped me remove the fuel from the bike. My Spanish was better than his, and his motorbike knowledge was better than mine so between the two of us we got both bikes shipped to Bogota.

The heat and humidity was so bad that I had to strip down to my lycra shorts while getting the bike ready. I think the sight of my rotund frame walking around in the pissing rain in a pair of lycra shorts that you'd normally expect to see someone wearing in a porno movie helped to speed the whole process up. Hiro and I headed back to Panama City to book the flights to Colombia, however with all the mad countries showing up on my credit card there was a stop placed on it back in Ireland. I had to sort that out by talking down a pay phone on a crowded Panama street with heaps of chicken buses and noisy trucks driving by at a hundred decibels, it was manic.

I eventually got it all sorted and it was time for a treat. All the American chains are in the city and I needed a dessert. The best dessert I'd had since crossing into Mexico was a tin of peaches turned onto a plate with some nuts on it, nowhere near enough for me to maintain my reputation as a fat bastard, so TGI Fridays had my name written all over it. In Panama, all the yuppies go to TGI, so it's a totally different buzz than in Ireland or America. Hiro and I chatted away for a while that night, his English was bad, so the conversation dried up rather quickly. He had travelled extensively at that stage, all through Africa and the Middle East on the strength of, what could best be described as pigeon English. It just goes to show the world is a very helpful place after all.

I had another two days knocking around Panama before I was due to fly out to Bogotá. I was expecting a torrid time since those IRA lads went to Columbia and suddenly made their way home with the help of Gerry Adams. I could see it now, back home on the news "Irish man arrested in Colombia" and all the people back home saying, "Well, if he's in Colombia he must be guilty, sure who in their right mind goes there?"

Panama for me oozed sex. All the billboards were stuffed full of women wearing half nothing. As a result, I was working my way to a hairy right hand and being a fully fledged membership of the Stevie Wonder club. The women walked around the city most wearing jeans and shorts two to three sizes too small for them. The typical outfit as far as I could make out was a vest and a pair of jeans borrowed from a ten-year-old child.

The cultural mix in the town was wild. They brought in laborers from all over the world to work on the Panama Canal and when it was built most stayed in the country, the result was a racial melting pot.

I pottered off to see the Panama Canal. If you go to "old" Panama City and look out to the ocean, you can see many huge boats all waiting to get in through the canal. Apparently, the backlog at that point was about four days so it was a complete surprise to find that I had to wait around drinking beer in the Mira Flores Cafe for about three hours before a boat showed up, something rotten in the state of Denmark me thinks!

The canal is full of tourists, it's "the thing" to visit when you're in Panama City and it's a good opportunity to meet people. When traveling, you have to force yourself to keep going through doors, in other words keep introducing yourself to people and saying hello and not be deterred from being the first person to say hello just because you think maybe the person won't reciprocate. I always told myself that I'd two choices, either keep going through the door and introducing yourself to others or sit quietly alone by yourself for the rest of the trip. When you're in good form it's easy to be outgoing, when you're not in the best it takes a bit for work, but for the most part, it always pays off. While I was there I met James and Kate a great couple from Camp in County Kerry in Ireland. James was over working with Digicell and invited me along to a night out they were having in a place called the Sky bar that night. From there we went on to a nightclub, which was heaving with people and we had a great night. I spent the next day nursing a wicked hangover. They have a beer called "Panama" which is exactly like "Harp" in Ireland, and it seemed like they copied the recipe exactly. The headache from it is wicked, in Ireland it's served with two paracetamol. It was fantastic to meet up with some Irish folks for a chat, somehow it felt like I wasn't so far away from home.

That night I managed to get trapped in the hotel elevator for over an hour with another guy and six women. We were all lumped together in this metal cage waiting for the power to come back on. Once the elevator stopped, two of the girls started roaring crying. As time went on two more started. If you can imagine the scene, eight people in a roasting hot humid elevator, with four people whinging and sniveling, two more of them trying to console the others and myself and this other guy. The noise in the elevator was like sticking your head into a blender. It was at that moment I realized that I'd never make a fire man. With all that whinging I was ready to just start throwing people down the elevator shaft and this was after only 45 minutes. I've no patience. I think I must have been hiding behind the rocks when they were giving out patience. Eventually we were hauled up to a home position, all drenched in sweat and as cranky as a bag of rattle snakes.

Later that night in an Internet cafe the Colombia prep went haywire over visas, I couldn't get any response on whether I needed one. Half of the websites reckoned I needed a visa, some didn't say and some said that I didn't. Those that said I did mentioned that the only way of getting one being to present yourself to the consulate in Ireland. Ireland was the only EU country that had this restriction, it was due to the IRA lads who were over here training FARC rebels. I had already shipped the bike there and was scheduled to pick it up the following morning. What would happen if I couldn't get there? Eventually I got the whole thing sorted by going onto the department of foreign affairs website, and the visa restriction had changed in November 2007. I was as high as a kite with the news.

The next day I was going to Colombia, everyone back home thought I was crazy. As I went into the hotel lobby to head up to my room for the night there was a guy from the US giving out that he'd had no sleep in three days with the noise in the hotel. I thought to myself, "Welcome to Central America buddy!"

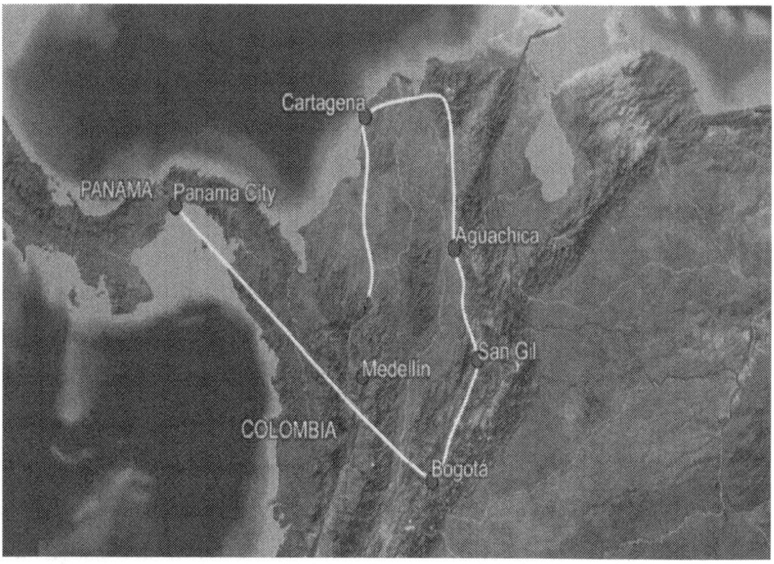

Chapter 7
Colombia

I met Hiro at the hotel before getting picked up by a taxi to take us to the airport to catch a plane to Bogota. The taxi was a complete banger and almost immediately started to overheat. As plumes of steam poured from the bonnet I looked over at Hiro and we exchanged a "WTF" glance. The driver didn't have any water with him so he used a milk carton to collect water from the side of the road and filled the radiator with the collected rain. In the end we made it to the airport with time to spare, but things like that left me feeling that something a bit looney happened every day, without fail.

Bogota

The plane took off and as we journeyed south I was constantly looking out the window at a world completely covered in dense rain forest. We got to Bogotá airport in a little over an hour. The decent into the airport is a wonderful experience as the plane flies in through a valley before it lands. The security was as heavy as you'd expect for Colombia, we walked through and got a taxi to a hotel, Hiro was on a tighter budget so he was looking for a cheaper place, and I went a bit more upmarket. My cut was, "I'm in Columbia, it's dangerous enough without staying in a shit hole as well." The taxi driver seemed to be ultra concerned with our safety, we told him where we wanted to go based on information in the lonely planet and he flat told us, "no way!" it was too dangerous. I really got the impression that he was concerned for our safety so I was happy to go with the flow. The result was I got to a lovely little family run hotel in the middle of nowhere.

The next morning was going to be our first attempt to get the bikes out of customs. I reckoned that it might take anything from one day to a week, "There is no point in trying to rush it, it will be ready when it's ready." It was such a relief to be in South America, I felt that the ugly part of the trip was over and from this point it would onwards and upwards. The plan was to head north and loop round to Cartagena one of South America's most famous cities, a three-day journey all told. We went straight off to customs to see if we could pry the bikes out and we used the taxi guy from the day before who spoke great English to help us out. I had asked him how much would he earn normally a day and just paid him that amount, if we were done early I'd pay him the same amount which really sped things up.It was $80 dollars well spent. Two hours later we had the bikes, much quicker than we could ever have hoped for. I said goodbye to Hiro at the cargo terminal, his road went south whereas I was heading north, he was a good lad. At the point we said goodbye he had done over 34,000 hard miles, he was a hardcore young fella no doubt about it.

Colombia is bigger than you'd think, as big as the UK, France and Germany put together so I was expecting to clock a lot of miles over the following days. This was as good a time as any to take a day off, so once I parked up the bike at the hotel, I headed off into Bogotá for the day.

The pedestrian pavements in the city were in a wicked state, anyone would think you were drunk as you're walking along as your stride is constantly interrupted by the uneven pavement. It was also very expensive, about 30% dearer than Ireland and that's saying something. Someone needs to tell them, "Hey you know this is Bogotá right?" The city itself feels like an eastern European City, it has some nice areas but also has sprawling square high-rise apartments in the suburbs, home to its seven million inhabitants. The people in the city are not that friendly, but that's the same in all cities I guess. It was obvious that people didn't seem to be happy. Hardly anyone seemed to smile. Now before someone chimes in with "if you smile at the world it'll smile back" I was in great form, I had the bike back so it wasn't me projecting a bad mood, but I was sure it would be a lot better in the countryside. After spending two days in Bogota I said to myself, "There is no way you'd ever come here if it wasn't because it's the only place in Colombia you can fly the bike into." My impression was that its a dark, depressing, miserable sort of place. The paranoia on safety was also bit off-putting, the taxi guy and another lad in the hotel had put the fear of god into me, both recommended calling into the police in various towns to let them know your there. I tried an Irish bar to see if there was anything going on, but no joy. On top of serving crappy food with Irish names, it had all the cheer of a freshly gelded bull.

The night before I got on the road I looked at the gear I had for the remainder of the trip. Over the course of the last eighty seven days, I had kept throwing away gear that I didn't need. At every place I stopped for more than one night I would ask myself "Ok, so you haven't used this piece of kit yet, so what makes you think you'll need it in the future?" The extent of the gear I carried now fitted comfortably into a tank bag, two panniers, and two hold all bags. As the trip went on this trend continued until at the very end I flew home with just one bag, I left for Canada with three. If I ever end up going on another trip, I'll know better. On the upside it made traveling very easy, on the downside it would have been great to pick up a few souvenirs but I had the consolation that I was on the trip of a lifetime and that was a small price to pay.

On my last night in the hotel, the bollix in the next room blared the TV into the wee hours as he snored the night away. The lack of peace and quiet I think is one of the things Westerners find hardest to get used to about Latin American cities, compared to the northern hemisphere its bedlam.

The plan for the following day was to head to a city called Medellin and from there up to Cartagena a distance of about 1100 km. Then I would take a couple of days to complete the 2000 km journey south to the border with Ecuador.

The following morning I left like the proverbial scalded cat

out of Bogotá, except Bogotá had other ideas. I spent the first two hours utterly lost and eventually decided to "Just head north" which was "kind of" in the general direction of Cartagena. As things turn out I found myself on the Venezuelan side of Colombia, not the side you'd be hoping for from a safety perspective, based on what I'd read in the travel advisories.

The weather was bad all day, it just rained and rained and rained. In the tropics, the rain is biblical, it always soaks you right through to the butt crack. Riding along with a small torrent of rain water flowing in between the cheeks of my ass was a new experience for me. The water always pooled around my meat and two veg and every now and then I'd have to stand up and let the deluge flow down my legs into my boots.

The scenery was dominated by dark green forests with an ever present mist moving through the tops of the forest canopy. I knocked out about two hundred and fifty miles but due to the roads twisting and turning through mountains and the large amount of trucks on the road it took me all day to do it. As a comparison, you'd knock out the same distance before lunch in North America.

The roads were full of soldiers, and during my first full day on the road, I comfortably passed fifteen checkpoints, but didn't get any grief.

It was the first time on the journey that I felt things coming to an end, believe it or not. I had over 20,000 miles done and I knew I was on the last leg. It was a silly thing to be thinking reflecting on it now, I still had over sixty days of riding to do, you'd be amazed the pure horse shit that jumps in and out of your mind as you drive along on a motorcycle.

I stopped in a small town for some grub and this Colombian guy came up to me and asked, "Where are you from?" I replied, "Ireland." The usual story followed, how I got there, how many CC's the bike was and where was I going. It turned out this lad used to work for the tourist board of

Colombia. (Yes there is one!) Towards the end of the conversation, he thanked me for visiting his town and Colombia with a vigorous handshake. I said to him "Listen buddy, I'm no one special or anything like that." He followed with, "When one comes, many will follow, I'm certain." I said goodbye and he left me feeling quite emotional. I was thinking about it for the rest of the day, and just couldn't put my finger on what the emotion I was feeling was.

San Gil

Having headed north I decided to pull in at a small town called San Gil. It was 4pm, normally I'd drive till about five but it was Colombia I said I'd pull in that bit earlier each day, better to err on the side of caution. The welcome I got at the hotel was very genuine, and I was stunned with all the smiling faces compared to Bogota. The girl working at reception was a knockout wearing a two-piece pink suit which looked like it had been painted on, my eyes were jumping out their sockets. Her boobs and backside look like they were going to spill out at any second. Colombian women have a look, its a fiery, sensual, dark, mysterious "don't mess with me or I'll cleave your goolies off" type look. I wanted her to spank me and say, "Your a naughty hardcore biker, and we all know what happens to naughty bikers!" Ahem, sorry about that, back to the story....

I had a cold shower and headed off into the centre of the town which was lovely, at its center was a lovely park surrounded by trees. Everyone I passed smiled and said hello and when I went into a restaurant for dinner, the people in there were made me feel very welcome. I got the distinct impression that a couple of the señoritas were checking me out, I thought to myself, "Maybe this is the place you'll get into the gratuitous sex part of the trip!" Oh God I hope so!

I sat in the restaurant sipping a beer and trying to work out a route to Cartagena, the big problem for me was that I was on the wrong side of the country, I should have been heading north through Medellin. Very few of the towns on the way to Cartagena on the east of Colombia were documented in the Rough guide or the Lonely planet so I'd be taking chances as I drove north on whether towns on the maps had places to stay.

The FARC (Colombian Leftist Rebels) were on the news that night, they had released a guy who they had captive for over a year. I was preparing myself for plenty of heebie jeebies moments until I hit the coast. It wasn't only FARC I had to worry about, the power of drug cartels in these areas was also a major concern for would be tourists, but I comforted myself with the fact that I was now in Colombia and I must therefore be a hardcore stud. The next day I celebrated my birthday, the 8th of October. It was thirty-eight years since I was dragged out roaring and screaming, I have not stopped since.

I hit the road early the next morning and about an hour out of San Gil I had a minor / major emergency depending on how you look at it I guess. I'd had something a bit weird for breakfast, a Colombian dish of potatoes and sweet bread mixed into a watery soup. Anyway, about an hour after I hit the road it felt like that scene in Alien where the monster jumps out of that guys chest, except this beast making a B-line for my bum. It was one of those situations where you get absolutely no warning apart from a couple of minor sloshes in your stomach. There was no place anywhere close with a toilet and I was driving on a mountain with sheer drops on one side and steep cliffs on the other. I kept saying to myself, "Hold on, hold on, hold on, holy bollix hold on, Jaysus hold the fuck on!" I got the signal that valve failure was imminent, I pulled the bike over to the side of the road, jumped off, dropped the tweeds and hung my arse over a metal barrier on the cliff and fertilized a solid acre of mountainside. The bike hid at least some of my shame from the passing traffic. I sat on my make shift throne for about ten minutes feeling at many points that I was about to launch for Tokyo, all the while listening to the beeps of traffic as they passed. When I felt the fresh air on the back of my throat, the only true sign that the chamber was fully purged I was left with a bit of a conundrum. With no toilet paper handy, I had to take off my motorbike boots and both socks met their waterloo.

Aguachica

From there I made my way, delicately, north to a place called Aguachica, along the Ruta 45A. For the first time since I left Costa Rica the sun shone all day and I was having a ball soaking up the wonderful Colombian countryside. There was a huge amount of soldiers and police on the road and I passed a checkpoint every ten miles or so but never got any hassle.

I booked into a hotel and was again taken aback by how friendly the people were, it really took me by surprise. How could a country with all these problems and such a bad reputation have so many wonderful people? As I checked into the hotel I was met by an apparition behind the reception desk. A girl with long wavy black hair, a damp see through red vest and a pair of white denim jeans which were spray-painted onto a body that just wouldn't quit. She showed me to my room, and it's these moments you pray that at least some of the stories in porn movies could be true, "Do you need some help undressing Mr Hughes?" I went in and had another cold shower, at this stage I was so horny I would have shagged the crack of dawn.

The women in Colombia were incredible. They've fantastic figures with long black hair and tremendous bottoms but I go the distinct impression that they were a cranky bunch, sure why else would all the lads in the country all be out fighting.

I went out in the town that night and none of the restaurants had any menus so I was back to pointing in the air with one finger with a high pitched "Si" when I heard something I recognized from the waiter. There were large amounts of soldiers everywhere I went and as I sat in a cafe looking out on the people passing up and down the road I got a sudden burst of homesickness, not surprising really, after all it was my birthday and I was a long way from home.

The next morning started great. As I was checking out of the hotel the owner and the furnace hot receptionist gave me a birthday present. You have to give your passport details in hotels there and sure enough they twigged my birth date and gave me a little bag of goodies, I was going to ask if there was any chance I could just marry the receptionist. I left and started to roll north. The countryside was a dreamy wonderland. The vast majority of the roads were lined with trees that grew over the road creating a green tunnel to drive through. When you can see into the distance, the mountains are always there, with swirls of mist constantly moving across them. I remember one stretch of road where on my right side clouds were passing up and over mountains so fast it felt like I was fast forwarding through a dream.

There are over two million Motorcycles in Colombia, most are of the smaller variety so when you stop for gas on a big 1150 invariably you draw a crowd of at least seven or eight kids, all with the same questions: "Where are you from, where are you going, do you like Colombia, how much did the bike cost, how do they get the figs into the fig rolls." It's enough to give you an ego. I hit the coast road near Santa Marta, close to the very northern tip of Colombia and turned left for Cartagena.

Cartagena

The road follows the coast and there are large amounts of makeshift restaurants by the side of the road with sea views. I pulled in for a bite and had shrimp cocktail about ten yards from the beach. The shrimps, only caught a couple of hours earlier were mixed into a cocktail right in front of me, fresh lime, mixed with veggies and whatever else goes into a shrimp cocktail. It was so good I had to have a second round. Sitting there supping a coke, eating shrimp cocktail with the sea at my back and a lovely cool sea breeze blowing all around me, I thought to myself "Man, these are good times!" A kid by the side of the road tried to sell me a live rooster, or at least I think it was a rooster. Obviously, poultry is about as useful as ashtrays on a motorbike so I said no. The kid looked like he was going to start crying. The rooster didn't seem too happy either. I asked him how much it was, about eight dollars, so I just gave him ten dollars and told him not to kill the rooster! I fully expect forty gold bars in heaven for this should God turn out to like roosters.

I rode all day and as the light was fading, I arrived in Cartagena. On my right side the sun was setting in a blue grey sky as I swept into the City, it was incredible. That day was so good, I had every experience imaginable: rain, sun, sunsets, wind, gorgeous scenery, mental drivers, gorgeous grub, roosters, presents, some really bad roads, and I was constantly meeting what were for me the best and most friendly people in the whole world.

It took me a good while to find a place to stay in the city and I booked into a high-rise hotel. As a rule of thumb I'd tried to avoid big cities on this trip, and my advice to anyone is, you get a better sense of a country by staying in the smaller towns and villages, cities are the same the world over. If you want to avoid the bottom feeders of the world, staying away from the big population centers is a good idea.

Cartagena is an attractive city, reputed to be the best-looking city in South America with vast quantities of colonial architecture and the old city is completely ringed by a massive wall that was built to defend the port from pirates, Sir Francis Drake used to plunder Spanish gold from this port. Many of the original cannons are still in the walls and it's very impressive to look at. The women were fantastic looking (I know I'm laboring that point) my final point on the matter is that hot pants were in fashion in Cartagena.

All over the town and I do mean all over, there were bakeries churning out roasting hot rolls, pasties, cakes, and every manner of pastry and bread. The smell creates one of those Scooby Doo moments where you get the scent of all the freshly baked goods, it tastes great and it's ridiculously cheap. Most people eat on the streets as the restaurants are pricey, but you can get a good breakfast for about $3 as long as you don't mind chowing down on the foot path. If your calorie conscious, it's not the best place to go as its all pastry, so you can feel yourself getting fatter by the second. I tried out a Chinese restaurant when I was there, I saw the sign and thought to myself "Yes, nice round of sweet and sour chicken!" When I'd ordered I looked at the price and said to myself, "Crikey that's expensive!" but when the grub arrived I figured out why. The portion was so large it had to be put on the plate with a spade, there was easily two kilos of grub.

On a down note, as a tourist you're targeted as having plenty of cash and therefore fair game. For example, that day I had about ten transactions where I was paying money, in at least seven of them I was ripped off straight to my face. There wasn't even a hint of trying to cover it up. Some examples were trying to give you the wrong change, charging you twenty dollars for a five-minute cab ride, pretending they had no change and leaving you waiting for twenty minutes in the hope you would just leave. In the hotel, they wouldn't give me a key so I had to keep going up to the room with the porter who was looking for a tip each time. On one occasion I felt like a complete dumb ass, I stopped a taxi and asked him to take me to a part of the old town, he looked at me funny and we drove for about ten minutes and pulled up to the place I was looking for, I paid him and said Adios. As I closed the door and he pulled away, I looked across the street and about two hundred yards away was the back of my hotel, I could almost hear the guy saying as he drove up the road "dumb gringo!"

The women seemed as cranky as hell, much like Bogota. Every time you order a drink, a coffee, or a cake or pay for anything they look at you like they just caught you trying on their knickers. They may be hot tamales, but cranky is too high a price to pay. This lot made Irish red heads look like baby kittens. They can keep their tanned hot bodies, fake boobs and bountiful arses, give me a freckly set of Irish boobs any day! It was becoming more apparent since I'd left the US that nobody seems to really care about the countries natural treasures down south. The fort walls, which surround the city, doubled as the city latrine with much of the feature stinking of piss. I saw at least ten lads all taking a leak up against the ruins of a wall that took two hundred and eight years to build. This fort is massive and is very striking, but there's rubbish all over the place, the stink is brutal and there is no planning control so all sorts of out of place buildings surround it. It's a shame. Imagine you went down to the pyramids in Egypt and the whole place banged of piss, or had a McDonalds parked right beside it. On top of that, the whole sea front and most of the other features are covered in garbage. There are many homeless people knocking around, with many folks missing limbs, apparently Colombia has one of the highest amounts of land mines in the world. Cartagena is definitely worth a visit but it has its warts.

That night I headed out in Cartagena for a bite to eat in a place called El Bistro, a German restaurant recommended by the lonely plant. While sipping a coke I met two Swiss girls, Vera and Annette who had been traveling in South America for the last two months and just got back from a seven-day cruise on the Amazon. Swiss women are a fairly confident tribe, they were both wearing vests with no bra's over bodies that had been tanned for a week sailing up the amazon. The sexual torment continued unabated. We had dinner and a couple of drinks and shared stories from our trips. I had a great night, the Swiss are a cool bunch and guess what, English was the girls forth language, after Swiss, German and Spanish. They would put you to shame. I said goodnight around 10.30pm and headed back for the hotel. When it gets later things get seedy in the busy spots, and as I was walking back to the hotel, there were tens of prostitutes all flogging their wares. Some of them were persistent and I summarized a quick conversation I had with one of the girls below. She was about forty-five years old and had a set of choppers that could chew an apple through a letterbox.

Charlotte: Hey you, Hey you, where u go? Oisin(jedi): Back to my hotel darling. Charlotte: Which hotel my lova,which hotel? Oisin(jedi): Ummmm emmmm, don't remember the name, it's a long way, a long long way Charlotte: You wan fuckee fuckee? Oisin(jedi): Emmm no thanks darling, I have a girlfriend y'know. I'm going out with Britney Spears! Charlotte: No you not, no you not, You wan suckee suckee? Oisin: I am. She told me to swing up to Los Angeles earlier and not to forget my tooth brush! Charlotte: you wan tug? (doing hand job motion, I was surprised she didn't call it tugee tugee) Oisin: No thanks, I'm grand, sure I better go, Britney will have the kettle on! After five or so more propositions, thankfully I was back in the hotel.

Medellin

I set off the next day with my chief goal being to get as close to Medellin as possible, not a town you want to ride to in the dark, lest you become a statistic. I ended up riding about three hundred miles and in keeping with all the time I spent out of cities in Colombia, it was brilliant. There was rolling green countryside, beautiful warm weather, and warm friendly people everywhere I went.

I was very quickly falling in love with Colombia, and I found it remarkable how much of it reminded me of Ireland. I stopped in a town called Caucasia and at first tried to check into a hotel that was actually a hospital, they never changed the sign outside. The girls at the reception were in fits of giggles at me trying to check in. That night was perfect. I carved my way through a great steak with lovely chilled beer in an outdoor restaurant on a beautiful summers evening. There was a lovely warm breeze blowing up through the streets and the whole place had a carnival atmosphere as Colombia played a World Cup qualifier. I sat back and watched the world go by, it was lovely. It was when I finished I realized I didn't remember the name of my hotel but thankfully remembered the general direction it was in and found it after about thirty minutes.

I was continuing to avoid big cities and stay in the countryside and small towns, with that in mind I was going to make for a small town just south of Medellin. I thought it would be about three hours away however I didn't realize the road to it went over the mountains. The roads had a good surface and the lovely warm sunshine had my spirits soaring. The people I met along the way were all smiling and everyone I met was unbelievably enthusiastic to meet someone from Ireland on a motorbike trip. There were military and police all over the place, and it seems like their favorite mode of transport was also on a motorbike, with one soldier driving and the other riding shotgun behind holding the gun in a menacing grip. I got stopped a couple of times and they were a bit picky but let me go after a couple of minutes.

It definitely did feel like the ante had been upped on the security front the closer I got to Medellin. Medellin is a city in a valley, surrounded by mountains so if I wanted to drive through it, it would mean making my way through two mountain passes back to back, I planned on waiting to see how I felt closer to the time, if I liked the look of Medellin I would stay a night. During the climb, the rain started to come down like it only does in the tropics and as I went higher and higher, the rain got heavier and heavier. There were rivers of water coming down the road and the whole mountainside seemed to be washing away. I drove through three separate landslides, and two floods over a foot high, at one point, I was afraid I would draw water into the piston heads. This continued for about ninety minutes, torrential rain and combined with lunatic truckers, landslides, floods, and cows and horses on the road. It all made for an insane morning. As I started to descend out of the mountains, the rain eased off and by the side of the road, people were funneling the rain coming down off the mountains to wash trucks, have showers and wash clothes. As I continued on the road to Medellin, I was kept company by one of the longest shanty towns in the world hugging the small space between the road and the river.

Medellin is a city of about two million people and you hit the sprawl a long time before the city so progress on the road was very slow. I quickly made up my mind up that I wasn't going to stay in the city and I'd push through. As usual in the big cities, I ended up getting lost and that's when the first problem happened. The scumbag element exists in every city, the difference is that down in South America driving a BMW with a BMW enduro suit you stand out like a sore thumb. The inevitable result is that these hombres are drawn to you. For the second time while stopped at traffic lights two muck birds showed up with robbery on their minds, although this time the outcome was different.

I had learned my lesson from the first incident in Mexico. I had left at least fifteen feet of room in front of me to give me somewhere to go, and I had a lump hammer in my tank bag. The first lad showed up under the guise of begging and approached me on my left side. I was watching his friend closer who was circling to the right. I had replayed this situation in my mind a thousand times since Mexico, what would I do if it happened again? The guy on my right was carrying a big stick, nothing more. I wasn't too worried about the stick, the enduro suit with gloves and helmet left me well protected. With the bike in neutral, I kicked down the stand in anticipation of the guy on the left pulling at my side, and with my right hand whipped out the hammer and swung wildly, "Come near me and I'll fucking do ya!"

The guy on the right then cracked the stick off my shoulder. I jumped off the bike and ran about ten steps towards him with the hammer lofted above my head, "Get the fuck away from me!" No sooner had I roared it when four of the folks who were in traffic behind me jumped out of their cars and ran for the two muck birds, who then ran off. There we were, me and a bunch of lads from Colombia shaking hands saluting our victory with about half a mile of traffic stopped behind us, it's a moment I'll never forget. As the horns started to go, we all headed off. As I was driving up the road at least ten cars beeped the horn at me as they passed, I felt like Thor!

From there I crossed the city and as it was only 1pm, I could easily make it to La Pinta, a town south of Medellin. The road took me back over the mountains and it was a case of rinse and repeat on the weather from earlier in the day although thankfully it didn't last for the whole journey. On the way to La Pinta I came across an accident, you always know there's one ahead when you have to filter through a mile of backed up traffic. The accident was between a biker and a trucker, with the bike in bits and the rider in the recovery position on the side of the road. There's an unwritten code that if you can at all, you have to help bikers in distress so I went over and gave the people helping him anything they needed out of my first aid kit. The poor lad was white as a ghost and looked in a real bad way. There was nothing else I could do to help so I hit the road.

It turned out that day was a bank holiday so the town, which is a river resort, was completely booked out. It was 5:15pm in the evening and I'd about forty minutes of light left. The next city was over two hours away, Manizales. I just had to pucker up and hit the road, driving at night is a really bad idea in Colombia so I was shitting bricks. I got lost close to Manizales and once more, this time in the pitch black, in the middle of nowhere I was lost in Colombia. No matter which road I took I was over two hours away from somewhere to stay. The rain started again and the next two hours were mental. Unable to see due to the rain on the visor I had to contend with horses and cattle on the road, masses of construction, people walking out onto the road and every type of road hazard imaginable, but it wasn't my first time, and apart from it being a huge pain in the ass, I took it in my stride. The best way to deal with these situations is to use a truck as your battering ram. If you nestle up behind a truck you don't have to worry about hitting any animals or people on the road, and if its pitch black it's far safer to do this than go it alone. I finally found a motel and checked in. The motels double as love hotels in Colombia, just like Mexico and Central America, you pay in four-hour installments. Knackered tired I was serenaded to sleep by the sound of couples shagging all round me.

Things really went crazy the next day.

As I was filling up with the usual hoard of kids around me, a really shady character came over. I knew he was odd because he wouldn't look at me. He asked questions of the kids that I had answered them earlier, where's he from, where's he going, how much is the bike worth and then he walked off, you didn't have to be Sherlock Holmes to figure out something was up. He went back to his car and sat there making some phone calls as I talked to the kids. I waited until I saw him drive off before leaving.

I stopped for breakfast a short time later on the side of the road. These roadside restaurants are temporary structures randomly placed on an area by the side of the road with a canopy covering some tables and an area where you can cook some food. As I was eating, the same guy from earlier drove by really slowly, eye balling the bike, but this time he had three other guys in the same car. "Fuck me, what the fuck is going on!" I took the registration of the car and said to myself, "Ok, go to the police, give them the details, it can't hurt." I went, and had a nightmare time explaining to them what I meant, lets just say there was ample use of the word bandito.

I told them I was headed for Popayan and would phone them by six that evening and if I didn't show, that car was the culprit. I drove off. Along the way, I thought, "So do they want me? Nah, don't think so, no room in the car, and they would have to butter me to get me into the boot. The bike? Hmm maybe? To rob me?" I had no idea.

Just then as I rounded a bend my heart instantly went to 199 beats per minute.

There on the road pretending to be broken down was the car. I could see it about four hundred yards ahead with two of the four guys standing out on the road. I had a truck behind me so couldn't easily pull over. My mind went crazy, "What the fuck am I going to do!" Acting purely on instinct, my right hand went into the tank bag for the hammer, I moved it over to my left hand and with the right hand wound the accelerator back as far as it would go. Very quickly my speed was almost 100mph and in my mind's eye one of these bandits was getting the hammer right in the head if they tried to stop me. The engine roared. I roared, "Me Bollllllliiiiiiiiiiixxxx!" as I passed one of the guys who had moved into the middle of the road into a blocking position. He had noticed the waving hammer and backed away as I shot by him. I switched the hammer back into the tank bag and looked into my rear view mirrors to notice the guys getting into the car and turning to follow me.

At that moment I was petrified, I have never felt fear like it. My whole body was instantly lathered in sweat and I was hyperventilating. With sixty-five miles to go to Popayan I put the hammer down like no one has ever done before and few will ever do again. I kept telling myself, "If you can't keep this bike at 5000rpm you are a fuck bag who deserves what he gets!" I screamed through army and police checkpoints, rounded bends on the ragged limit, rallied over ramps, overtook on the hard shoulder, you name it I did it. Anything to get away from my pursuers. My thinking was to try to get the cops to follow me, If they did I'd be safe then.

Thinking about it now, I should have just stopped at one of the police check points but with fuck all Spanish these guys could have made out that I had robbed them, or at least that was how I reasoned. The reality is I could have just as easily been shot for rallying through the checkpoints. It wasn't exactly a moment of clarity.

I made it to Popayan in well under an hour, and with the maneuvering I did on the road no one in a car could have kept up with me. I never saw the car again.

I pulled into a police station and spent an hour with the police explaining to them what happened. They have federal and local police so I had to wait for the federal guys to show up. They even sent around a guy who spoke some English so that made things easier. He was the second guy in Colombia I met who could speak English and his name was also Carlos. He said that the number plate I gave him was Venezuelan and that he thought that they were probably going to rob the bike and any valuables, but nothing more.

We chatted for a good while about what I was doing in Colombia, where I'd come from and in his owns words, "Man your fuckeeen crazy traveling alone in Colombia with no Spaneesh, no phone, alone and no fuckeen clue!" When it came to giving descriptions I was useless. Average height, tanned, black hair, tache, the whole country looks like that! I told them I didn't want to take things any further and I was going to head south the next morning. Carlos gave me a route to take which took me off the beaten track in case they might be waiting, they knew from talking to the kids that I was heading south which could only mean Ecuador, the main road being the Ruta 25.

When I got back to the hotel I was laying on the bed thinking about everything that had happened and kept running it over in my head, my mind was caught in a big loop. My heart was going like a jackhammer. I was taking my pulse and resting it was running at 140 and wasn't getting any slower. I think it was some sort of a reaction after having burned so much adrenaline on the sixty mile bull ride through the countryside.

This next part isn't particularly macho, but it's a warts and all account so I said I would include it. I sat on the floor in the corner of the room taking really deep breaths to try to slow my system down but it wouldn't work. The walls in the hotel started to close in on me and it felt like there was no air anywhere and although I've never suffered from claustrophobia, or had a panic attack, I really felt like I was going to get crushed where I sat. I was certain I was going to have a heart attack. My chest felt like it was going to burst and I couldn't breathe. With the help of my trusty Rosary beads, over the course of the next two hours slowly but surely I got myself back in order. I was a mile away from getting to sleep and just packed up my stuff and sat in the dark looking out the window of the hotel room waiting for the first sign of the dawn. "This sort of thing never happens to Indiana Jones!"

The dawn came and I hit the road, the goal being to get to Pasto, about 140 miles south of Popayan. I was ragged leaving, I hadn't slept a wink, and felt like someone had let the air out of me. I ended up spilling the bike while trying to take a picture while driving by some mist covered mountains. I wasn't going very fast and neither the bike nor me were damaged although my pride was severely dented. So by 8am I was completely in the horrors.

When you're surrounded by the Colombian countryside it's hard to stay in bad form for long. The roads weaved their way through stunning valleys, up and down the side of mountains and as is seemingly always the case in Colombia, the distant mountains were always covered with a beautiful mist. The roads had sheer drops on one side; with steep cliffs on the other and I travelled through several tunnels cut through the mountain.

I must have passed five hundred soldiers, the average age being no more than twenty years old. There's something wrong about a young lad that age standing on the side of the road in all weathers carrying a loaded machine gun or rifle, when you talk to them you can tell their just kids and nervous as hell but all of them were genuinely interested in me and the bike and we had a great laugh.

I stopped for lunch at a small roadside restaurant in the mountains (four tables with a tin roof) and the family took me into the back, sat me down at their table and made me lunch. None of them had a word of English but we got along great! The amazing thing was that these people survive on way less than fifty dollars a week and there they were sharing out the grub refusing to take any money from me. The Colombians are amazing. Imagine that, you're as poor as a church mouse and you're still sharing with a complete stranger. I just had to do something to return the favor so I made an excuse that I was meeting "mucho amigos" down the road and bought ten bottles of diet coke, crisps and chocolate bars from their shop. About twenty minutes down the road I met some folks on the side of the road and gave them the goodies, they looked as though all their birthdays had come together.

From there, I went up over some more mountain passes, which felt like being on top of the world. At one point I jumped off the bike and sat there on the side of the road, looking down at the valley and vast mountain ranges all around me, sipping a bottle of water. It was a perfect moment, you get them every other day on a trip like this, I was back on a high.

Most people who ride a motorcycle always say that they spend a lot of time looking at the sky. The main reason is to see whether you're about to get soaked, and in Columbia, given it's in the tropics the cloud formations that dance across the sky have to be seen to be believed. All through the journey I had become increasingly fascinated by the sky, I wondered whether it was always like this but because I normally drove a car, I just never noticed.

When you're driving in very remote areas, sometimes a sliver of light appears through a huge bank of clouds and you imagine that the light is a beacon showing you the way home, that the light is just for you and it was made by your guardian angel. The next day I was supposed to cross into Ecuador, but I was worn out and did not have the heart to do a border crossing, so I said I would take a day off and take some time to do nothing. I took the bike up for a spin around the mountains and volcanoes that surround the town and in the process took a bit of time out to reflect on what I'd done so far. In ninety-five days I'd knocked out over

22,000 miles. By the time I would finish I'd have done more miles than the Long way round and the Long way down combined, which was always the intent anyway so no big surprise there. I was in my tenth country (USA, Canada, Mexico, Guatemala, El Salvador, Honduras, Nicaragua, Costa Rica, Panama, Colombia) and the rest of South America was coming soon and I had done all the hard miles alone. I allowed myself to feel good about it, hopefully it would be onwards and upwards from here.

I did what limited touristy stuff there is to do in Pasto, probably the most notable thing about the town is that it's surrounded with active Volcanoes and keeps being destroyed every now and then. The shops and people as a result have a fatalistic sort of attitude from what I could pick up e.g. the driving on the roads is suicidal. It's almost as if the attitude is, "Well it's better to die on the road than get scalded alive by molten lava from the volcano!" You cannot get diet coke, or diet anything in the whole town, "Sure what would you want to be on a diet for, don't you know we are all going to die any minute! Have a cream bun!" The beggars were as aggressive as hell. They weren't big on playing the pity card or putting on a sad face so you'll feel bad and cough up some readies, nope not there. It was more like, "Hey you, yeah you ya big rich gringo bollix...give me some money or I'll breathe on ya!" The people in Pasto were a mix of Spanish, Indians, Creoles, Whites, blacks, and some other stuff not necessarily walking on two legs. There was seriously not a looker in the whole town, when it comes to restocking the herd, they won't be coming down there for samples although I doubt they'll come my way either. Pasto was a place to go to sleep in, but not much more.

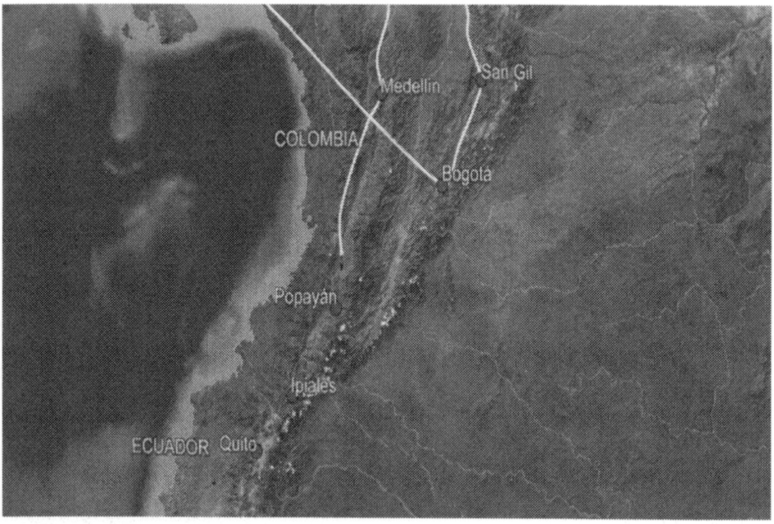

Chapter 8
Ecuador and Peru

Every time you have a border crossing you should always plan to be there really early so you don't run the risk of getting caught there over night, also to avoid getting caught behind big busloads of tourists. I had no idea what to expect but given it was the Colombia Ecuador border, I was not expecting a good time.

The road there continued to wind a path through massive mountains, this part of the world is raved about in the motorcycle overlander fraternity and it certainly lived up to its billing. I arrived at the border and 8am and parked up the bike and for the first time since I crossed into Central America, the crossing went like clockwork. One of the border guards took me under his wing and the whole thing was over and done with within ninety minutes. Now, while in the western world a ninety-minute border crossing might have you penning a letter to your public representative let me assure you in this part of the world its cause for celebration! I was elated, and setting out for Quito at 9 30am, I said to myself "Fat boy, you've earned yourself some nosebag!" The chow never lasts long when I'm around and before too long I was back on the bike haring for Quito.

The early difference between Ecuador and Colombia was that Ecuador was completely deforested, near the border at least. It's much poorer than Colombia too, many of the small towns on the way to Quito were in a terrible state.The road was littered with checkpoints and there was a massive police presence. In Ibarra, a town in the north of the country, I came across the aftermath of a mini riot with debris all over the ground and there was tens of riot police wearing gas masks. They must have used tear gas to break it up and while there was no gas visible in the air, in two seconds flat my nose and throat and eyes felt like someone and taken a garden rake to them.

It was a fairly trouble free journey after than and along the way I stopped off to take some pictures as I passed the equator. I was giggling away to myself as I imagined that one of my balls was lying on the northern hemisphere and the other on the South with my lad lying on the equator. Hey, I'm a guy, that's what we do.

Quito

Eventually I got to Quito. The main reason for going there was to get the bike (renamed to Sam Gamgee) serviced and tarted up after a grueling time since Phoenix Arizona. Quito is a big city and very spread out so I was worried that it was going to take a long time to find the BMW centre, but as I was driving into the town I spotted the dealer on my right hand side. When I went in to the reception, they took the bike straight in, not only that, they said that they would have the bike ready for the following evening. They even paid for a taxi for me to a nearby hotel, they were awesome! The hotel was very plush, for $38dollars you get some style down in Ecuador, it even had lovely soft and fluffy toilet paper not like the tracing paper I was used to in Colombia.

That afternoon I headed into Quito City, for what I promised myself, was my last ever look at colonial architecture, I had seen enough "colonial gems" to last me a lifetime. That night I hooked up with a fellow biker, Steve Barnett from the USA who was also riding through South America. We met in Finn McCool's Irish bar, which was run by a girl from Ireland, Ursula. She was very friendly and introduced me to the whole bar when I got there. We had a heap of pints as one must when introducing oneself to a countries beer and I woke up the following morning not unexpectedly with an atrocious hangover.

I went off the next morning to do all the remaining touristy stuff in the city. Quito is vast and the traffic insane so I hired a taxi for the morning and got him to take me around all the hot spots. Doing this normally works out at less than $20 and saves you having to figure it out for yourself, yes that's right, I'm a lazy bastard. The taxi driver sported a pair on leather gloves and drove like Mario Andretti all over the town when the traffic permitted. The dude was a font of nervous energy, changing the radio station every two minutes, beeping the horn as if he was being paid for every beep and continuously shouting at the whole world.

There is a code to the beeping that goes on in South American Cities, and I think I've deciphered just a bit of it, here are some examples: One beep: Heads up! That light will be green in a minute Long beeeeeep: It has gone green. Go will ya! Really long beeeeeeeeeeeeeeeeeeeeeeeeeeeeeeeeep: It's been green for a full second, move it Tonto! Two short Beeps - Bep Bep: Nice bum (passing girl on the street)

During the tour, we came across two student riots. The basis for the rioting was that the city had put up the price of bus fares so much that it was beyond the student's means to pay it. It was all turning to violence and on three separate occasions, we saw police running away from hundreds of youths. I've never been witness to a riot before but your first clue its all kicking off is the deafening whistles and shouting. There was definitely an disgruntled undercurrent in the city and I remember thinking it wouldn't be too long before Quito makes the news at home soon, apparently several people had already been killed.

In Finn McCool's, a bunch of expats and myself talked about the things you never get used to once you leave the United States and head south. The common denominator we all arrived at was the noise. A good example was the hotel I stayed in. It was right beside the airport and as the planes landed and took off, you could feel the vibrations in your bones, on top of that, it set off all the car alarms on the street. Sleep south of Tucson is fleeting at best.

Someone turned on the rain that night in Quito, turning the city into a parking lot. There were knee high floods everywhere. Despite the obstacles I collected Sam Gamgee from BMW and from there it was a quick dart back to the hotel and from there back to the touristy part of Quito for a couple of pints and a bite to celebrate my last night in the city. On the way there, the taxi the driver was blaring salsa music, I don't mind a bit of Salsa but it was all I'd heard now for nearly two months and after a while it starts to sound like someone scraping out the ashes from a fire. You know those people who always scrape far more ash out of the heart than they need to while you sit there clenching your teeth so your fillings don't drop out? I hate them.

At the end of the second pint, the whole town had a power cut leaving the Mariscal area of the city in total darkness. Everybody paused for a second and continued drinking as if nothing happened. Ursula from Finn McCool's was telling me that a pub owner was shot dead the previous day. I had seen the shrine the night before and was wondering what it was all about. She was also saying that most of the expats who run businesses carry guns, the city isn't for the faint hearted. I bailed out with two fellow Dublin lads who were on their way to an all night rave and we jumped in a Taxi. Both lads had been on the lash for a couple of months solid since both breaking up with their girlfriends and had been on a drugs and drink binge.

Steve had talked to me about riding together on a section of road as we both headed south. I explained to him that having come this far on my own I really wanted to complete the rest of the journey alone. To his credit, he completely understood, and we have kept in touch since. I got a taxi back to the hotel but when I got there, I knew something was up. The whole street was empty and there was two police cars making announcements. Apparently, there was a curfew due to fears of more student rioting. The city had that vibe running through it, when you can feel that something bad is going to happen.

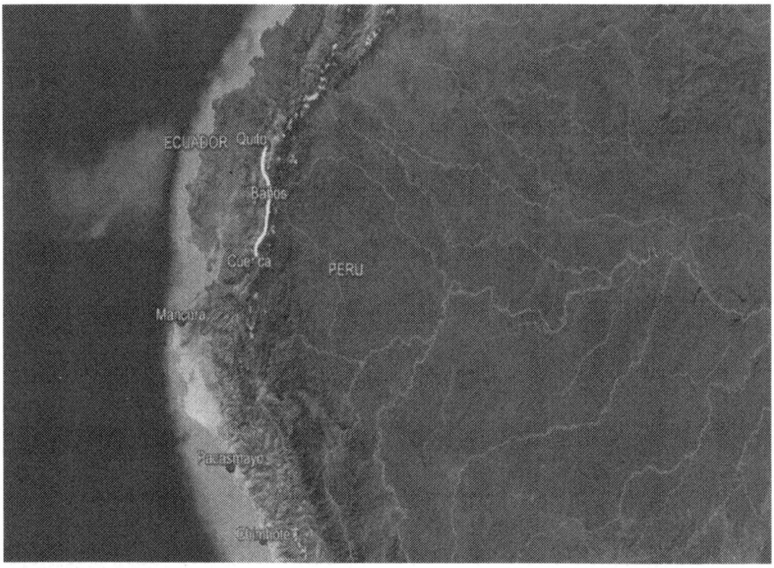

It was time to leave and under a cloudless sky, I drove out for a town called Baños. The first task was to find my way out of Quito which is really just an exercise in relative failure. I got lost as usual, but sixty minutes spent lost in Quito's urban sprawl was a massive victory compared to the two hours I'd regularly spend lost in the towns of Central America. On the way south, the route runs parallel to the spectacular Andes Mountains. One mountain in particular was snow capped, and as I was only a hundred or so miles from the equator, I found myself saying, "Kilimanjaro how are ya." I was armed with a brand new set of intermediate tires instead of knobbies and it was the smoothest ride I'd had since Arizona.

Banos

Baños is completely hemmed in with green mountains and a volcano. There's hot springs, waterfalls, hundreds of markets and of course the ubiquitous colonial church. The town is the adventure capital of Ecuador, and not surprisingly was full of back packers, no problem as long as I didn't meet any gap year types, I secretly prayed that when it came time to trim the herd that they would be first.

In that area there seemed to be quite a large Indian community, I'd seen at least five Indian women no bigger than hobbits, all wearing really cool hats. Most had unbelievably crooked teeth, bad enough to make a dentist reach for a brandy. Using Baños as a base, I took Sam Gamgee up into the mountains to do a bit of exploring. This was the first time since Costa Rica that I'd taken the bike off the beaten track, up until then it had been a bit too dodgy. In total I covered about fifty miles on gravel roads which bended and twisted as they climbed their way through the Ecuadorian Andes. I spent most of the time off the bike acting the maggot and generally enjoying the countryside. The road initially cut across a bridge over a river many hundreds of feet below. As I peered over the side, several people were walking across a rope bridge a hundred feet below.

I met a Danish couple on the way up the mountain, Ryan and his girlfriend (can't remember her name for the life of me), from there they were heading over to the coast to do some diving. I would have done that too but I look too much like a bull elephant seal when I wear a wetsuit, it would only draw great white sharks, and it simply would not be fair on everyone else.

I found a spot to sit down on the side of the mountain and I can't describe how good it felt to be sitting on the soft ground with a beautiful cool breeze sweeping up from the valley below. This was all going on at about 10am in the morning (-5hrs GMT) and my thoughts started to drift to friends and family all over the world.
I wondered what they were doing as I sat and soaked up the moment for about two hours. In Los Angeles, it would be 7am and Helmar, the guy I met in Alaska would no doubt be still in bed hopefully nursing a hangover with vague memories of the night before. The folks I knew in Portland, would be starting to get the first hour of their Sunday sleep-in over with, I hoped they enjoyed it. In Phoenix it was about 8am and the tens of people I knew they would all be about to head out for Sunday morning breakfast, everyone does that in Phoenix. In Atlanta, the same time as Ecuador, they were no doubt combing their way through the Sunday morning broadsheets. In New York my brother probably just had the kids up and washed and was about to head out the door with Shannon to do some family stuff. Back in Ireland it was 3pm and folks were no doubt tucking into a Sunday dinner with gravy flowing left right and centre, the men all chasing the grub down their necks so they can go in to the sitting room and watch the sports on television, the women all saying to themselves "well he can piss off if he thinks I'm cleaning all this up!" In Germany it would be 5pm, Twisted Robot is helping himself to a bit of dinner and would be in the shower soon, he'd a hot date with a full-bosomed Fräulein and in Australia it was already tomorrow and the Fosters were all fast asleep, wherever they were, I

really hoped their Sunday was as good as mine!

Baños was turning out to be a trip highlight. It had a really relaxed buzz and was full of travelers and kindred spirits. That night I went out for pints with Carina (German) and James (English) a couple who I met in Quito and were traveling their way through South America. While we were out eating dinner, we met Jake and Jemma also from England who were off doing an epic two-year traveling spree all over the world. I had planned to leave the following day but Jake and Jemma talked me into going canyoneering and bridge jumping. Canyoneering for the unenlightened (which included me until we started it) is where you take a section of rain forest where there is a canyon and fast flowing water and you hike, abseil, and repel down the canyon through the river. On the way, you're absolutely drowned by waterfalls and spend a good four hours in the water. It's a brilliant experience, it lashed rain for large parts but as you're soaked anyway it just adds to the event. The whole day we were treated to beautiful butterflies flying all round us and with the steepness of some of the descents we built up lots of camaraderie as we gave each other tremendous moral support. For the decent, you have to put on a wetsuit. These things never seem to fit me and the suit I was given for this adventure was no different. It was final proof if any was needed, that you can get six pound of crap into a five-pound bag.

A bridge jump is where there's a rope tied to the underneath of a bridge and you jump off an adjacent bridge over the canyon and swing back and forward over a mountain river. The last time I did something like this it was about ten years previous and the feeling as I initially jump was terrifying. I stood there and the guy who was supervising says to you "on 3, 3..." Then, through your mind flashes "Jesus these ropes look awful thin, will they hold my weight!" 2..., "Is this buckle latched properly, holy fuck, holy fuck!" 1 is where you jump but instead today Jake started roaring, "No don't jump, don't jump, not yet!" I started roaring, "Is it the ropes are they broke? What the hell is going on?" Jake turned around and said, "Sorry about that mate, hadn't got the camera turned on mate, now you can go!" "You bastard!" My heart was doing cart wheels and then, once again it was 3, I'm not ready, 2, I'm not fucking ready, 1, Go! As you initially free fall it feels like your stomach is going to pop out your arse, after which it's just like being Tarzan in a movie, that is, as soon as you figure out you are not going to die.

When I came to Ecuador I really thought the highlight would be getting the bike serviced and riding through the equator with maybe a couple of mountain passes but it had exceeded all my expectations. In keeping with the trend of outrageous swings in fortune and mood, the following day started crap, I woke up with eleven mosquito bites around my left ankle and the itch was brutal. At that moment, cutting my foot off with a spoon seemed a good alternative to the itch. After that, as I was walking down the three stories of the hotel with my bags, I fell down the last four steps, about as graceful as a bull in Wellington boots. As I picked both myself and my dignity up off the floor, the oul one working in reception, about 80 years old muttered, "Mas despacio, no problemo!" In summary, slow down and you'll have no problems. I resisted the temptation to take out my hammer but took comfort in the fact that no doubt, she'd die of old age fairly soon.

I left Baños with a knot in my stomach after having such a great time there. Jake and Jemma and everyone else was first class. The British are the best swearers and cursers in the whole world, a great quote from Jake, "Mate I'd give my right bollock to be on this trip with ya!" it sounds so much better with a Bristol accent! Jake was a man's man, the son of a Vicar he had a mouth like a sewer. I asked him how long he'd been into motorcycles, to which he replied "Since I shot out the vagina mate!"

From there I headed back to the Pan-American Highway to head south to Cuenca, another colonial town, it had been recommended many times to me. Up until midday, the road continued to cut through the Andes as it wound its way towards Cuenca. With about a hundred miles to go I stopped for petrol and the guy asked me where I was going. I told him. I then asked how much longer to get to Cuenca. He said four hours more or less. I said, "For 100 miles, you must be joking!" He knew what he talking about, the road was awful and the weather was crap, a mixture of fog with pissing rain and lunatic drivers. The whole country was addicted to over taking no matter where it was on the road. Say if the top speed of your car was sixty and you were an Ecuadorian and say you were driving at 58mph and there was a guy in front of you doing 59mph. Well, to not try and overtake for an Ecuadorian is like saying, "Would you not like an extra two inches onto the end of your John Thomas?" They just can't resist.When I got to the hotel, they told me to park the bike in the lobby. Awesome!

The following day the plan was to cross into Peru.

Ecuador is quite small, only about the size of the state of Nevada in the USA but seeing as I had to cross a border I set off very early hoping to cross through to Peru for 2pm. When I'd a border to cross I'd always wake up grumpy and that day was no different. The other part that was on my mind was that all the cool stuff to do in Peru was in the south of the country. The Nazca lines, Machu Pichu, Lake Titicaca, all of them, all in the South. Peru is over five times the size of Britain so there would be many miles to get through to get to the sexy stuff.

During the last miles in Ecuador the countryside turned schizophrenic. One minute I was in lush green tropical mountains, and seven miles down the road, I was in a Mars like red desert landscape. The variety is on account of the Andes, according to the guide books they block water ever getting to certain areas and that's where all the contrasts come from. At one point it was like someone found the green and brown switch as I moved from brown mountains to green in the space of three or four miles. Not long after, as I approached the ocean the whole world turned into a massive banana tree plantation. The plantations all seemed to be owned by large multinational fruit companies, with the brands you would normally see on a banana peel when you're out shopping. The area covered was vast, and I started to see why the rain forest was under so much pressure. At home we get told to eat 5 portions of fruit a day, I wonder if the subtext of the advertisement read "and it will help clear the world of rain forest" would people be as keen on it.

As I approached the border with Peru and the town of Huaquillas, every gas station was dry. Petrol is over twice as expensive in Peru compared to Ecuador, a lad charged me $10 dollars for two gallons in Peru versus $1.79 a gallon in Ecuador, all the Peruvians not surprisingly go across the border to fill up their cars. The best way to think about a border to get an idea of what its like in these parts of the world is to think about a lovely lake, but at the sides, there's loads of pond froth and scum. The countries are lovely but the borders are full of scumbags and people of lower virtue than crocodile shit.

In every country till then, the process has been the same. Stamp out of the country your leaving then stamp into the one you are going to and then import the motorcycle. Well, in Peru, they like to do it differently.

In Ireland a two hundred yards distance can mean anything from two hundred yards to a mile in the countryside, well in Peru three kilometers has the same rough application. I stamped out of Ecuador very easily even feeling confident enough to tell a few fixers to piss off. I should have gleaned something from the way they were smiling at me. Next, I went down the road (3 km) and instead of getting to stamp into Peru first, you import the bike first, magic stuff, this was the hardest part done, "woo-hoo!" I thought. So I asked the chap where I stamped the passport into Peru. Note you can't get out of the country or into the next one without these stamps so it's a big deal. He told me 3km up the road on the right. So that so that puts me right back at the start. I asked are you sure? "Si Si" he said. Off I went feeling like a ping pong ball back to where I started. "Señor where do I stamp into Peru?" "4km down the road" and I said, "Oh 4 km down the road, ok must be just past where I was the last time."

I went back down the road and this was the routine for the next hour, back and forward, back and forward. Eventually I figured out I needed a stamp on one of the sheets which I got after four pings on the tennis table, and then I had to go over to a bridge. There sat Jabba the Hutt with a mustache. If you asked someone how could you make Jabba the hut uglier? I would say give him a mustache. There he sat delighting in his ugliness. I had watched a video of guys who did this border crossing a couple of years earlier and it was the same bottom feeder doing the stamping through. No bigger bollix exists on earth I can guarantee you. From there you head off and stamp into Peru another 3 km down the road.

Peru

I didn't expect Peru to look the way it did, the early part being primarily desert, coast roads and small fishing villages. There were many occasions when I passed a secluded beach with a couple of beach shacks standing empty on golden sand, and out at sea in the distance a couple of fishing boats were busy hauling in their nets. All the petrol stations on the Peru side of the border were closed down because everyone not surprisingly heads for Ecuador to fill up. I started banging out the Hail Mary's so I wouldn't run out of gas. On fumes, I arrived into a town called Máncora, a small coastal town beset with surfers. All the grub was seafood on the menu, which is great but as a result of my microbial Spanish dialect I ended up ordering octopus for dinner; it was like chewing a tyre tube.

Peru started bad, I was ripped off several times and anytime I went near a city or town I got lost. Next time I see a charity box which says, "Buy sign posts for developing countries"

I will gladly throw in a weeks salary. The Peruvians are a strange bunch and my first two days traveling in the country left me thinking they were inhospitable, especially compared to the folks in Colombia and Ecuador. I never really felt in the least bit welcome since I arrived and I had been doing the whole smile at the world and it will smile back at you routine. It's not like I'd been asking them to do much more than take my money.

Pacasmayo

I left Máncora and drove south to a town called Pacasmayo. I decided to jump off the Pan-American Highway to go and ride through some of the Peruvian desert, you would be amazed at what seems like a good idea when you are just after eating a nice breakfast. The world slowly turned a Magnolia color as I hit the desert, first the bushes and trees thinned out, leaving just scrub and gradually that thinned out as well to leave just sand. The landscape was completely flat in all directions and not since Montana in the USA had so much of the horizon been visible. Given that we do not see much of this sort of thing in Ireland and I had spent so much time in the tropics, a desert was a welcome change in scenery.

In the afternoon, the wind picked up ferociously and for the last four hours of the day, I thought Mother Nature was trying to rip my head off. As the wind picked up it stirred up the sand and filled the entire sky making the world seem an off peach color. Because the sand in the air blocks the glare of the sun, it appears as a red disk in the distant sky. While I was enjoying the change in landscape, I was ran off the road three times by oncoming trucks.

I got to Pacasmayo as the sun was beginning to set and the

world had turned utterly pink, a mix of a red sunset masked by the wind blowing the sand from the desert into the air. In my life, I never thought I'd live to see such a sky. As I got closer to the coast, the sun turned a red orange as it dipped behind the horizon out on the Pacific Ocean. I had a stroll down the pier and bought some necklaces and good luck charms from some stalls. The place I stayed in the town was right on the beach and as I was drifting off to sleep I remember thinking to myself that there is no better sleep aid than the sound of the sea lapping up against the shore, I'd still have swapped it for a good shag. I had completed over five hundred miles in Peru, and to use a sexual analogy, I hadn't even got the hand up the jumper yet.

The next morning I woke up and after all the fighting with the wind the previous day my body was in a heap. I decided to stay an extra day and relax. I spent the following day aimlessly wandering around Pacasmayo and it was quite an experience. On the face of it, it's a lovely little sea side town on the North west coast of Peru. Elderly men meet for early morning coffee and discuss the comings and goings in the small town. On the pier, people drop lines into the water to catch crabs to bait their traps for bigger fish, and out in the distance you can see small boats fishing, albeit in crafts that look far too small for the height of the seas around them. On the beach near the pier local fishermen work on repairing boats, it all feels very wholesome. Along the beach front people sell ice cream as they do all over the world in similar locations, with stall sellers selling every manner of trinket imaginable.

It seldom rains for whatever reason. As the town is on the edge of the Peruvian desert and the wind never let's up, there are decent size waves breaking onto the beach for most of the day, a surfer's paradise or so you would think.

As the day dragged on a thought grew in my mind until I found myself saying, "Where the hell is everyone?" I know in these places they have siestas but the town felt completely empty. I went to a restaurant which was recommended by the locals as being the best fish restaurant around and for about $10, I got a whale sized portion of white fish, not sure what type of fish it was but it tasted mighty.

I walked down the beach and saw just one person, a young boy playing with his puppy, and started to see why no one was attracted to the beach, it was full of rubbish. The further I walked I saw that the towns sewage was running untreated via an open shore directly into the sea where people would be swimming. Still further on down the beach, a large gathering of vultures and gulls were feeding off the waste material from an abattoir where the effluent was pouring untreated into the sea. It is hard to believe that the folks there do not get the linkage between pumping raw sewage directly into the sea and people not coming there to swim in the water. As it is a fishing town, don't the fishermen know that fish prefer water thats clean? I asked myself why they don't do something about it.

As I walked from the beach along the sea front, kids were playing barefoot on the pavement. The children's park was empty, all the swings were long since broken. Its only when you look up the side streets where there's little more than rocks and mud for paving you see that, if barefoot is the way you have to play, the paved area is preferable.

I passed a guy who was catching crabs, if they were too small he didn't throw them back, he threw them behind him on the pier where they quickly died in the heat of the sun. It seemed like he didn't want to have to catch the same small crab again, better to let it die. He seemed to have no sense of tomorrow, "Survive today, tomorrow's tomorrow." I walked up to a statue of Jesus which most towns have overlooking them in these parts. Beside it was a graveyard. There was no one to be seen either up at the mirador looking down on the town or in the graveyard. Strolling around I saw that the graves were above ground, and for a headstone some people just have their name scratched into the cement. I stood there and thought about it for a while. What if at the end, that is all there was to remember you? How would I feel? Do people just live on in people's memories anyway and the headstone doesn't matter, I couldn't decide.

The sad thing was that Pacasmayo could be brilliant. It could be a Mecca for surfers, beach goers, or for even just people who love fishing, or even just eating fish and it could be done very easily. How do you inject pride into people, or a sense of passing what they have now onto future generations? From a natural resource perspective the thought process on everything seemed to be, can I eat it? If not, can I sell it? That's where thinking about the consequences for future generations stops and starts.

As the day dragged on it was hard not to feel that the town was doomed and that if folks in these countries don't imbibe some national pride in their natural treasures, there won't be any left, I couldn't help feeling that the clock was ticking. Later, a pair of dweeb surfers turfed out the environmentalist mood in me and replaced it with Machiavellian malice! I talked to these two lads for about five minutes and slowly felt the life force begin to ebb from my body. I finished up talking to them and was secretly glad that the abattoir was pumping its gunge into the sea maybe it would draw in some sharks and trim the herd of these two numpties. That night in an internet cafe a girl the size of a hippopotamus chatted me up in Spanish. I was never happier that I knew the phrase, "No Hablez Señorita"

I was glad to leave in the end and I tipped south. I left the town and immediately I was straight back into the desert and wind. It was such a strange feeling driving through that landscape. As with the previous day, the wind picked up and threw the sand up for miles around. Mountains and any visible shape become silhouettes of themselves and driving through it felt like driving in a black and white movie.

It goes without saying that, you need to keep your wits about you. As I was driving along a truck which was carrying big sticks started to shed its load stick by stick, it left me doing a slalom behind it to avoid the debris. The desert was full of rubbish, and the houses and buildings I passed were little more than shacks. I passed a desert town where all the houses had a strange looking receiver sticking out of the roofs, it looked like they were all dodgem cars parked together in the middle of the desert. The vast majority of the shops serve out goods to you through iron bars, I guess most are worried that the place will be robbed, not too much spontaneous shopping done here, "Oh I just went in for milk but passed the cookies and just had to buy them!" When your Spanish is as bad as mine you do a lot of pointing, "No up a little, down a little, yep that's it." Out in the desert miles from anywhere some sadist had put up massive Pepsi and beer signs. Driving through one of the driest landscapes in the world with your mouth feeling like a camels heel a sign for Pepsi was a cruel torment. My mind started to think about it, "Mmmm, a nice cold Pepsi, mmmm, the feel of the cold bubbles hitting the back of your throat, mmm. and a lovely belch at the end of a long slug." However, can you buy a Pepsi in the desert? No. Are you even within fifty miles of a Pepsi? No! These signs were pure torture.

I made it to Huanchaco, a surfer town which is famous for the weird sea crafts that the native folks surf out to get their fishnets in. It was wall to wall backpackers, and it seemed to be very far off the beaten track to be so popular.

I went out to the beach and caught another gorgeous sunset. While in the town, I met a couple of really cool people, Andy from the states who let me know that you can't weld aluminum and Flo from France who was over my left shoulder eating a huge pastry as I watched the sun setting.

I knew the next day would be very long, I was going to try to get from Huanchaco to ANY town past Lima, well over 400 miles away. It would be the longest day in the saddle since I left the United States. In case you didn't know, Lima is where they insert the enema for the world, its famous for having a crime committed every three minutes. I left Huanchaco at dawn with four hundred miles ahead of me. Lima, as I mentioned above has the reputation of being one place that no matter what, you don't want to end up. However, if you want to go to Cuzco, Nazca, and Machu Picchu you have to pass that way.

I was straight back into the desert but in a much grander

way than previously. That day was, in my mind anyway, somewhere between riding a bike on Mars, and taking a bike into the Sahara to chase down a couple of camels with Laurence of Arabia. The road stays very close to the coast so at regular intervals you get to see the desert run right up to the sea. The weather started the same as it had for the last four days, high winds with loads of sand in the air with the mountains and oncoming traffic all just vague shadows of themselves. As the day went on, the clouds burned off and the wind dropped to reveal more of the surrounding landscape. The sand had swept across the road making driving conditions treacherous and when the wind gusted, at times you couldn't even see the tarmac. In the desert you can feel completely alone, and you are. There is absolutely no one around for miles and when you drive through it your mind starts to wander in all sorts of directions. Things you have said and done, things you shouldn't have. It's weird how you have to force yourself to think of the good stuff, whereas the not so good stuff just floods in all by its lonesome.

Driving on the roads can also be like a turkey shoot in the busier sections, and guess who the turkey is. Two or three times a day I'd get run off the road by trucks and was continuing to run into incidences of them shedding their loads. All day horns were going, lights were flashing but I think one of the biggest pains in the arse was the fact that many of the buses have a horn that is very similar to a police siren so as you are dodging through traffic you constantly think you're getting pulled over. If that wasn't enough, red lights seem to be just something to consider, not follow, on multiple occasions in small towns I had to swerve to avoid a guy who had gone straight through a red light.

En route I was stopped twice without reason by the police for speeding, completely bogus charges. They didn't even have speed cameras, they were just stopping me because I was a gringo and they reckoned I had money. On both occasions the routine was the same "Mucho Rapido, blah blah." They leave you sit by the side of the road while they do their best to put on a concerned face. The other thing that became apparent is that they phone ahead to each other to let each other know there is a sucker coming. The annoying part about having to bribe these guys is not the money that you have to part with, it's that if something did happen where you needed their help, if the opposition drops a couple of Benjamin's you lose. The Police in Peru are pure scum.

I wasn't having a great time in the country so far. The Peruvians up to this point were not in the least bit friendly. I'd stopped for gas three times, had three meals and stopped for some water another three times and not once did I walk away with the impression that these guys were happy to even get the business. There is an old saying when it comes to traveling, it is "people not places" make the destination, well that's not true for Peru unless you're meeting other tourists there. The only sign of caring at all I'd seen in four days was when two lads helped me find my way to Chiclayo. The rest of the time was like selling rosary beads to Protestants. I wondered when I'd meet nice Peruvians. Most backpackers or normal tourists probably don't see this side as they go straight to the touristy spots which are well catered for.

After over three hundred miles, I arrived in Lima and as it was a Sunday, getting through was straight forward. There's a three lane highway which runs through the city the whole way reconnecting with the Pan-American Highway to the south of the city. So as things turned out it was handy.

I got to a town called Chincha about three hours south of Lima and headed out for a steak. After almost five hundred miles on the road, a hundred more than I thought I'd have to do that day, I earned it. I was the only one in the restaurant. Half way through the steak I looked up and the movie

Titanic was on the TV. It was the scene where Kate is letting poor oul Jack go and he sinks away into the abyss. There wasn't a dry eye at my table. I looked around and two chefs were standing leaning over the counter with their chins on their left hand complete with big tufty chef hats all glassy eyed, it was a lovely moment.

I was lying in bed the following morning and noticed that there were about twenty or thirty holes in the roof, not a problem when it never rains although when you forgot to put on deet the night before it's a big deal. I looked like a teenager after too many Easter eggs with all the Mossie bites. Thankfully, I didn't go to sleep in the buff and all was well with the frankfurter and town halls, so no major damage done.

Nazca

I set off for Cuzco but gave up early, it was just too far away and I was knackered after the previous day's efforts. The road turned inland towards Nazca and all of a sudden, someone hit the heat switch. To be fair it wasn't a massive surprise given that the sun was directly over that part of the world when I was there but I was amazed at just how cool the coast was versus inland. I started to hit serious desert again, and it was so vast I just had to stop and try to take it all in. I pulled well off the road and followed a track a couple of miles out into the middle of nowhere. About five miles out I had an argument with myself; not something you would like the lads in the white coats see you doing. The subject wasn't new. For some reason the biker crowd of which I'm a member are a bit touched. I was in the middle of the desert, alone, with no mobile phone and not a soul for miles and miles. I'd about 250 ml of water in my bag, a dozen sentences of Spanish and to cap it all was about 12000 miles from home. Like a lunatic, I was heading off into the desert on some track which was last trekked by some Inca with a dose of rabies who was thrown out of the tribe for interfering with the village basset hound. I won the argument as you'd expect and said to myself, "Dude just do the miles leave the trekking for the camels." Seeing as I was in a remote spot I decided to do a bit or roaring. The desert is unbelievably quiet and for some reason it seemed that a good roar was an appropriate thing to do. I played Jack Nicholson and Tom Cruise in a Few Good Men, "You want me on that wall!" and finished off with a bit of Samuel L. Jackson in Pulp fiction.

I made my way to Nazca, where the famous lines are. The lines were made by removing the stones and rocks to leave just sand beneath. It's the usual story, no one knows who or why they made them. Well, I have a theory, they were bored. There's nothing else to do in the desert. I headed into the town and stopped at a cool restaurant where they

were playing traditional Peruvian music. At the next table a retired American lady from Dallas Texas introduced herself, her name was Grace.

Oisin: So what brought you to Peru? You on holidays or vacation as you'd call it?

Grace: Oh I'm down here with my family showing them the sights, I worked here for over twenty five years on and off as an archaeologist.

Oisin: Nice one! Wow, Nice one! Indiana Jones or what! There is plenty to keep you occupied here I'd say. Machu Pichu, Chan Chan, the whole Inca thing - you could be here for years and not see it all.

Grace: Oh you don't know the half-of-it sonny! This place is just awash with history.

Oisin: Still they couldn't have been that great, a couple of Spaniards on horseback killed off the whole thing right?

Grace: Oh your just an ignorant SOB ain't ya! (laughing loudly)

Oisin: Still, the people are very friendly though eh? (both of us laughed)

Grace: So how come your here...?

Oisin: Blah blah blah, motorbike trip, blah blah. Grace: Wow sounds fun!

Oisin: Yep, having a ball.

Grace: So are you married? Oisin: Why you looking for a date? You're a bit old for me! (Grace didn't laugh, I threw out a "Haha" to show I was joking which didn't land) Oisin: (bringing in the recovery JCB) So how many of you are down here?

Grace: Don't think you can waltz round that, "Old" remark sonny! (thankfully smiling)

Oisin: Don't mind me, I'm an ape at the best of times.

She went onto describe how Machu Pichu is sinking my 1 cm a month (I made a joke, that's fairly slow eh? Another arrow that missed wildly) and how much was lost to conquistadores and private collectors. I got a heap of tips where to go and what to see, but mostly it was brilliant to chat to someone in English again. I left Nazca not bothering with the plane trip to see the lines. The place was too hot and my mossie bites were itching like I don't know what. My most vivid memory of the town is the incessant beeping of Taxi horns, they never stopped. If the taxi driver sees a foreigner he just beeps the horn so you see him and then you make eye contact and shake your head. This happens five or six times an hour.

The next morning I headed for Cuzco and was on the road a little before dawn. The sign on the way out of Nazca said 561 km which given the route I was going was over mountain roads I knew I had at least nine hours of driving ahead of me. With 200 km done, I passed a sign that said Cuzco 472 km. What the hell? It meant that I'd have to ride almost 500 miles before I'd get to Cuzco, I wondered if I'd gotten lost or something. The road had very few gasoline stations so I filled up at every opportunity, never passing a gas station. It was hard to get any gas above 84 octanes which is one octane above baboon piss, but Sam Gamgee lapped it up and kept going.

The road gradually carved a path through the Andes changing from desert to rocky planes and finally into mountain farmland and altiplano. All day I was treated to steep climbs and descents through the Andes, high mountain planes, deep canyons, rolling rivers, lakes, snow capped peaks, and a stunning sunset. I really thought I was going to burst, I didn't realize that anywhere in the world was so beautiful. The most spectacular thing about it is was I was completely alone, it was like it was all for me. I stopped for something to eat in a remote village and sat outside under a parasol chowing down on rice and chicken. As I was eating the grub, three pigs two sheep and a chicken walked by, I swore the chicken gave me a dirty look, "You're eating my brother!"

Cuzco

With over twelve hours gone, I ended up out in the Andes with sixty miles still to drive in complete darkness. The hazards when it's dark are many and varied. The amount of cattle on the road made me think Noah was up around the corner, at one point I almost plowed into a herd of cattle, I'm sure my pannier caught a tail, my heart was all over the place. I was taking my life in my hands and I'd no one to blame but myself. I made it eventually and pulled into a hostel in the middle of Cuzco.

That night I tossed and turned all night in the bed, I could not stop thinking about the altiplano, which I had seen that day. In my mind I'd seen the best scenery that I was ever going to see and I had an uncontrollable urge to see it again. The great thing about having such a long journey is you can do just that, so the next morning I set off at 5am to go back. It took a little over two hours to get to what I wanted to see and then two hours back. I was afraid that it would look different or wouldn't be as good as the day before but it was exactly the same. The place is haunting. When you pull off the road and step out onto the trails it feels like your stepping out onto an endless plane. I said already that the silence is the most striking thing. The only audible sound is a cool breeze blowing in your face. I saw in the far distance a grey blue motionless lake, and beyond that steep snow capped mountains. The roads stretched off into the distance without a bend, and the clouds painted shadows on the yellow plane, and as if to cap the experience you can see them drift across the sky and altiplano in unison.

I think it's only in the most remote and quiet places of the world that a person really relaxes and unwinds, sitting there thinking about things you never normally take the time to. As I drove on, the hills rose imperceptibly at first but before long I was shaken out of my trance by sweeping right and left hand bends as I made my way back to Cuzco.

Cuzco is very touristy, and with that, expensive. You can't sit anywhere but you're beset by people either begging or selling something, so it's not a comfortable place to go out and walk. A lot of the bars sell T-shirts with the words "No Gracias" printed on them as a way of showing solidarity with the beleaguered tourists. The altitude has some interesting side effects. First, if you do anything at all you're out of breath. Second, the altitude gives you brutal wind, for a while I was farting like an officer's horse. (Well, it was either the altitude or someone put farting powder in my grub)

Thankfully, all my chamber pressures equalized and I booked up for Machu Pichu the following day, after that it would be time to head south to Puno and Lake Titicaca, however all of Cuzco was awash with stories that the road was blocked by farmer protests and you couldn't get through. With an afternoon and a night before the train to Machu Pichu I went out and about in Cuzco. I met a great Irish couple, Fergal and Aoibhann in an internet cafe and we headed around to O' Flaherty's pub, a real Irish bar. Fergal was probably the biggest Liverpool fan in the world and we were both anxiously waiting to see if Liverpool held out against Portsmouth. Thankfully they did and we went for some grub and beer.

There were many negative stories about Bolivia doing the rounds and if half the tales were true the country was starting to unravel, with civil war apparently a certainty in the next year. There were several horror stories both on the news and getting told by the backpacker fraternity. One was about people getting kidnapped and taken to an ATM every day to empty out their cards until they had no money left. Apparently three Irish folks were kidnapped and held in this way for over two weeks, and when they'd no money left in their accounts they were released. The other I'd already heard something about, namely that in the south of Peru there was a massive strike, and the roads are totally blocked with no way through. The same was apparently starting to happen in the North. At that moment everyone was flying to La Paz in Bolivia thus bypassing the problem, that wasn't an option open to me on a motorbike. I decided to stay another day in Cuzco while I tried to plan a route which allowed me to get to Lake Titicaca and to the salt flats in Bolivia.

We met Fergal's cousin Dayna, (It was a guy, he knows it's a girl's name too) and slowly but surely the amount of pints in the system climbed. Later, I met Sam from Australia, the same guy who I met in Antigua and he also came to join us. More folks kept showing up and at one stage there were Germans, Canadians, English, Australians, Irish and Belgians all swinging out of pints at our table. We went to a nightclub and got absolutely hammered, it was a great night.

Machu Picchu

I got back to the hostel at 4am. I was rotten drunk. I was getting collected at 6am to go to Machu Pichu. It felt like I just blinked and the door was getting hammered down by the tour guide. I just had time for a wing wash (can't beat the Boots Cucumber wipes) and off we went, the world was still spinning. Machu Pichu exceeded my expectations and with everything I'd heard about it, I really thought that would be impossible. Even though the place is full of tourists it's still possible to find places where you can be alone and soak up the whole experience. As I was sitting looking off the side of the mountain into the yawning chasm below, a girl from Slovenia came along and started eating a sandwich while sitting up against a rock about five yards away from me. She was a cracker and was working as a tour guide. We chatted for about two hours and really hit it off but we were both heading dramatically different directions so we said our goodbyes.

On the way back to Cuzco on the train I met a couple from Uruguay who I took an instant liking to. They were always laughing and joking and telling stories, I wrote in my diary that a good sense of humor is one of the best qualities you can have. I think it draws people to you. I guess no one wants to be hanging around a bunch of moaning Michael's. In the main square in Cuzco I met a young lad of about eight years of age called Nino. He was a shoe cleaner. Normally I wouldn't get my shoes cleaned not because I'm tight but because I have a problem with kids cleaning shoes for people at such a young age, but in this case given he was so persistent I told him to go ahead. The care and attention he put into cleaning them was amazing. He carried a box the size of a small dollhouse with him and it was full of little doors and presses. Every now and then, he would take out a little bottle of some potion or other and use it to clean off a blemish and then very carefully pack it away and get another potion for another blemish. We ended up having the coolest of chats, which started with him saying to me, "Do you like Snickers bars?" I replied "Yep, but there not as nice as a Double Decker." He said that he'd never heard of one so I described it to him in detail. I also said its best out of the fridge and served with a cup of tea, I said that I'd post one over to him. So it went for the next half an hour just chewing the cud about which type of chocolate bar was nicer and did they have this type of bar in Ireland, and did I prefer Mars to Milky way or Twix to Snickers.

The night before I left I met up with Sam again for a couple of beers in a bar. While we were there chatting we bumped into Vanessa from Belgium. She was touring South America on her own and she was a vision, she could nail a pint of beer as quick as any guy, the Belgians are notorious for having hollow legs. We were in rounds and although she kept saying, "Just get me a glass" we kept getting her pints. She always was the first to finish and look over with a glance that said, "Dudes the tide is out, your twist!" We went back to a party in her hostel, I considered trying to kiss her but decided against it, she was too hot, and too cool. She had worked in Ireland for a few years, so unbelievably spoke English with a semi Irish accent. I should have tried to kiss her, I didn't and regretted it every single mile and minute from then to now. I did however meet her again, but that is a story covered in another book.

It was time to leave Cuzco, and it was harder than you might think.

The previous night it was Halloween and the Peruvians really go on the slaughter. The car park where I had my bike parked didn't open till nearly 10am, it was supposed to be open at seven which is when I showed up to collect it. The lad who was working there, was so hung-over looking when he showed up I didn't even bother to moan at him, he was suffering enough. Before I'd got to the car park I noticed one of my Mossie bites had become very inflamed, or at least I thought it was a mossie bite, maybe I'd scratched it too hard during the night. Some people really flare up if they get a bite, I normally don't so given it was unusual I used the time I was waiting for the car park to open to pop down to the surgery off the square, and get them to have a look at it. The attendant looked at the bite and started making a weird face, the sort of face you make when you think one of the lettuce leaves in your salad just moved all by its lonesome. He took the arm under one of those magnifying glass platforms and then started a round of shaking his head. Next thing I knew he had gotten a needle, popped the lump and sucked out the gunge. Then he said a word, a word which turned my face green in 1 second flat, "Huevos" Eggs, I nearly turned inside out. There was an American guy there who spoke English and they asked me was I trekking or camping in the desert? Some nasty beast had laid eggs into me so next thing the doctor got me to strip off to check the rest of me, I hadn't had a shower so I was cringing. The doctor did a full check from head to toe and there were no more around the place, thank God. "Unusual" was how he summed up.

I logged onto the Department of foreign affairs website to see if the roads had cleared to the south of Cuzco and it said the following: Protesters are currently blocking the main road, near Sicuani, between Cuzco and Arequipa. Travelers should avoid this route. In recent weeks several political and labour-related strikes have been occurring across the country. These demonstrations may lead to violent outbreaks at any time, especially in the departments of Apurímac, Ayacucho, Arequipa, Cuzco, Huancavelica, Huanuco, Junin, Lambayeque, Piura, Puno and San Martín. The armed forces and the national police were recently deployed nationwide in an effort to control civil unrest. Roadblocks may occur on main roads and cause traffic disruptions. Irish citizens should not attempt to cross blockades, even if they appear unattended. Curfews may also be in effect and airports may be closed in response to further unrest.

If I did manage to get through the protests in Southern Peru, it said the following of Bolivia: Currently the situation within the country is very tense and there is potential for social unrest, particularly in the eastern provinces. It is possible that flights to these areas may be cancelled. It is recommended that travelers exercise caution and monitor the media for developments. We are advising against travel to Tarija and Santa Cruz regions for the present. There is also the risk of violent protests in Pando and Beni regions I went anyway.

The initial part of the journey followed the course of a river through green valleys hemmed in by massive brown mountains. The roads started to climb and I was back onto another section of altiplano. I've never felt as at home in any landscape in my life. For me this was a mirror image of Rohan in the Lord of the Rings and instead of riding a horse it was me and Sam Gamgee the bike. I like an old ruin as much as the next guy but natural beauty is what I really love. It was like my feel good meter was absolutely maxed out. The only thing that could have made it better would be watching Liverpool win the European cup while getting fed marshmallows by a nude Britney spears.

By the time I got to the blockaded area, the road was clear of protestors but full of rubble, you could tell things had got nasty as the area was heaving with police. I continued down the road and got to Puno, the last town I would visit in Peru. I went out for dinner in a lovely restaurant on the square and just above the church you could see the moon and a very bright star, it was all very romantic but it was just me and Sam, man I needed a woman.

Lake Titicaca

The tour bus collected me at the hotel at 6am to head to Lake Titicaca. To be honest I wasn't really expecting much, a big lake at high altitude with some people living on funny islands, not really my bag but you can't come to this part of the world without doing it, and so off I went. The trip started poorly, the boat that was taking us stunk of a mixture of crap and diesel fumes so there was a scramble to get up top away from the stink. They only let ten people up top at a time so with ten hours to go on the trip, the atmosphere on the boat was going downhill quick. Early on in the trip before everyone was either barfing from the smell of crap or unconscious from diesel fumes, we pulled into one of the reed islands.

The islands are built on the roots of these reeds that float like corks. They then pile reeds and weave over it. It's squishy to walk on and it was all very different from anything I'd met with so far. The initial part felt unbelievably touristy as the family on the island sang a couple of songs, but it was cool at the same time. As it went on it got a lot better. Apparently the people who live there suffer terribly with rheumatism and after the age of fifty most can't walk. You can't help but notice that the people's faces are etched from hard work. They all have unbelievably deep wrinkles on their faces with most people very bent over looking. They took us out on reed boats which were propelled by only one guy and a large paddle. Even carrying twenty tourists, he still managed to keep up a good gallop. We then went to an island where with the altitude was over 4,000 meters above sea level, I was out of breath just tying my shoe laces. The island was touristy but still worth a visit. We had a trout lunch and the locals put on a couple of dances, the sort of thing my Aunty Mary would love.

As the air is so thin you can see for miles and the sun is unbelievably strong, and because of that, the lake is unbelievably blue. On the way back the sun was setting in the distance through a storm, I felt so calm I could have given Buddha a run for his money.

I went out for dinner in the square and ended up talking to a girl from Russia who was also traveling. Her English was about as good as my Russian so the conversation was mainly taken up with polite nodding. I thought to myself,

"Which nationality of women have a penchant for hairy arsed Irish bikers out on a world trip with a beard that Jesus would be proud of?" The answer was no more apparent than on any of the previous 114 days and 25,000 miles.

The next day I was going to Bolivia.

Chapter 9
Bolivia and Chile

Have you ever had a near miss accident in a car? Most people have and it's enough to keep them talking about it for a week afterwards, "Oh you just wouldn't believe it, I really thought I was a gonner!" I can see a caring partner sitting beside you with the arm around your shoulder saying something comforting like "Oh you've had a lucky escape, really makes you think about how lucky you are to be alive." Then you'd reply, "Oh your right, any chance of a cup of tea and a couple of chocolate biscuits, I've had a hard day." Well, driving in second and third world countries you end up having as many as four or five of these moments a day, eventually you just stop thinking about them, you expect them and if they don't happen it almost seems like the day was a bit of a bore. It must be the same thing that kicks in for adrenaline junkies, when they feel the need to get into increasingly dangerous situations.

I left Puno and drove towards the border with Bolivia keeping Lake Titicaca on my left side as I circled round for the town of Copacabana in Bolivia. All morning I was spoilt with views of Titicaca and a mixture of altiplano and distant snow capped peaks. Along the road, old native women tended small flocks of cattle and sheep, no one appears to own the land by the side of the road, so it's free to pasture. All they do is drive the cattle up and down the roadside and it struck me how simple a life it was. I didn't see any guys doing it, it seemed that the vast majority of labour in these countries was carried out by women.

As I drove along an old man was throwing bricks and stones out onto the tarmac and I happened to be driving by him as he threw out another causing me to swerve while uttering "What the hell was his problem?" Further along the road just in front of me a truck went straight off the road for some reason, it didn't hit anything, and I guessed the driver fell asleep. The incident seem to happen in slow motion, I could see the truck on down the road about half a mile in the distance, then there was a shattering of glass and then the truck went off the road, I can't tell you how many times I said, "Holy shit!" in that couple of minutes, but if there was swear jar around, I'd have been broke after it. The last couple of days were some of the best of the trip and I even found time to meet some lovely Peruvians.

I have to say overall it's a great country, and I really enjoyed it. Along the way I passed 25,000 miles, a hugely emotional milestone as its approximately the distance around the world at the equator. As an aside, for some reason I always felt that the moon was about the distance round the world away, 25,000 miles. That felt symmetrical, however its 250,000 miles away.

I hit the Bolivian border at what I thought was 11am, plenty of time to get the whole importing the bike routine done before the lads went on lunch, but I forgot about the time difference, once you cross the border you lose an hour. In fairness, the customs guy was great and got me through. Surprisingly the whole border routine took less than thirty minutes. The whole thing put me in great form about Bolivia, I found myself saying, "What a great country! I love it!" Soon after the border I got to Copacabana, a town on Lake Titicaca and an interesting place. The Virgin Mary appeared there and it's been a place of pilgrimage since. There's a really cool tunnel where you go and light a candle and graffiti the wall with candle wax. At the end of a dark tunnel lit entirely with candle wax is a statue of Mary, its eerie. Somehow writing, "Oisin was here" just didn't seem appropriate.

That night I had a dose of the itches in bed. I got up and turned on the light to figure out what the hell was going on. The bed had about two hundred ants rummaging around in it. The only thing to get rid of them was to get some damp soap so as you give them a smack, they stick to it. After about an hour I thought I'd got them all, maybe I did but spent the night scratching either way. The next morning I went in for a shower and had an alleluia moment; the water was not only hot but was also high pressure, I must have washed my balls twenty times to celebrate. My second day in Bolivia turned out to be one of the toughest of the trip. I crashed the bike four times and ended up in hospital again. It was like someone upstairs said, "That guy has been having too much of a good time, let's throw him a couple of kicks in the bollix!"

I left Copacabana early, I knew it was a short run to La Paz and I wanted to get there early and do a bit of sightseeing. As I was leaving the town, I was "clothes lined" by a police chain. I saw the check point but normally they just wave you through. It was cloudy and I was wearing sun glasses and as I hit the check point the chain hit the wind shield, then popped up off it and hit me knocking the crap out of my chest and throwing me off the bike. I wasn't going too fast but it hurt like a mother! I did my usual systems check, wriggle toes, ok, wriggle fingers, ok, put hand on lad, I can still feel it. I got up slowly, it felt like someone had dropped a cavity block on my chest. Sam Gamgee was fine as usual despite falling over on its side about eight yards down the road. After catching my breath and agreeing to go "Mas Despacio" (Slower) I set off but there would be no cuddling of any women tonight, no change there so.

The road continued to hug Lake Titicaca and I couldn't help thinking the whole place had a magical quality. When I first saw it, I wasn't that impressed but the blueness of the water and how it sparkles in the sunshine starts to grow in your mind the more you look at it. The second surprise of the day was that to get to La Paz you had to take a ferry. The ferries are tiny and don't look in the slightest bit lake worthy. The floor of the ferry was missing whole lats of timber, so much so you could see the lake water and to top it all off, the only way off the ferry was to reverse and there was no metal plate to act as a ramp to the shore. Luckily, there was a gang of Finnish bikers on the other side so they gave me a hand getting the bike off.

On the way to La Paz, you get back onto the altiplano and in the distance you can see the massive white caps of the Andes. The city however, is a massive ugly sprawl, with only one main thorough fare, which on the plus side makes it difficult to get lost in. The city reeks of car fumes and is wedged with people so I just kept the hammer down and burned right through it, heading south for the next biggish town called Oruro, on the way passing a statue of Che Guevara. On the way from La Paz to Oruro, every gas station was out of gasoline. I didn't know the reason but I tried at least ten over a hundred-mile distance with no joy. All along the road there were cars parked up which had run out of gas. The implications to my trip were huge, if I couldn't get gas I risked being stranded or at best I'd have to cut across to the Chilean border and miss out on the salt flats in Uyuni. As it turned out there was a strike which was going to last the next four days, you could only get gas in major cities and towns, not a disaster but meant that I'd have to plan my miles carefully through the country.

I eventually got to Oruro on a mixture of prayers and fumes and filled Sam up till there was petrol flowing out the overflow tube, I was sure I'd need ever drop. It was still early so I had another idea that I wish I could take back, "Sure its only 320 km to Uyuni, let's go!"

Uyuni is famous for its massive dried out salt lake and it was the main reason I came to Bolivia. Either I took a wrong turn, or a Bolivian bollix gave me the wrong directions but I ended up in the middle of nowhere. The road ended, which wasn't initially a concern because it had been crap before and had turned to autopista before too long, so I was ok with struggling on. After forty miles of sandy gravelly crap, the road turned to just sandy crap, and I can't ride an 1150 on that much sand. At times, it was so deep I had to strip the bike of all the gear and panniers and walk it to firmer ground just to make any progress. Three times I fell off the bike, each time hurting a different part of my body. The first time I was doing about 30mph and the front wheel washed out, the bike went straight over on its left side on top of me. My left wrist was the only area that took any impact but I was sure it wasn't broken. It took a massive effort to get the bike back up off the ground; one more time having to completely strip it before lifting it. The bigger problem came because of where I'd fallen, there was nowhere to stand the bike as the whole area was deep sand. Eventually I rode the bike over to some scrub about thirty yards away and then carried the gear over to the bike and then rode on again. It's worth bearing in mind that all of this was done at serious altitude so any effort at all and it feels like your lungs are bursting. The second time I fell, I hit a deep patch of sand and the bike slid out from under me. This time I went straight down on my left hip. I took about ten minutes to get myself back up off the ground and then began to start to strip the bike again, find a hard patch of ground to stand the bike up in and they carry all the gear over to the bike and start all over.

I was starting to get in a bad place mentally at this stage and was stared to descend into a terrible mood. I was completely and utterly lost. I had no idea where the road was supposed to be but was certain that I was in the wrong place. I was too far out. I had a choice to either go on or go back. The choice was seventy miles of crap to go back, and then a further sixty miles to go back to Oruro, or hope that the track turned to road further on. I had only about 200 ml of water left so said to myself, "Better the devil you know, turn around." The thought of having to refight a battle I'd just lost was a crushing blow.

Just then, I saw a truck in the distance. I went cross country over the desert to see if he was on a road and could see that one was in construction about a half mile off. I managed to keep the bike up and got to the edge of the road without crashing again. As I tried to go up the bank of the road to get onto the gravel the whole bike went into a wheelie and threw me off the back of it, the bike then proceeded to slide down the bank clobbering the leg I'd already hurt in Mexico. I lay there in the blackest mood of all time cursing the whole of Bolivia, but chiefly the road network. The gravel was too soft and too thick. I couldn't get the bike up onto the road and was killing myself trying, and burning the back tyre in the gravel to try to get some traction. By this stage I had stripped the bike and taken off the panniers. I'd done everything and I just couldn't get it up onto the gravel. I was starting to panic.

No one used this road, and anyone who might do, would not have any gas in their cars because of the strike. I was seventy miles from a town which I only thought I knew the direction of, I was completely out of water and or the first time on the trip I genuinely thought, "This is it, you are fucked." I sat down on the side of the road, sore all over, dying of thirst as the sun was setting behind me. I told myself, "You have 2 choices, walk towards the town and hope you meet someone on the road, then get some water and get some help to get the bike out." I really didn't like that plan because it gets dark in a heartbeat there, in all likelihood I'd end up just walking aimlessly in the dark, or the other option was to "Try again to get the bike out."

I really started to give myself a hard time,"Why cant you get the bike out of there? It's fully stripped, so it's a 250 kg weight, why can't you drag it up onto the gravel?" When I was younger, I dead lifted 220 kg, so I used this as the spur to tell myself that it was possible to get the bike out of the hole.

I allowed myself to go completely berserk with the bike. Slowly dragging and pulling for all I was worth I got the bike up onto the gravel surface. I nearly collapsed panting for air, I was sure my lungs were going to explode and I spent about ten minutes sitting on the ground trying to catch my breath. I loaded up the bike, jumped back on and rode like a man possessed through the gravel and finally back up onto the autopista to get back to Oruro. As I drove up the road, and I guess as the adrenaline wore off, the parts of my body which had been clobbered gradually got sorer and sorer. By the time I was thirty miles from Oruro I could no longer change the gear on the bike, both because my left wrist was so sore, and my left ankle was locked up with swelling.

I booked into a hotel and the guy at reception looked at me like I was a ghost. I caught a glimpse of myself in the mirror, I was destroyed with sand, with my face caked in a mixture of sand and sweat. My lips were so chapped and burnt from the sun that it looked like someone had stuck green cornflakes all over them, and my mouth was as dry as peanut shells. I bought a large bottle of water and drained it in one, while I was drinking a scene from a movie came into my head, "Drink it slowly Tarzan, a great thirst is best cured slowly!" "Silence, Me Tarzan, Me Thirsty."

The guy helped me up the stairs to the room and I went in for a shower. My body was in bits. I felt my back and I'd a lump where I shouldn't have, I needed to go to a doctor. The guy in the hotel drove me to the emergency area in the local hospital where they told me to come back tomorrow after strapping up my wrist. That was after me making sure I had a clean pair of underpants on me before I left, what a waste. I went to the hospital the next morning and things checked out, nothing was broken, just some soft tissue damage. The only thing that was really bothering me was my chest from getting clothes lined by the chain the day earlier, but nothing was broken so I pushed on.

Potosi

I looked at the map and tried to figure out what was the best way to get to Uyuni. I could get within a hundred and twenty miles of Uyuni if I went back to the route I tried yesterday before I hit the sand. Looking at the map I judged that if I headed southeast to Potosi, the highest city in the world, at over 4000 meters, that I could then head south west to Uyuni on what looked like a road on the map. It was two hundred miles away so I hit the bricks.

The road to Potosí was very much like riding in Zion Canyon Utah, everything was red and orange mountains and canyons. The difference was the road was cutting a path through the Andean altiplano so it had a more "in the middle of nowhere" feel to it. With the gas shortages there was hardly a soul on the road so you could throw yourself into the bends and take up both lanes, at times I was really putting the bike through its paces and loving every minute of it. I think it was God's way of giving me a break after the torment of the previous day.

When I got to Potosi my first task was to find out about the road to Uyuni. The total distance was about a hundred and sixty miles, which was less than a tank of gas which took away the risk of running out of petrol. I found out the road wasn't paved, none of it! I think the taxi driver who was explaining it to me thought I was going to kill him, "What are you talking about, not paved, are you kidding me!" The net result of that days two hundred miles was to move me over thirty miles further away in "sandy road miles" from the target, yesterday I was a hundred and twenty-five miles away, now I was a hundred and fifty-five. I sat down and thought it through. I totally stripped the bike and went through my gear with a rapier. "Do I need it today, why do I think I'll need it tomorrow" The goal was to drop the weight of the bike, I knew I could expect to be picking it all up off the sand a lot the following day.

Why was I so stressed?

Riding on sand is a huge mind melt because if you go slowly you definitely come off, but if you go fast and you come off you'll injure yourself so in your mind you're trading those two alternatives all the time. Instinct says slow, what you know says go fast; that sweet spot in the middle is managed by your nervous energy. If I was to make it, I promised myself that I was going to have a three course meal, all deserts and woe to the restaurant that didn't have a good desert when the conquering hero darkened the door. All joking aside I was very afraid and I was certain that I'd bitten off more than I could chew. I really didn't know what to expect but as Sam Gamgee's gaffer used to say, "It's the job that's not started is always the hardest." I needed some inspiration to get me through what would no doubt be a huge physical test.

I left Potosí around 7am with about a hundred and fifty-five miles of "who knows what!" ahead of me. The one thing I knew for certain, there wasn't a millimeter of asphalt along the way, the road would be terrible and I was pushing myself beyond my limits. As I was getting ready, I prepared my gear with great care. I took extra special attention to the boots, taking time to fasten the buckles and pull all the straps as tight as was comfortable. I put each ankle into an ankle strap which I had from the accident in Mexico. I tied each wrist up tight in Buffs, double buffed my neck and zipped the suit jacket top and bottoms together so if I slid the jacket wouldn't slide up my back or if going the other way so my trousers didn't slide off and destroy my pristine arse, already the proud bearer of mucho blisters. I was ready and roasting hot. I just had to find the road to Uyuni, sounds easy eh?

The Bolivians are a very polite bunch and tend to give you the answer they think you want to hear so when you say in Spanish "Excuse me, is Uyuni this way?" You'll nearly always get a yes. So, every two hundred meters you double check with the next person you meet on the road so you don't trek off into the middle of nowhere. I stopped for a gallon of water on the outskirts of town knowing today I'd need it and asked for the last time "Is this the road Uyuni?"The woman replied, "No, the bridge is bad" you need to take a diversion and meet the road a couple of miles out the road, so off I set.

The first part of the road was in atrocious condition with six to eight inches of sand everywhere. I struggled along in first gear with my two legs outstretched like stabilizers, and kept this up for about four miles. The road then started to climb into the mountains where thankfully the sand had for the most part been blown off the road so I was left negotiating a route through a gnarly rock and gravel landscape. Gravel and rock is infinitely more doable than sand so my wellbeing took a major shot in the arm straight away.

I started the countdown at 155 miles, and broke the journey up into six twenty-five mile stretches allowing myself a break after every twenty-five miles. With the first twenty-five done, it had taken almost two hours and I knew it would be dark by the time I got to Uyuni if I kept this pace up. It probably goes without saying but there's one thing you don't want to do and that's drive on a terrible road after dark, so for the next twenty-five miles I took a lot more risk keeping the hammer down, it only took me one hour.

The road alternated between deep sand, deep gravel, corrugated gravel, heavy riveting as it bent and swept through red, brown and yellow mountains like a snake. I took over five hundred pictures of the scenery along the way. It was all just so out there, and so different to anywhere I'd ever been before. On many occasions the road was only a car width in size with sheer drops at your side, and with the surface as unpredictable as it was, at times it was terrifying.

With almost seventy-five miles gone in four hours I hadn't fallen off and was starting to feel good. Coming over a hill, I met a bike going the other way driven by an Australian couple. I had only passed a couple of 4X4's all day and it was surreal to be out in the middle of the Bolivian desert having a chat with a guy from Australia. They had some great news for me. First, it was only another seventy-five miles to go, and second that the next fifty miles weren't too bad. The other thing that gave me heart was that there were two of them on one bike, if they could do it with two on the bike and not come off, I should be fine, or at least that's what I reckoned. I headed up the road brimming with confidence, and about five miles after leaving them I had my first spill of the day. I took the wrong line going round a bend and the front end of the bike swept out, as far as falls go it was a good one, I didn't hurt myself or damage Sam Gamgee. Sand was the culprit and for me at least, the word sand was quickly becoming a byword for all that was evil in the world.

To go through a road with sand on a bike is very hazardous, much more so than in a car. The critical differences are 1) A bike has only "1 wheel" drive, the back wheel does all the work, 2) the wheels are round at the road contact point so you've a lot less contact area with the road 3) If you hit the brakes at anytime other than when your perfectly straight up, you'll probably slide and come off. When you hit sand with a road tire, on a bend with a small contact area, made even smaller because you're leaning to turn, you're off the bike before you know it.

The biggest problem with my first spill was picking the bike up, it was facing the wrong way down a hill so I was foaming at the mouth from exertion trying to get it back upright.

Everyone always says, "Practice makes perfect" or the other molten bronze droplet, "You learn from your mistakes" but when you come off you don't learn till the next day, when you've had a bit of time to think about it. On the day that it happens in it just etches away your confidence. You start to look at every bend as having hidden peril and you start to vividly imagine that you back tyre is washing all around the place.

I set off again and after eighteen miles I came upon a construction zone. There was absolutely no organization to the work. Crews had dropped heaps of materials on the road and appeared to be flattening it utterly randomly. You can't drive on it till it's flattened because you just sink into the gunge. There was a path up the side of the road where they were working so I burned off up this stretch. About halfway up, there was a dip in the road full of deep muck created by the work crews, as I went through it my front tire stuck deep and threw me over the handle bars. Out of pure instinct I had retracted my hands in time, as typically

when this happens you catch your hands or fingers under the break or clutch lever and break the bones in your hands, luckily I was just thrown off and landed on the flat of my back after somersaulting through the air. I was lying on the flat of my back on the ground looking up into the blue sky and went through the usual routine "wiggle wiggle" etc.
I picked myself up of the ground and I've never been so winded, just standing not to mind breathing was done with huge difficulty. I looked at the bike perched in the muck like a stick in a toffee apple and said to myself, "Screw this." A work crew came along and gave me a hand getting the bike out of the mud. For the next fifteen miles or so it was on and off construction, the whole thing had become a complete and total nightmare. I had lots of little monologues with myself, "You'd think they would finish one part of the road before starting another!" I was driving up the road like an oul one with piles and then, as if a gift from heaven, the road straightened out and hardened up for about twelve miles or so.

I was over nine hours on the road and had only twenty miles to go. I was doing about 40mph when once more, the bike washed out. As it was washing I pushed myself out of the saddle to avoid getting hit by the bike, but as myself and Sam Gamgee impacted on the road, the right pannier clobbered my right calf. I was lying on the ground with the bike a mixture of beside me and on top of me at the point of despairing when my camera fell out of the side pocket of the tank bag and hit me right on the schnoz, the second time it happened on the trip. I just started roaring laughing and had a mini conversation with the man above, "Ah yeah as if I'm not bad enough! Throw the camera at my beak! Any kitchen sinks up there!" I couldn't get the bike up off the road, I was too tired and any time I tried, as it was sand on gravel, when I tried to push the bike up my feet kept sliding out. I lay down at the side of the road, I said I'd wait till someone came along. That plan was scuppered when I noticed petrol coming out the overflow line of the bike, the angle of the bike on the road was causing it to pour out onto the road. I didn't have any spare juice and not getting to Uyuni wasn't an option. So with the last piece of energy in my body and with a roar heard for many miles I pushed and pushed till the bike was back up. I was panting like a dog on a roasting day after a run, sore all over, feeling like a bag of shit when I jumped back on the bike to tackle the last leg. I was determined not to come off again, I couldn't take it.

There was no way I could have lifted the bike again and I was certain that if I fell one more time that I'd do serious damage to myself.

Every mile was a struggle, the first fifteen miles of the twenty five took over an hour. When I was just five miles from Uyuni I came up what I judged would be the final mountain pass before my decent to the salt flats. I reached the summit of the mountain and looked down onto the most eerie sight I've ever seen. The town of Uyuni sat on the edge of what looked like a red lake. The salt reflected the red of the sunset, and all through the red lake mountains appeared to be floating as the sun set in the distance. I kicked down the side stand, got off the bike, took off the helmet and gloves and walked over the mountain edge. While looking out onto the vast valley, with the road I'd just driven behind me, I roared at the top of my voice with a mixture of joy, relief, and above all exhaustion, "WHO'S YOUR DADDY?!!"

As I drove into the town the noise of millions of plastic bags rustling in the wind all caught up in rocks and various desert plants was the first thing that struck me, like most deserts I'd come across, there was rubbish everywhere. The town exists to bring tourists out onto the salt flats and that's it. The whole place feels like it just shouldn't be there, it's a horrible place really. People arrive, go on the tours and leave. When the lake dried up, this town should have gone also.

Uyuni

The next day I decided to go out on the salt flats by myself, another in a long line of bad decisions. Unlike the salt flats in Utah which have layer upon layer of compacted salt built up, this lake has only about 3 or 4 inches and in the wet season it gets rain. I drove out and got stuck out in the middle of nowhere with the bike having gone through the salt into the mud. It took me three hours to go one mile, constantly having to push the bike over onto its side, lift it back up and then try to start again, whereupon I'd get about twenty meters before I was stuck again. After about four hours struggling I stripped the bike fully down(again), and walked it out of the muck and shite for about a mile then had to walk back to get my gear, then obviously walk back to the bike again. All told I'd walked about three miles at altitude in motorcycle boots and an enduro suit, across pure muck. I gave up, totally knackered I headed back to town to see if I could catch one of the organized tours but they were all gone.

I keep a bag of "I told you so" just for myself. "I told you it was a bad idea to go south in Bolivia." "I told you to go on a tour and not go by yourself onto the salt." "I told you not to use carbolic soap to wash your bollix." "I told you she'd say no if you asked her out for a dance!"

In the end I spent the day arsing around Uyuni, which is all there is to do in the town and got ready for the run to Chile. When everything was all packed up I went out to find an internet cafe. While I was there the same group of Finnish bikers all showed up, we said Hi, none of them could speak English, but they were there for the same reason I was so we all hung out checking email. One of my mates back home had sent an email, innocently titled but when I clicked the link my whole screen was taken over by a video of a guy getting shagged by another guy leaving absolutely nothing to imagination. It was one of those booby trapped joke mails where you cant clear your screen and it also turns the speaker up really high. I was scrambling to close the window surrounded by a posse of Finnish bikers. Eventually to clear the window, I just plugged out the power. Right up there with my most embarrassing moment ever. Can you imagine what they must have been thinking?

The run from Uyuni is 165 miles to the border with Chile and it's all unpaved. In my mind it couldn't be worse than the day before, as it turned out I was only marginally right. It was chiefly incredible rocky desert with brutal roads but all that day I managed to stay upright. A new vector to deal with in tandem with the sand and gravel arrived in the shape of savage wind. It kept blowing sand in my face, even with the visor down it was coming up under the helmet at a savage rate. The hardest part was when I had to lean the bike into the wind and try to keep as much of the tyre on the ground as possible, all day I battled to keep the bike out of the ditch. On gravel roads there is typically only one or two good lines through normally the track made by a big truck so if your pushed out of your line, which is easy with bad wind the chances of you coming off, go up exponentially. At either side of your line is a build up of gravel and sand depending on the traffic and wind it can vary greatly in height. If you have to cross out of your good line you have two choices, either be going like the hammers of hell in which case you just blow through it, or slow down to a crawl and bump through it.

All day I drove in constant fear that by leaning into the wind to keep your direction straight that I wouldn't have enough thread on the road and I'd slide off. Having started at 7am I arrived at the Bolivia Chile border at 6:49pm. The Bolivian side was crazy. You have to first stamp your exit out of the country as normal, but have to climb through trains and walk across three train lines to get to the office. From there you have to go back across the trains and the train tracks to another office to complete the paperwork. From there it's up to the "efficient" Chile side. I was knocking on the window to try and stamp into the country. I pushed in a door and said, "Hola, Buenos tardes" (hello good evening) to which I head a huge chorus of banging of knives and forks off plates, as if to say piss off and wait, we are having a bit of grub."

After a bit of a wait I was through and got to the town of Ollangue, a town without a gas station, one of the most windswept and godforsaken places on earth. I'd about sixty miles of gas in the tank, and it was about a hundred and sixty miles to the nearest gas station, I was stranded. Even If I did get gas it was almost another 160 miles of unpaved road to a town called Calama in Chile which is when the asphalt would start.

I set about finding a place to stay and first tried the only hostel in the town which had two bunk beds in the dorm where everyone slept. When I walked into the room there were three dudes all lying on their beds with hefty bellies and bald heads with their shirts off. It all seemed very "midnight express" so I headed back to another bed and breakfast type place, I didn't fancy having an eight ball strapped in my mouth that night. It was as humble a lodging as I've ever stayed in but I had a bed and a door between me and the night which was the main thing.
I went to the dining room for a bit of grub, and asked what they had. The reply was comida de la casa (food of the house) which turned out to be a shin of mutton and rice (think of a sheep, now look at one of its legs, more meat on a budgies wing) The town lost electricity at around 9pm and didn't come back, but it didn't bother anyone in the place. Cooking still went on over an open heart, and it seemed like it was a daily occurrence.

The plan the next morning was to try to bum some gas, maybe go down to the customs station or see if anyone passing had some. I'd work to do, it was time to make myself a sign. I solved the no gas problem early in the day by knocking on doors in the town and eventually found someone with some. I went around the back of these two old women's house and there it was, a big fifty gallon drum of Texaco. I bought three gallons off them at war time prices but was delighted to be back on the road so I wasn't complaining. I must have asked them five times "Gasoline Si?" to which they always replied "Si"

If it wasn't, this was going to be a short trip. I was deter-

mined to conquer my fear of the sand, so I kept remembering all the things I knew about how to drive in it and kept repeating it back to myself as I was driving along. One of the most important things to do is to stay loose in your arms and let the bike sway underneath you. Now the feeling of a bike swaying under you is enough to send the heart beating up into the 200+ range but you have to get over it, stay loose. Here's the rhyme I told myself:
Stay Loosey Goosey, Loosey Goosey,
Look at Hughsey staying Loosey Goosey
Up in Canada saw only one Moosie,
Stay Loosey Goosey, Loosey Goosey
The whole trip I haven't kissed a Flusie,
Loosey Goosey, Loosey Goosey

Very bad I know, but it worked and I just repeated it over and over for hours on end. A number one its unlikely to be, but it's all about staying in the zone and keeping yourself there, for that it worked a treat.

The last eighty miles of sand were the worst because the wind picked up where instead of just doing the loosey goosey routine I kept saying, "Piss off wind, piss off wind, piss off wind."

After over six hundred miles of gravel and sand, the asphalt was back, the most gorgeous, beautiful and sexy substance in the whole world. When it came, if you had offered me a steam room with a nude Britney Spears sitting in it with Sharon Stone on the way over with a tub of rum and raisin ice cream, I would have taken the asphalt.

Once I got to Calama it was a short run to San Pedro de Atacama, a famous oasis in the Atacama desert. I was going to hold up there for a couple of days to recharge my batteries. The town has the feel of a town on another planet. The road descends to it from the mountains and altiplano and the scenery, much like most of Bolivia was like riding on Mars, which is how almost everyone who's been there describes it. It was the first time I noticed the difference in price, everything hiked up incredibly. For example it's about five times as expensive in Chile for a room, compared to Bolivia. On top of that, because you've dropped from high altitude the heat is brutal. The following day I got up at the crack of dawn to head out to the Valley of the Moon near San Pedro. It's so hot there that if you don't go early, you'll boil alive.

It wasn't long before I was back off-road knee deep in more sand and gravel. This was slightly different though, it was like a day trip, which was fun. The difference for me was that when you don't absolutely have to get through it, if you don't like it you can just turn back and head into the town and have a cup of coffee (and a bun) The only trouble I had was when the back wheel got trapped in deep sand (again) and had to tilt it out and pull it to good ground (twice), but given it was a day trip, I'd no luggage so it was much easier to deal with. After beating around the desert and the valley of the moon I went out for some grub. I met three Irish girls, Laura, Orla and Sarah. They were all in their mid twenties and were off dossing around South America for six months. I hadn't talked with anyone really since Cuzco and the conversation felt awkward at first, I think conversation is an art that you need to practice, I think maybe you forget how to do it. In the end we'd a good laugh, nothing like a few pints to get the chins wagging. In a bar later a guy offered Cocaine to me and the girls, which I gave back to him. I'm sure the average Chilean living in San Pedro handing out free cocaine is an alright sort, but I decided not to take any chances.

For the previous three nights I'd been having a recurring nightmare about the desert. Every time it was the same, I crash the bike and break a bone and end up getting stuck out there. I always woke up with a jump and in a sweat and struggled to get back to sleep. In my reckoning the cause of it was that I was terrible at driving on the sand and used to get myself all worked up about it, especially knowing the Ruta 40 was coming up in Argentina. I decided that the only way to cure it was to go back out onto the sand. I went about forty miles outside of San Pedro where I spotted a track through the desert, and I said to myself, "Ok, time to conquer your fear. There's no point in having one of these recurring dreams back in Ireland, it'll be too far to go the desert, so fix it now." I'd really no clue how I was going to do it but I found the track and said to myself, "Ok Oisin, just keep riding till you fall off." The whole time I stood on the pegs and did my whole "Loosey goosey" routine and just let the bike move around under me. I kept driving and driving and when an hour had passed I stopped, "Ok, not bad, a full hour out in the desert and you didn't come off! Nice one." For the way back I just used a slightly different line and again made it the whole way back to the road without coming off, I wondered whether I was cured.

I'm asked a lot if this sort of journey is lonely or if being in these sorts of locations is lonely and I always give the same answer. If you are in the middle of the desert on your own, you feel completely and utterly alone but surprisingly not lonely. I think it's because you don't expect anyone to be there. However if you're in a city and maybe go to a restaurant, then you do feel lonely. It's no different than when I used to go on business trips. There is nothing worse than being in a strange country sitting down to a bit of grub on your own especially when all around you are people with their partners and family.

I left the desert and headed south for a town called Mejillones on the coast. On the way, I passed the Tropic of Capricorn for the second time in my life. I passed it previously in Australia. Somehow, I felt a whole lot "lower" in the world when I was in Australia than I did in Chile. When I think of Australia I think of "down under" but here I was, at the same point, it didn't seem that long ago that I passed the equator just north of Quito. After taking some time to digest the moment, I felt very far away from home and I was overcome with the feeling that the journey was coming to an end. I got to Mejillones, all I wanted was to get a room and go for a kip, the hangover from being out with the three Irish girls the night before exacerbated by the dry desert air left my mouth feeling like an old sock. Even though the town appeared to be empty of people, there were no rooms. I drove further south to Antofagasta to find the same thing, no hotel rooms. I looked at the map and it meant I'd another two hundred mile drive south to Tal Tal, a fishing town on the coast to find a place to stay. It was 5pm, and I was hung-over as hell with 200 miles to go, I groaned loudly with an audible "Bollix!" as the carrier wave, and proceeded to burn south. Would there be somewhere to stay in Tal Tal?

The memory of driving through that terra-cotta desert as the sun was setting from a clear blue sky will stay with me forever. On my left side, the moon started to rise and I felt my senses bursting. Despite the fact it was getting dark I had to pull over to try to take it all in. I took over fifty pictures of just that location and when I look at them now I can feel the warm desert wind blowing in my face as I watched the moon rise over a distant hill. It was dark by the time I got to Tal Tal but the twenty decades of the rosary said in hope that there would be somewhere to stay there worked. I didn't bother with a shower, popping on my jeans and a beanie cap and paced off out for some freshly caught fish. After over five hundred miles I slept like the dead

Chile was very different.

There was no cattle grazing at the side of the road, no pot-holes, or cars or trucks coming for me on the wrong side of the road, no one running red lights, everyone obeyed the rules. When I went to the ATM there was no friendly security guard armed with an AK47 or a sawn off shotgun, I missed those guys! There's no incessant beeping of horns, I was beginning to think my hearing was damaged because in an entire day there was not so much as the smallest beep. There were no plumes of blue smoke behind every truck and bus, and I didn't have to bribe any police officers, I hadn't even been stopped by one. There were no military checkpoints to drive through, no hidden ramps to smash your goolies into next week, no guessing and hoping for hot water in the shower, it was always hot. On the news the previous night, it didn't catalogue a hundred murders and finally there were no beggars putting on mealy mouthed expressions to help you rid yourself of your loose change. I guess it's the "little" things that let you know your back in the first world.

I pushed to within two hundred and fifty miles of Santiago to a place called San Lorenzo. I was supposed to go to the space observatory but it was as cloudy as hell so no joy. I had finally passed through the Atacama, the driest desert in the world, everything since Uyuni had been part of it and it had taken well over a week. As you drive south towards Santiago you come through a valley which is one of the places where the Andes stops the moisture from heading north and east to the Atacama. There was such a dense build up of cloud overhead, it feels like you could put your hand up and grab a fistful.

Santiago

For the first time Sam Gamgee was starting to suffer. I'd a small oil leak ever since I left Ecuador and it was becoming a big one, not really a surprise when you consider the bike had been down ten times so far. There would be a BMW dealer in Santiago so it was only a matter of nursing it to there. I arrived in Santiago after slicing through the Chilean countryside like a knife through butter in a hot dish. To be honest it was too easy, I never thought I'd miss the hardship. I know it sounds a bit mental but I relish the test, doing something because it's hard. If it's handy and I know I can do it I say, "What's the point?" The previous three days had seen me cover almost twelve hundred miles without a moment's difficulty.

There was however one massive barrier still to cross on the trip, The Ruta 40. This is renowned as one of the toughest roads in the world for two reasons, 1) it's mostly gravel and 2) the winds seldom drop below 40mph as it roars across the Argentinean plane. It would be the last big test of the trip but it was still a long way off.

For the next two days have I did the whole Santiago thing. I met my cousin Eileen (if right now you're breaking into a round of "C'mon Eileen" by Dexy's Midnight Runners, might I suggest a brandy) who took me round the tourist spots in the city. So how come I have a cousin in Chile? Well, my uncle Vincent met a Spanish woman here in 1973 and the rest is history. I never met my uncle Vincent, he died in 2003 and I had never met any of the Chilean branch of the Hughes household, so the reason I came here was to say hello.

We went for a great sea food lunch in the central market in Santiago. In your mind's eye picture every manner of fish from mermaids to squid for sale and then being cooked in restaurants right in the centre of the market, all accentuated by lads walking around playing the guitar and singing, its a great way to spend an afternoon!

We then went out to a city near Santiago on the coast called Valparaiso and met two friends of hers who have an apartment with the most spectacular view of the bay you could possibly imagine. Eileen missed her calling, she should have been driving formula 1 cars, the one liter vroom vroom we drove out in seldom dropped below 100mph the whole way, and the rosary beads never left my fingers till we stopped. We sat in the apartment talking till about midnight and outside the moon seemed to be larger than I've noticed before as it cast a yellow highway across the bay. The lights from the buildings arced around the bay to the right, the scene was definitely filed under "Top moon moment" (apart from when yer one showed her bum in the film Clash of the titans)

That evening I headed out and around Santiago and went to see James Bond and I got a total boner because it was set in Bolivia, Bond was in Bolivia, I was too, that makes me Bond, follow my logic?

On the way back to the hotel a guy walked up to me and introduced himself. This guy was about sixty and was missing every second tooth, with the rest clinging on for dear life to dodgy looking gums. He had a Bee Gees hair do, except it was black and grey, and had a serious mustache. He wore a grey pin stripe suit (Oxfam vintage), with a blue tie, and a shirt which looked yellow, but no doubt had at one stage been white, and a pair of black shoes with more mileage on them than Sam Gamgee. He walked straight up to me and said hello in a very gentlemanly way, I said hello back he smiled which is when I caught a glimpse of the choppers, they looked like a set of piano keys. He said to me straight up, "You're from Ireland." Blown away I said to him "well spotted"(You got that from a hello!) Then he said to me that I was an engineer (which I used to be). Then he said to me that he knew my face. I was quite taken aback, but not stunned it wasn't like he'd given me a slip with that night's lotto numbers yet. He then went on to tell me that he was schizophrenic and that he was trying to get to a town called Antofagasta which is north of Santiago and that he didn't have any money and could I give him the fare. He showed me his wrists as if to prove he was sick, both had huge amounts of scar tissue on them where it was obvious he'd tried many times to commit suicide. Now this guy was a very gentle mannerly man, so I asked him why he needed to get to Antofagasta. He said that he would be admitted to a "unit" there, but that he had slept of the streets of Santiago for the last eight nights while he tried to get into a place in Santiago or beg for the fare back to Antofagasta. I asked him how much he was looking for and he said 40,000 pesos, which was about $80. I told him, "Listen buddy, no chance I'm giving you that much money." He then said to me "Its ok, I understand." He shook my hand and went to say goodbye and then I asked him was he hungry? He said he was so I told him to wait. I popped into Burger King and got both of us a double whopper with Cheese meal and we both stood there tucking into the grub while chatting.

While we chatted, an old man dressed as Santa was playing a haunting tune on a tin whistle funneled through a megaphone. I thought I was in Roman Polanski movie. I popped over and dropped the change from the burgers into his mug at which point he stopped playing and came over and started talking to me and Mr. Wilkinson sword. I offered him my fries, which he gratefully accepted. There I was chowing down on fast-food with quite probably the two craziest guys in Santiago, something mental happened every day.

I put Sam Gamgee into the BMW dealers to get his final service before taking on the Ruta 40, I told them anything that looks even close to marginal, swop it out. There was no point skimping now and then being stuck out in the middle of Patagonia broken down for the want of a couple of hundred dollars. That afternoon I found the best internet cafe ever. Why I hear you ask? Was it because it had new PC's with rip-roaring bandwidth, flat screen monitors, ergo keyboards, comfortable seats, air conditioning, nice aromatic plants sporadically placed around the building or just the right lighting? No, it's none of these things! It's because it was built next door to a strip club and although I'm not one to visit such dens of iniquity, there was a window right beside my screen and every now and then women clad in nought but a G string would walk by. Obviously I'd report this to the police and the Catholic Church, em, after a couple of hours. I also thought it was a good time to reread every email I'd ever received. Someone needed to stand guard at this window lest a child walk by and be forever damaged by such wanton debauchery. The Chilean people could sleep safe in their bed knowing Oisin was staffing the wall tonight and maybe for a good portion of the next day.

I spent the rest of the day walking around Santiago people watching. There is more Visible Panty Line in Santiago than there are arses. On my road where I grew up when I was young, a woman complained that the tinkers were robbing her knickers off the line. I now know these types of jocks to be called roll-ons, and I can testify that the entire "stolen or lost" roll-on underpants that ever went missing anywhere in the world have all made it to Santiago where they are being sported by women between the ages of thirty and forty. At least the Chilean army is sure to never run out of tents. When does a pair of knickers become a roll on? When it takes three pegs to hang them up on the washing line. Large portions of the people in Santiago spent the whole day kissing, I never saw anything like it. I was going to get a t-shift which said, "Get a room already!" It wouldn't have been so bad I guess If I wasn't on the biggest barren patch since Robinson Crusoe got left on the Island, I was dying for a bit of woman Friday. Benny socialists had a couple of the parks and visitor attractions shut down with protests so there were limited enough places to go and see. I can just see Che Guevara now rolling in his grave, "Nice one ya pack of bennies, you shut down parks! Ze favorite hangout of ze capitalist dogs! NOT!!"

I was starting to get a bit lonely in Santiago. If you want to talk to people in cities there is a lot of mistrust knocking around with good reason I suppose. On top of that, I'd spent so much time on the road on my own and had talked to so few people that when I did meet someone, I was like a fire hydrant and didn't stop talking, so people ran to the hills quickly. Maybe I bring it on myself. It's not like when you go up talking to people, that you pick out that mad bitch from Misery, no doubt that mob would talk and talk and talk. It's always people who kind of look like you might have something in common with, fellow tourists. If they're early into their travels, they are so full of urban legends about them having to be "so careful in South America or they'll have their kidneys cut out" that they get spooked when anyone approaches them. Similarly, many folks travel in their own groups with three or four pals and likewise aren't receptive to a fifth beetle. Woe is me! There I was, Hughes, once counted amongst the mightiest of conversationalists in Christendom reduced to chatting politics with Mr Fluffykins (my toy rabbit). I really wanted Sam Gamgee to get well soon and bare me to the wilds!

I went off to see some vineyards. It was the usual story, lots of tasting all the different types, however there was no spitting back with the big fella and I ended up having about three bottles of wine. They offered a lunch and all the wine you can drink for thirty-five dollars and as always when you bring the big fella to a buffet, they made no money. I'd beef for lunch and was drinking white wine with it. This French bollix said to me "White wine with meat?" I gulped the glass of wine down in one, turned, looked at him and said, "Wines wine, it's all the same." He looked at me like I was taking a piss on the Arc de triumph.

Merrie and Pippen Sam Gamgee was returned none the worse for wear and Merrie and Pippen arrived from Ireland. Both are college buddies and are great friends and we spent a few days partying, flying is thirsty work apparently. We went out to Valparaíso and had a great day acting the maggot and ended up going out for dinner with my cousin Eileen and her friends. Pippen and Eileen spent the night winding me up that they were going to get married. After kicking it with the lads for a few days I said goodbye, we were meeting again in Chiloe, an island off the South west coast of Chile. I rode off south to a town called Chillán, about seven hours south of Valparaiso. There was no real reason for me to go there other than it was about half way between Valparaíso and the island of Chiloe. The road I took was called the Ruta 5 and it carves a path through the Chilean wine growing region. The road was too easy, too straight, and too predictable and the only battle I had to fight was against falling asleep, I can hear you now "you can't keep that bollix happy, it's too hard, it's too easy, I wish someone would cut his throat in six places!"

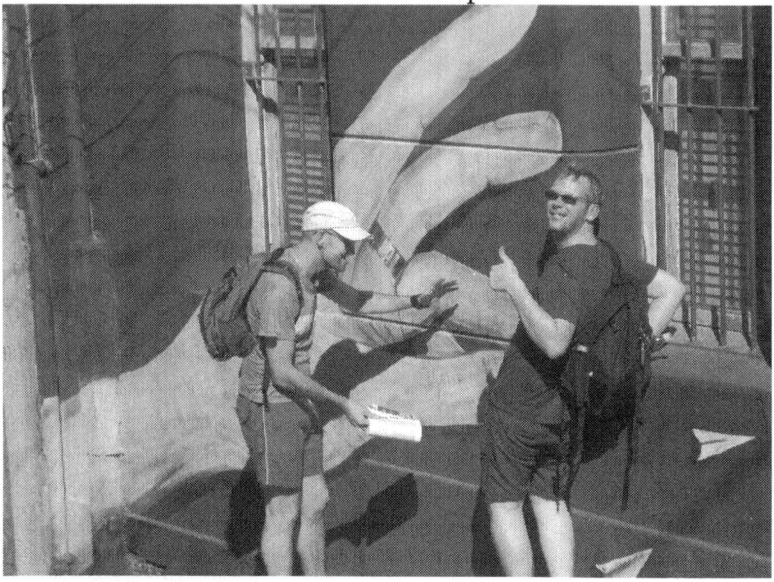

I crossed the 29000-mile barrier just as I got the ferry to the island of Chiloe. The first impression I got of Chiloe was, "Wow this could be Ireland!" It was springtime so the roads were awash with color and a wonderful spring freshness was in the air, it was a real tonic. The place was full of mad dogs. I was starting to get the impression that no dog on the island has ever seen a motorbike, every one went Hezbollah as I passed them.

I noticed when I looked down at my boots and pants they were covered in oil. The bikes oil leak was back, BMW in Santiago just succeeded in moving the leak, and making it worse. I pulled over and started checking where the leak was coming from and how bad was it. I reckoned I was losing about a liter of oil for every six hundred miles, so not a disaster yet but there was definitely clouds on the horizon. It was another thing to worry about. Where was the oil going on the bike? Would it start to make its way towards the back wheel, or into the clutch and maybe onto the back brakes? In Chiloe, it rains a lot, "So what?" I hear you say? It rains everywhere. "Well, in Chiloe it really really really rains a lot. This place took rain to all new levels, it came down in sheets, it was like being stuck under a waterfall. The locals are used to it and no one seems to mind.

Outside the hostel window that night, there were people talking until 4am, and it pissed rain the whole time, they weren't even bothering to shelter. No doubt, whiskey played some small role. I hooked back up with Merrie and Pippen and we headed off on a mixture of sightseeing and hiking, which chiefly involved being part of a human experiment for how much rain water can you take getting fired at you before you turn into a fish. The lads were mad to do stuff which suited me grand and we'd a good chat about whether doing nothing counts as doing something from a holiday perspective, know what I mean?

Puerto Varas

At breakfast I talked to an American couple who told me to be sure to go to the penguin colony, Merrie and Pippen were taking the bus to Puerto Varas so wouldn't be able to see it, but me and Sam Gamgee with no such constraints decided to head off in search of the wee cuties. The road takes you north and then west looping around the North ring of the island. This part of the world is battered by the pacific and looked just like the West coast of Ireland with the notable difference that today it was sunny. Once you get about twenty miles west of Ancud, the most northerly town in Chiloe the asphalt stops abruptly and your back to gravel roads. Along the way there were plenty of cows and farm animals and I asked a couple of farmers for directions to the penguin colony, let's just say there was much pumping of the right hand in the direction of where I was going "Guess it's this way huh?" Every time I'd come to what looked like a beach I'd get off the bike and go for a quick walk in search of the elusive colony. I wondered if it was not that big or maybe it had moved. I stood there listening half expecting to hear the sound of millions of the little fellas roaring for nose bag, but nope, all that was to be heard was the sound of the waves. I gave up and headed off the Island in the direction of Puerto Varas, in the Chilean Lakes region.

On the ferry I had my photo taken with about twenty kids who were on a school tour. They all wanted to get on the bike and put on the helmet which I hadn't washed for five months, no doubt their mothers would be delousing their heads when they got home.

I got to Puerto Varas, which is an old German Colony built on a gorgeous lake, and right at the end of the lake sit two Volcanoes. I was now officially in Patagonia and whatever you've heard, its better. Snow capped peaks, gorgeous blue lakes, wonderful plant life, it's hard to imagine any place nicer in the whole world. I hooked up with Merrie and Pippen and we hired a car and headed off exploring the Volcanoes.

When you go to an area that has had "recent" volcanic activity, it's a strange experience.You can see where the activity cleaved a path through the mountains and the vegetation. It's like someone spilled a bucket of black paint on the landscape. The older the activity you can see where plants are starting to grow again. It starts with lichen turning the mountainside red, and then weeds can get a foothold and from there the plants and eventually trees come back. It's magic to be able to see all the phases of recovery happening at the same time in different parts of the mountains. On the way back the exhaust fell off the car, it was a Peugeot, say no more. We ended up having to tie it up with our shoe laces. By the time we were done exploring, all three of us were burnt alive, our faces glowing like a two bar electric heater.

It was nearly time for the Ruta 40.

The road has several names. In Europe, we call it, "The Ruta 40" In the UK they call it, "The 40", in Yemen, they call it "The Ruta Fuck story", and in Poland, they call it "The Ruta Wherethefuck?"

The following passage was found in the pocket of a biker who was found in a hysterical fit lying by his bike on the Ruta 40:

Woe to You Of Earth and Sea;
For the Devil Sends his Road with Wrath
Because He knows that the big fellas Time is short
Let Him Who Hath Understanding
ReckonThe Number of the Road
For it is a Human Number
Its Number is 40

I said goodbye to Merrie and Pippen the next morning.

The original plan was to take a four day ferry south but I couldn't for two reasons, first the thoughts of being cooked up in a boat for that length was getting to me and secondly it would short circuit about three hundred miles off the Ruta 40. So what's bad about that I hear you say? Well, it's a guy thing. It goes something like this. When I'm asked "So Oisin, did you do the whole thing on a motorbike?" I can't say yes because of the ferry. Yeah I know, no one cares about that but secretly every guy in the world knows exactly what

I'm talking about. You either did or did not go the whole way on the bike and are therefore "a big girls blouse or not a big girls blouse!" Moreover, there is a sub level to that which is if I'm ever invited to the hard-core bikers Christmas ball, the question will come "So Oisin, did you do all of the Ruta 40?" Again I can't say yes. I will have to answer, "Well except for the bit..." and I'll get all those derisory "Harrumphs!" and let's face it nobody needs that.

At that moment I didn't realize that the Ruta 40 starts at the border with Bolivia, and not at Bariloche in Argentina so riding the entire Ruta 40 would have to wait for another trip. For my last night in Chile I was treated to a terrible dream. I was in college and I got a paper back from a lecturer with the assessment written on it "You are dumb, dumb, dumb!" It was one of those dreams that long after you wake you just can't get it out of your head. When you're driving a motorcycle there's nowhere to hide from your thoughts. Your head is stuck inside the helmet without a radio or someone to talk to help drown it all out. I figured out a bit about myself while thinking about it over the hundreds of miles that passed. It was important to me that people respected me and that I was thought highly of. I started to wonder if the only reason I came on the trip was so people would think I was cool.

Even while I'm writing this I'm doing it I guess, I could put some shit down here that I'm doing it to inspire others, to show people what's possible, the reality is that I'm doing it to tell everyone how cool I was by doing the trip. It's one thing being a prick, but when you know your one too, now that is hard! The other point I realized was that I talked too much, especially about the journey. I realized that I wanted to talk about it more than people wanted to hear about it. I couldn't believe that people didn't want to know every detail and that there wasn't a queue of hot birds lined up around the corner waiting to make me tea and biscuits. I was pretty sure this was one of those moments where you find yourself, only to find that you weren't really worth finding in the first place.

Chapter 10
Argentina

I drove north from Puerto Varas to Villarrica and cut east towards Bariloche in Argentina. I had reached my fifteenth and last country and the border crossing was a doddle.

The drive towards Bariloche would make you want to leave Ireland and move there instantly, the people living in this part of the world were spoilt rotten with incredible scenery. Snow capped mountains, rivers, blue crystal clear lakes, blue skies, no matter which way I looked I was confronted with an awesome display of nature at its finest. I was feeling like everything I'd done up to this point was merely,"existing!" At last I was living, and I wished this day would never end. Sure, I was on my own, but I was happy.

I then started to wonder how was it possible to be so down in the morning and so up by the afternoon. Do the ups always follow the downs? The darkest hour is just before dawn I suppose, but I wondered if I wasn't just a bit mental.

Bariloche

I made it to Bariloche, a town sitting on the banks of Nahuel Huapi Lake. It is completely hemmed in by craggy rough looking snow capped mountains, and sits on a beautiful lake, even the hedgerows were ridiculously colorful, it was like a garden show along the side of the road. It all feels very like the Alps in Europe except everything seems more rugged, more extreme, and its obviously infinitely more isolated. The forecast for the coming days was good. It was time to get going on the Ruta 40 while the weather was with me. It's one thing to take on these gravel roads in dry and windy conditions, but in the wet it would be brutal, so as the old saying goes, "Get going while the goings good!" I talked to one biker who said he drove through 70-80mph side winds on the Ruta 40 a couple of weeks back, he said his neck was like a coat hanger after it.

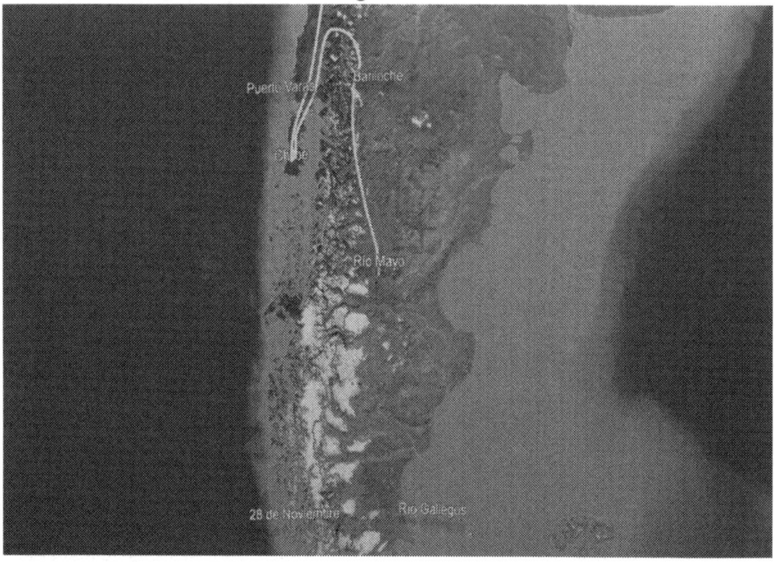

I was hoping to make it to Ushuaia in five days assuming Sam Gamgee and I could stand up to the battering by the wind and gravel. At this stage, I felt like I'd seen everything I wanted to see and now I just wanted to get to Ushuaia, I was itching to finish. When I look back now I wish I could go back, smack myself in the head and say, "Dude! Cop on, when you go home it's all doom and gloom and there's a recession, treasure every second you have left."

The 40 takes you through one-horse towns so it was back to cold water and no TV. I wrote in my diary that night "nothing like a bit of old, to make you appreciate the new, good oul days my eye." The four things I had consistently heard about Argentina were 1) The women are gorgeous, 2) The steaks are unbelievable, 3) It is expensive and 4) The Patagonian region is great. My buddies back home had sent me a couple of emails threaded, "What are the women like in Argentina?" The answer is: It is very like the relationship I have with the average Robin Red Breast (it's a bird) Namely, they are lovely to look at but I can't understand a word they are saying and they fly away if you get too close to them! The Argentineans, were a very friendly bunch, mad into Soccer and Rugby. I did three hundred miles on the Ruta Diablo (40) on my second day and was still around to tell the tale. I knew what was ahead wouldn't be so easy.

The further south you go, the more remote the areas and the less maintained the road would be. This area stood out for me because it was all in bloom given it was mid spring early summer. The average ditch had more flowers than fifty gardens put together back home. It all smelt somewhere between vanilla and honeydew and as it rolled up under the helmet I couldn't help thinking, "You could drive forever in this place!" I saw lakes with perfect mirror reflections of the mountains that lay on their banks and while I was parked up taking it all in, a yacht with a huge white sail passed me by as it moved from right to left, it was paradise.

As I drove further and further south on the Ruta 40, lakes and mountains were gradually replaced with rolling hills as you start to arrive on the Andean Foothills and just like Alaska and the Yukon, there was absolutely nobody there. I drove the last seventy miles that day without seeing a single car. Most of the tourist traffic takes a right into Chile at a town called Esquel and heads south on the Caretera Austral and then hooks back into Argentina further south, thus bypassing some of the shittier windswept sections of the Ruta 40.

If I was to get my hard-core biker merit badge I'd have to do every mile so there was no "handy number" for me. Again, at this stage I was under the impression that the Ruta 40 started in Bariloche and was about 2000km long, I since found out it starts at the Bolivian border, running for over 5000km right down to Rio Gallegos on the Atlantic coast. I had a mad experience while lashing through the country-side. The wind was about 50mph or so (how I know that will become apparent) but I noticed when I rounded a bend the noise of the bike seemed to get a lot louder, almost like the bike was "choking" itself only louder. It took me a while to figure out that it was the wind. What had happened was that the wind had become a tail wind and when the speed of the bike matched the speed of the wind the only sound was the engine of the motorbike, eerie stuff and one of those "you'd have to be there" moments.

On the road I passed a good few Gauchos herding thousands of sheep. The noise of that many sheep was manic. When I got to Gobnorado (not making the name up) on the Ruta 40 I asked the service guy was there any good hotels in the town, he replied "Más o menos." It means "more or less" in English. Well, let me tell you there was a whole lot of Menos and not a whole pile of Más, the hotel was shocking. The town was quiet, all you could hear was the odd bird chirping, and even the noise my feet made in the gravel seemed an intrusion. Everywhere was closed, I guess the whole place was doing the whole siesta thing. As I walked around wondering if everyone had been kidnapped the only thing I came across was a chicken walking along the street.

By 6pm things had livened up a bit. I wondered if they were off having a secret meeting to decide how they were going to cook the gringo.

That night I lay on the bed looking up at a fan spinning on the ragged edge above me while the rain teemed down outside. That's Patagonia for you, the weather changes constantly, but I couldn't complain, the last two days were amazing so I was due some hardship, and I was nervous as hell about what lay in store for me. Many years after being here, Charles Darwin said of this area in Patagonia in his memoirs of the Beagle voyages, "Why is it that this place so haunts my dreams and every waking hour?" Charlie, a big Ditto from me to you. The following day I rode over three hundred miles, this time all of it on gravel, muck, crap, sand with a hefty helping of brutal wind and driving rain. The only highlight was that I saw some Emu's and road runners, Emu's are fast, road runners are, well I don't have to tell you. I saw three trucks and cars out on the road in all those miles, the only time I came in contact with people was in the tiny towns to get some gas and grub.

Perito Moreno

Finally, I made it to a town called Perito Moreno. Halfway there I went through a town called Rio Mayo which happened to be paved for about five miles either side of it. It got my hopes up that maybe the Argies had spent a few bob and finally threw down some asphalt between there and Perito Moreno, my hopes were dashed as soon as I left the town, it was back to gravel. Perito Moreno also happened to be the first town on the last page of all my maps. If you can imagine, I left Ireland with over twenty different maps of all the different countries, and to be on the last page of the last map felt really good, not as good as a good shag mind, but in the wilds one has to take what little pleasures one can get. I had also crossed over the 30,000 mile mark.

Argentina is quite a poor country. Most of the shop shelves were empty or half stocked at best, a combination of low demand with a sparsely populated countryside but mostly due to the really bad infrastructure. None of the restaurants had Menus, the woman rhymes off what they have and you say "Si", for some reason always accompanied with a finger in the air. Then it's on to drinks and you really hope you recognize something she says. For breakfast every day, no matter where you stay, its bread, jam and tea or Coffee. My mother had two words for tea or coffee that was either too strong (Moonlach) or too weak (Sulach). If you have coffee you get Moonlach, if you have tea you get Sulach. I'd been opting for Sulach, the Ruta 40 is no place for a dose of heartburn.

I left the next morning at about 8am very apprehensive about the road, I'd so much gravel ahead, about 1100 miles.

Every gravel road has lines. A line is a place you can drive your motorbike on, I touched on this before but it's worth spending a bit of time on. What happens is the traffic moves gravel around the place on the road and over time tracks appear. Most roads have three, one on the left, middle and right of the road and every car or truck follows these tracks. The tracks only disappear when you come to bridges, which they have a lot of, or when two trucks meet and have to pull over to let each other by, thus destroying the lines in a section of the road. So, as long as you have a line, you can go along at a good clip, the problem is keeping your line. The line sometimes runs out into the ditch, or the wind constantly pushes you across the road making it really difficult to keep to a line. If you go out of a line you have to cross what may be a gravel build up of ten inches or more which is easily enough to make your front wheel wash out and put you on your arse. Note falling on gravel and rocks is much more risky than on sand, every time you go down your, "Gonna lose some meat!"

The rules of the game are simple enough, for an amateur biker at least, or for someone who hasn't ridden that much off road. 1) If you use the breaks and you're not going straight you are almost guaranteed to come off so you have to break with the engine i.e. pop her down a gear and only go up a gear when the bike goes over 4000rpm 2) If you go too slow you'll definitely come off, anything under 30mph and your pissing against the wind. At speeds that slow you're just not hitting the obstacles in the road hard enough so you'll end up washing the front or back wheel. Anything over 70mph and you'll kill yourself if you do come off. 3) If you drive in the wrong gear and the engine idles, chugs or free wheels you won't be able to react if something happens, the bike will be too sluggish. The engine has to be hauling ass the whole time, 4000rpm. 4) If you tightly grip the handle bars and don't stay loose, you won't be able to compensate as the bikes rolls around on the gravel and you'll end up overcompensating, pulling the bike back too hard. Loosey Goosey is the name of the game, it's good to wobble, it should feel like you're riding a jet ski when on this junk, or that's what you keep telling yourself. 5) Accelerate is your only way out of any problem, hit the obstacle hard and burst your way through it. The bike wants to go straight so more gas will give it the best chance of getting through whatever it is on the road. 6) If it's raining it's impossible to see your line so you're screwed, its better to just stop and wait for the rain to pass. 7) Do not put your feet down to act as stabilizers, if you're traveling too fast when your leg has an impact on the ground there's only one thing that's going to happen, you'll break it.

By this stage I'd moved into a part of the world that was unchanging and completely flat. My whole world had become flat barren pampas. The road seldom changed, the only thing that did change was the sky.

Rio Gallegos

I ended up doing over six hundred miles the following day, leaving at 5am and not getting to Rio Gallegos until 8:30pm. I had originally planned to go to Calafate and from there onto the Perito Moreno Glacier and Torres Del Paine, but I was tired and really just wanted to get to Ushuaia. If I felt good I'd go and see them on the way back up from Ushuaia to Buenos Aires. I had completed 2000 km of the Ruta 40. The only answer one expects from a fellow biker upon telling them that you did this is "Here is my wife, please pleasure yourself with her!", that is the sort of street cred you get.

I burst three blisters on my arse before I got into the shower that night only to discover I'd no clean jocks and went out and about in Rio Gallegos Commando. Apart from the length of the ride, the wind was terrible at times making it feel like pure torture. For a guy the best way to describe dealing with the wind would be to imagine you were lying in bed asleep and your next door neighbor came into the bedroom and kicked you straight into the bollix with a pair of hob nail boots. If you're a girl obviously the above doesn't sound so bad so just imagine someone pulled your top lip up over your head till it was touching your shoulder blades.

The only way to deal with the wind is to lean into it; you end up taking a position on the bike to compensate which is about as ergonomically friendly as someone hanging a nine inch cavity block off your left nut. I went to bed that night never realizing it was possible to be so tired. I thought I had a chance at getting to Ushuaia the next day and wondered if they'd have a parade for me or line up some women. I'd tell the parade organizer, I wanted Britney in the red latex suit, Kylie in the gold hot pants, Sharon stone minus the ice pick and underpants, the bird from the club orange add with the nice arse, and the one who worked in the cafe in Taxco in Mexico with the white trousers. I knew it would all come true.

The next day was frustrating. I didn't make it Ushuaia. The amount of border crossings was always going to make it difficult. Assuming no problems I had to cross from Argentina into Chile and then from Chile back into Argentina to get to Ushuaia, stamping in and out of each country. When I got to the first border it was closed, it turned out that for the first time in thirty years the Argentinean Prime Minister and the Chilean Prime minister were meeting to shake hands and guess where they were doing it, at my border crossing. It meant having to wait from 10:30am to 2:30pm, by which time a huge Queue had built up making the crossing even slower. It took away any chance of making Ushuaia that day. There would always be tomorrow.

Even though the sun shone brilliantly all day, the wind was appalling.

One near death experiences happened while I was overtaking a truck. If you can imagine a straight stretch of road about a mile long with a truck ahead of you throwing up bits of rocks hitting your wind shield and visor with a savage cross wind blowing from the right. There was another truck a good distance up the road on the left side. This was the sort of overtaking maneuver you would do twenty times a day out on the road, and even in the wind it wouldn't normally be a problem. As I passed the truck ahead of me on its left side and was coming round to go back into my "lane" the wind picked up a massive gale and I couldn't get myself back into my lane with the other truck coming right for me with the air horn blaring. There was nothing else I could do but gun the bike into the ditch on the left. Normally putting the bike in the ditch would be followed quickly by a ride in an ambulance, but the ditch on a gravel road is a gravel hollow with tons spare gravel knocking around. Acting purely on instinct I rode the bike down the ditch at about 50mph, scooted along the bottom of the ditch gunning the bike down to second gear in the process, and steered it back up onto the road even taking the time to indicate and continued down the road. About a mile up the road, I pulled over and kicked down the side stand. I took off the helmet, glasses and gloves and as the realization of what had just happened came to me, it was all I could do to not throw up.

Straits of Magellan

I made it to the Magellan straights and took the ferry over to Terra del Fuego. The seas were so high I was certain the ferry would be cancelled, but they're used to it down there. Black and white porpoises followed the ferry over, I've never been so close to so much violent water. If you fell in, you wouldn't last a minute and the ferry was rocking about so much that the bike fell off its stand. The northerly part of the Island of Terra del Fuego is very flat and you can see forever. With the delay at the border earlier in the day, combined with the fact that the entire Chilean side of the Island is all gravel roads it was late in the evening by the time I made it to Rio Grande. The whole way into the town the sun was setting on my right side as you'd expect if you're driving due south, it would have been a very special moment if mother nature didn't have my head in a vice grips with the wind. If the wind can do that to a fat bastard like me driving a 250kg BMW I'd hate to think what it would do to people driving lighter machines who were a little less rotund.

I hung out there for the night and then pushed on to Ushuaia the following morning. I was so worn out from battling the elements that I was really looking forward to the end. It was a 230 km run from Rio Grande to get to Ushuaia. I felt so weird the whole way. I kept replaying Brothers in Arms by Dire Straits on my iPod, it seemed to fit the mood. For some reason best known to God, as you reach Ushuaia you leave the flat lands behind and once again you're back into the mountains. As you get closer to the town, the forests start to return, in places whole sections were destroyed by the wind. The closer I got to Ushuaia I kept expecting that the excitement levels in me would grow and grow and grow and that any moment I'd be punching the air with excitement and roaring crying with happiness having completed my goal. It never happened.

Ushuaia

Along the way I bumped into Graham, a Scottish biker also headed for Ushuaia. When you get to Ushuaia it's not clear where to go to get to the end of world, or the "Fin del Mundo" as it's called. I thought to myself "You'd think they'd have a sign!" I asked many people did they know where it was, they all said they weren't sure what I meant. Worn out from traveling and very tired, I was starting to get frustrated and was saying in my head "How the hell can you not know where the sign is, it's what every biker comes here for. Everyone in the world who comes here wants to have their picture taken up against this sign, how can it be no one knows where it is?" I eventually got to the end of the Ruta 3, which had merged with the Ruta 40 in Rio Gallegos. Just two miles from the end of the road I came within an inch of being killed by a Taxi overtaking on the wrong side of the road on a bend. He was so close I thought it was game over. I eventually got there in one piece, parked up the bike, and stood looking at the sign. This sign is one of the biggest draws for the world's list ticker travelers of which I'm a member I guess otherwise I wouldn't have been there. My camera had packed in one mile from the sign so I got a girl to take a picture of me and send it on. She was lovely and had the worst lisp I've ever heard, eventually I figured out that she was saying her name was Isis. I waited till everyone left and sat up against one of the tree stumps. I stared blankly at the sign. The sun shone and the trees shook in the gale that was blowing into my back. I tried to take it all in. I tried to remember the places I'd been, how many days and miles I'd travelled, how many times I'd nearly been killed on the road, the different conditions, the different landscapes, I was done. I was waiting for the sense of accomplishment to kick in but it never came. I could not understand it.

I emailed Rafael, the guy from Venezuela who I'd met in Alaska, to tell him what I was feeling and he told me to chill out and take a couple of days in Ushuaia and most importantly to go for long walks to set things straight in your head. I do think that in some ways I wanted to be treated a bit like a hero. When you watch the Long way round, when the guys made it to New York there was almost a carnival and a big party with all their friends and family waiting for them. For me there was no one, just me and Sam Gamgee. I found a hotel and booked in for three nights. Something unusual happened to my psyche because in the three days I spent there, I couldn't even look at the motorbike. I don't understand it, because up until that point every waking hour was spent constantly either riding the bike or thinking about it.

I spent most of the next days ambling around Ushuaia. The town itself has many snow covered mountains nearby and the weather was very changeable, not altogether a surprise when you consider how close it is to Antarctica (Reason why most people go there is to get a boat to Antarctica). It's very expensive and full to the brim of tourists, most of the ones I talked with were from Holland, much like the tourists I'd met in Alaska. The first two days I was overcome with fatigue and spent the day sitting in restaurants drinking coffee looking out the window at the world going by. If anything I felt worse the second day than the first, I really felt empty inside. I wondered what the hell I did the trip for. Does anyone care? It was such a waste of time, is this what people meant when they say "You've the ladder against the wrong wall"

As I was sitting there bluer than the ocean, Isis walked in. She looked completely different today, her hair was down and if possible, she looked even more gorgeous. We had lunch together and chatted over a couple of coffees. The weather had taken a turn so it was a great excuse to stay chatting to a fine looking woman. Her lisp was hilarious, if anything it made her more attractive, but she was far too young for me. I'd met an Aussie couple earlier in the day and we all arranged to hook up for a couple of pints that night. The whole town was talking about a ship that had run aground on an Antarctic voyage, everyone had to be rescued off it, and luckily, no one was killed. I walked her back to her hostel. It turned out she was a high profile engineer with a Japanese company. I told her she could have been a model to which she replied that she used to be a model but left it behind her to become an Engineer. She wanted to be known for her brains and not her beauty. "Confident Bitch!" I giggled to myself. On my last full day in Ushuaia, I threw my copy of the Lord of the rings into the sea. I had read it three times on my trip and it had been my companion through many a dark moment, but it was time to say good-bye.

Ruta 3

The night before I left Ushuaia I sat in my room looking at the route to Buenos Aires gloomily. I knew it was going to be a killer on the ass, and most of it bar the early section would be mind numbingly boring. I went in to brush my teeth and noticed that I was going bald at a savage rate, I put it down to the length of time my head was in the helmet each day, "Air not getting to the scalp" and all that crap. I thought I looked old as hell too. Leaving Ushuaia to head for Buenos Aires didn't feel good. I knew that I was capable of doing every mile between here and there. I knew the first part would be hard as it was all gravel and wind, and that the second part would be flat straight roads combined with incessant gales. It's hard to motivate yourself when you know everything that's ahead and that no matter how hard I pushed it, I'd be on the road for at least four days.

The first day started well, I left a little before sunrise. As I swept down towards the marina in Ushuaia the sun was beginning to rise pouring a peach light all around the harbor. I had set myself many little milestones to try to build up a sense of accomplishment as I was riding along. For some reason the wind always gets worse in the evening so it was important that I get as many miles as possible done before midday. I burned off at a savage pace in the freezing cold with the town of Tolhuin in mind. It was to be my first gas stop of the day and I wanted to be there by 7am. It was the first and last place I could get gas, before I would cross in and out of Chilean Terra Del Fuego. I stopped on the Chilean border for two roasting hot cups of coffee and a couple of cheese sandwiches. Next stop was ferry at the straits of Magellan, and given the wind hadn't picked up yet I was making great time despite the gravel road. When I went through the Argentinean border, I thought it was very noticeable how young they all looked. I got to the ferry and boarded the boat. The bike had fallen over when I crossed a couple of days previous so this time I stayed with it. I sat down on a metal step holding the bike with one hand. Unknowingly I had fallen asleep when I was woken by an Irish couple who had spotted the Irish registration. They had just got engaged and were about to finish traveling after two years, they were on the way home. The ferry was short so the conversation was short lived but it was nice to meet people from home.

Puerto Julian

I was starting to get very worried about my tires, the gravel had taken its toll and my back tire had very little thread left on it. I wondered if I'd have enough to get me home, and if I didn't what town on the coast would I'd be able to change them in.

Once you leave Terra del Fuego, it's the end of the gravel riding for the whole trip, that was it, I had beaten my nemesis. I wondered after all these miles and all the experience how would I fare if I were to take on the Dalton highway again, I reckoned I'd kick its ass. I made it to Rio Gallegos by lunchtime and already had three hundred miles under my belt. I put the head down and kept the arse up and didn't stop till I came to the town of Puerto Julian. It's a lovely little sea side town with touristy stuff all along the sea side promenade, penguin tours, a Spanish galleon, it was a lovely town to spend a night in. When I went for dinner in one of the town's only open restaurants, I met Graham from Scotland, the same guy I'd met driving into Ushuaia. Both of us were stunned at the odds of the two of us bumping into each other in this restaurant in this town at this time. We'd a decent steak and a couple of beers and wished each other well for the remainder of our journeys. You might ask why you didn't continue the rest of the journey together, that was my fault, at this stage I was so accustomed to being on my own that I didn't want to ride with anyone else. I had less than nine hundred miles to go till I got to Buenos Aires so I decided to shoot for Bahia Blanca which was more than halfway, just short of five hundred miles.

My ass was so sore from the riding I was certain I'd need an ass transplant in Buenos Aires. All day I saw bikers going south, no doubt with Ushuaia as their destination. Every year there's a major motorcycle party in the town for New years with many folks starting the Pan American Highway heading South to North. For some reason the two bikers John and Rafael who I met in Alaska came into my head as I was looking at all the passing traffic. I remembered how desperate I was to meet some kindred spirits, when I thought back on it I realized I was very lonely, whereas riding up the Ruta 3 just wanted to be on my own, I think over the course of the last 33,000 miles my personality had completely changed.

Sometimes serious bullshit crosses your mind as you drive along in these ultra boring stages of a trip. I kept thinking that people would undermine the achievement. They would say it was easy and that anyone could do it. The truth was that anyone could do it, and that I'd met far more hardcore people on the trip than me doing things in a much tougher way. I comforted myself by saying that when I started I never thought I'd get as far as I had, and it doesn't matter that other people had done it a harder way, that's not the point, it was about testing myself. I'd passed the test and it was time to allow myself to feel good about it. I had to keep reminding myself that I did this trip for me, not for anyone else and therefore the glory or the lack of it would all have to come from within. The chances were that people who liked me before I left would continue to like me, and the people who didn't would continue to not like me. Why was I so obsessed with people liking me in the first place? So it went for every mile up the Ruta 3 that day, continually tormented by the raging wind.

Along the way, I'd see the occasional motorcyclist in a town or a small village and he might have his girl on the back or maybe even his son or daughter clinging on for dear life. Taking your girl for a ride on a bike is a very romantic and intimate way to travel I think. I was headed for Puerto

Madryn when my back tire finally wore right through to the canvas. There was no rubber left on it at all in places. I was at the town of Caleta Olivia and asked for directions to any motorcycle repair shop. The town had one, and not only that when I pulled up they stopped working on the bikes they had, brought me in and changed my back tyre there and then. I was so happy, it seemed like my back tyre had dominated my every waking thought for the last day or two so it was a huge relief to have it changed. They didn't have a front tyre but I reckoned I'd have enough thread to get me home. The guy who ran the shop was very friendly, as almost everyone was who I met in Argentina. While they worked on the bike, I nipped around to a bakery and bought the lads in the shop a big box of cakes.

Buenos Aires

The last days riding had come. I looked in the mirror before I got on the bike and I don't remember ever looking so tired. The road for three days had been flat, straight and boring with incessant gales, I was worn out. The last leg was over four hundred miles and part of what made the journey so tedious was the fact that every mile of the journey was counted down for me by marker poles. They counted down from 3200 in Ushuaia, it was like an extended version of ten green bottles hanging on the wall. My oil leak continued to spew oil out onto my left leg and boot and I was certain some of must have made it down into the clutch or at least was making its way to the back brakes, I really got the feeling I was limping across the finish line. It was only when I'd about a hundred miles to go that I finally started to relax and enjoy the ride. For the last two hours all I did was reflect on the entire journey trying to remember every town that I'd stayed in, the more I thought about it, the more I smiled. A friend of mine was meeting me in Buenos Aires and I'd arranged to stay in the Wilton Hotel. I pulled up to the hotel and parked the bike and checked in. I must have looked a state. Gone was the pristine blue enduro suit and brand spanking new boots, the freshly shaven corporate goon. He was replaced by a completely filthy bearded tinker who had just completed a trip of a life time.

Epilogue
Going home

I thought my adventures were over as I took a taxi to the airport in Buenos Aires. I checked onto the flight and flew out for Miami on the 19th of December 2008 exactly one hundred and sixty two days after I left Ireland.

I had a four-hour layover in Miami so treated myself to a western breakfast in the Airport hotel, my first since leaving Tucson over a hundred days earlier. After picking up some duty free, it was time to board for Chicago. In December flying in or out of Chicago is a lottery at the best of times due to the severe weather, and while we were landing the plane was getting blown side to side so much that the pilot got a round of applause from the passengers when we touched down. I'd only one more flight, Chicago to Dublin, it wouldn't be long now till I was tucking into a pint with the lads in the Laurels in Clondalkin.

The snow was falling very heavily as I waited to get on an American Airlines flight, and it finally taxied down the runway eight hours late. As it went into takeoff mode the right engine failed and we had to taxi back to the terminal. After another three hour delay with babies roaring crying and stranded passengers roaring and shouting we were all sent to a hotel for the night. We all had to book onto an Aer Lingus flight scheduled for the same time the following evening.

The passengers were all chucked out of the hotel for about twelve and headed to the airport to wait for the flight which was supposed to leave at 5pm. At 10pm we were once again taxiing for the runway to take off when the most unusual thing happened; the wing of our plane hit the tail of another plane which had unexpectedly reversed or been pushed out. This flight was made up mainly of the people who had been stranded the previous night and another bunch that were scheduled to fly out on this night anyway. The dynamic on the plane was crazy, the folks who were already stranded 24hrs were all saying, "I hope he chances it and takes off" The folks for whom this was their first flight were saying. "No way I'm staying in this plane!" Once more, it was off to a hotel to return the following evening to get an alternate flight.

It was getting on for sixty five hours since I'd left Buenos Aires but as people were getting stressed out all around me I didn't even feel remotely pissed off. It all felt in control, I knew I'd get home eventually, when you've gone through Central American Borders where so little is in control and you are at the mercy of bandits, getting delayed in a US City is a piece of cake. I ended up making some great friends at the airport and myself and four of five folks who'd been stuck for the same length of time as me ended up having a great time. We headed out for a walk in the Chicago weather, it was the first time in my life I felt my nostril hair freezing in my nose, it was as if someone just stuck a whole pile of newspaper up it.

With eighty hours on the clock and at the third attempt the plane finally left for Dublin, I wondered if there would be anyone other than my Dad to meet me at the airport, I wondered if my friends would have a surprise party for me, the returning hero!

As the plane approached Ireland I looked below the plane to see a layer of grey black clouds as far as the eye could see in all directions, it contrasted drastically with the blue sky above and the dawn sun beaming on the horizon. We descended through the clouds and landed in Dublin on a miserable wet and windy Irish December day. While we were waiting for the bags to arrive, a pink bag kept on going round and round the baggage track, I made a joke to Joel, one of my comrades from the three day stay in Chicago, "Do you think the owner is waiting till everyone leaves before he picks it up?"

My Dad collected me and drove me home to Portarlington. I dropped my bags at the door and went up to bed to catch some Z's. I lay on the bed on the verge of sleep, my eyes held open by the realization that it was all over.

About two weeks later, Sam Gamgee arrived at the airport, I unpacked him and drove home and put him in my conservatory never to be ridden again. Sitting on top of the motorbike as he was the whole way with me through the trip is my pet rabbit cuddly toy named Mr Fluffykins, a gentleman rabbit if ever there was one.

Adjusting to life back in Ireland was hellish, the economy was in turmoil and it seemed like the whole world was imploding. I was back in my original job and it was like I'd never left, I finally understood why people were telling me to enjoy every last second of the trip. People's moods in Ireland seemed to be very low and lots of my friends had lost their job, in fact there were few if any whose jobs seemed to be safe. It all seemed a million miles away from the splendid isolation of the Ruta 40.

All in all, was it worth doing? Absolutely, I rate it as the best thing that's ever happened to me. As to whether I'd do it again, well, as it happens I did, but that story is for another time. A glimpse of that story is in the opening pages of the book, the page about the bridge at the Honduras border.

My strong advice to you If you are considering doing something like this, just do it, don't live your life saying, "If Only."

I'm often asked whether the trip changed me, and the answer is definitely, although not in the way I was expecting.

I have always been a very social animal, very outgoing and happier with groups of people rather than being on my own. After the amount of time I spent by myself on the trip often going weeks without having a conversation with anyone, I'm now completely comfortable with my own company, happier in my own skin I guess. I look back now and realize that I was on that road searching for what we are all searching for, happiness. I didn't find it, but I know now, you have to bring it with you.

I often wonder how I survived so many near death experiences on the trip; I can only guess that someone was looking after me and that friends and family were praying for me. A final thought. Were you ever driving down the road and saw a guy riding an overloaded bike and thought to yourself, "Where's he off to I wonder?" Well, maybe it was me, and now you know!

The End.

How much does it cost to do the Pan American Highway?

I don't think its possible to do it well for less than $30,000.

Before I start, let me say that the internet abounds with stories of people who travelled the world on a shoestring, its possible but I don't advise it. The chief costs come from shipping the bike. If you have to go across the Atlantic twice for example, that will run you $4000. Shipping the bike from Panama to South America will run you $1,000. Allowing for inflation and unforeseen import taxes, budget $6,000. As your prepping you'll hear stories from guys who have friends working down the docks who can get a bike into a container for nothing and then you can just pick it up when you get to wherever your going, its all horse shit.

You will likely need 3 sets of tires and 3 bike services with oil changes and maybe two break pad changes. If your riding a BMW, you'll need to budget $4,000, this will give you some headroom for any unforeseen repairs and cost of parts that you may bring with you up front. Do research to find out the most common parts which fail and if you have the room, bring them with you. Again, if your riding a BMW - the labour alone on the bike is $100 an hour. They are a good bike, but they ain't cheap to maintain!

Gasoline is relatively easy to calculate, just work out your total miles and take an average cost of $5 per gallon. Budget: $4200. 30,000 miles / 30mpg = 1000 gallons * 5 dollars.

If your doing the Pan American you'll end up doing about 25,000 miles - anyway you get the gist - its pretty easy to work out.

Bike insurance (Third party), Travel Health insurance and border insurance for the bike: Budget: $800

Flights: This really depends on where you are shipping your bike, working from Ireland or the UK: Budget $2500 to cover 2 transatlantic and the Darien gap hop.
Already, were up to $17,500.

Now, Calculate the excursions you want to take while traveling. Whale watching, Machu Picchu, National parks, theme parks, boat rides, museums, attractions. In 6 months your going to do plenty - Budget a minimum of $2500, if it sounds a lot, its less than a $100 a week on activities and day trips, its not that much. There is no point riding all the way to Cuzco and then skimping with your coppers and not going to see Machu Picchu.

Now the variable component of the trip starts.
Traveling in Canada and the USA if you want to stay in hotels and motels I think you need to budget $80 a day. In Mexico about $50 a day, In Central America, $40 a day and in South America about $50 a day. If you go to hostels its a lot less and if you plan to camp (not advisable in Central America), its even cheaper.

Similarly when it comes to grub, most folks touring in the USA would do $10 for breakfast, $12 for lunch and $20 for dinner to include some beer, make sure the budget includes beer! The same would go for Canada. It's a lot cheaper in Mexico, Central and South America so you need to work out your durations. How long will you stay in each country.

I've met some folks who ate out of tins the whole time they traveled, it really depends on if you want to travel with a bit of comfort or not.
Maybe your thinking of couch surfing, think wisely. If you get a name as someone who is bumming his way round the world looking for free food and accommodation, you'll be found out, people don't like freeloaders.

Maybe your thinking of using charity to pay for the trip. I've heard of people raising $20,000 for traveling and only donating $5000 to charity, using the rest to pay for the trip - Karma will catch up!

Realistically the only way you'll pay for the trip is to work very hard for a long time and save up the money to go. Along the way as your saving pick up all the stuff you'll need and research your route properly. Most people will take up to 10 years to save up for something like this, its worth it! The best commitment I can give you is that you'll do your trip 3 times. Once while your planning it, once while your doing it and again when you come home. So take the time to plan it well. You may meat some loonies who'll tell you "oh no just go with the flow, let the road take you where it will" - but every trip has a start, middle and end. If you don't at least have a route with some rough durations you'll miss out on seeing some of the worlds great destinations and you'll make a complete balls of your budget.

How long did it take to prepare for the trip?

If its your first ever trip and your doing a Pan American, at least 6 months, thats assuming you have a day job. You could do it in less than 2 months if your at it full time.

Which country did you like the best and why?

For the ease of it, its hard to beat the USA. You could spend your life touring around it and never run out of things to see. Valdez in Alaska, and the Bonneville salt flats are two of my favorite places on earth. Mexico would be the cultural highlight with so many ruin sites. For being utterly different, Peru, Bolivia and Northern Chile stand out because at times it was like I was on Mars, and the friendliest people by far were in Colombia.

Do I need Visas?

For your country you'll need to check it out for specifics. The countries along the Pan-American highway require no visas other than the normal tourist visas that you would have to get if you were traveling there (assuming you are staying less than 90 days in any one country). That's the same for anyone in North America or Europe. Do the research, use websites like Horizons Unlimited, UKGSER's and ADVRIDER. They have forums which are very helpful but only take advice from people who've done it.

Should I learn Spanish before I go?

Yes, it will help enormously. Just being able to order food or get directions will make your travels much easier.

What is the best bike to take on the trip?

Any of these will do the job: BMW 1150 / 1100 BMW 1200 (Don't recommend the 2005/6 Models) BMW 650 Paris Dakar KTM 990 Adventurer Kawasaki KLR 650 Suzuki Vstrom That being said - You can do it on any bike. Remember - a lot of people cycle on push bikes around the world including up and down the Pan-American highway - if they can do it on a bicycle - you can do it on any motorbike.

Can you recommend shipping companies?

I've used three companies on multiple occasions and always found them very good. For Outward bound from the USA - Shipmybike.com For Outward bound from the UK, Ireland or mainland Europe - James Cargo, London. For Panama to Colombia, or Panama to Quite - Girag. Note they fly out of Tocumen airport and its much cheaper to get to Bogota than Quito.

How much did it cost to ship the bike?

Budget $2200 for transatlantic, and $1000 for Central America to Colombia, $1900 for Panama to Quito.

What Medical provisions did you have?

I had multi-trip travel insurance - it covers for 180 days of travel. I also had a first aid kit and 2 doses of general purpose antibiotics. Loads of companies offer this type of cover to capitalize on the world wide backpacker market. (Try www.vhi.ie)

What about insurance for the bike?

I used motorcycle express. Note - you won't get anyone to cover theft or fully comprehensive. This is just third party liability so you can drive in the countries legally that you want to pass through. In some of the South American countries you also will have to buy third party insurance at the border, but don't worry its quite cheap. Its critical to understand, if your bike gets robbed or your in an accident, there is no insurance in the world that will cover the replacement of you bike, especially in south America. I've had people pester me for months on travel advice and then not go because they were afraid of their bike getting robbed. This is the primary reason I seldom stayed in big cities, there is far less chance of hassle in the countryside.

What type of Panniers did you use?
Touratech Zega Panniers- in general they have very good gear, its expensive but its well made.

Where did you get your maps of Russia and Mongolia? Stanfords - UK - Do not go to Russia without a good map! Beware with Stanfords, they cost a fortune to ship maps outside the UK - so start with Amazon.com

What sort of Rider gear would you recommend? I would whole heartedly recommend BMW rider gear (Rall-eye 2 or 3 suit) While its very expensive - it will save your life and last you a very long time - that isn't true of other gear I've tried - e.g. I went through 3 different pairs of pants which ripped at the crotch. My friend Tom Victory put it best when he said that they are a ten year suit. Another point to think about is that if you look at a lot of the folks riding the Dakar, even though they aren't riding BMW's, they are wearing this rider gear.

If I was to do a trip and write a book and make a documentary would I make any money?
No! The genre is way too small, but don't let that deter you.

Can you recommend a good camera?
If your going on the trip of a lifetime I highly recommend buying a camera that will take high quality pictures - you are going to need to spend a few quid. For best results / price ratio, I recommend the Nikon D5000 - excellent pic-

tures - and you can pick it up for under 500 quid.

How did you backup your images while you were traveling?
I brought a 1TB WD Portable drive and copied the images onto it. These days you can also buy space on Google Drive and upload your pictures and videos to the web as you travel if you can get an internet signal. This is obviously way better than people have had to deal with in the past. They key thing to keep in mind with your pictures is that you need a physical backup and a geographical backup - for example so that all the photos aren't just stored on the hard drive of you PC - Use Google Drive or Picassa and make sure you upload them full size.

For the videos you posted online, what camera did you use and what editing s/w did you use to cut the movies together?
The videos were shot with a Canon HFS100 and Canon HFS200. I used Final Cut Pro X to put the movies together. The action shots were filmed with a FLIP ULTRA HD.

Can you recommend any websites for people who are thinking of doing more research and planning?
These are the ones I continually use. http://www.advrider.com http://www.ukgser.com http://www.horizonsunlimited.com

Would you do it again?
In a heartbeat!

Is there anything you should have taken but didn't?

I'd recommend bringing a kindle. You can load hundreds of books onto it and they don't need much power, they stay on for days. You'll end up in a lot of places where there is little to do and a kindle would be a great way to spend the time. Second, I'd bring some tubes for the tires.

Do you recommend camping?
In Canada and North America you can camp as much as you like - there are facilities near all the big parks so if you have the room to bring the gear, go for it. In Mexico and Central America I don't recommend it. In Central America it's not safe but the other point is that accommodation is very inexpensive so why would you bother? It's better to get up and have a shower than trying to find a river to hang your balls in. In South America, there are no facilities but there are such huge empty spaces it shouldn't be a problem, except for Colombia and Bolivia.

Do you have any tips for prospective motorcycle travelers?
Always have $1000 dollars somewhere for emergencies. Pack it in a place where no one can find it. If the shit hits the fan, it can save your life.

Scan all your important paperwork and have a copy of it online for example on gmail or google drive. If you lose your documents these will be a life saver. This includes copies of all your credits cards front and back. If you lose them and you need to book a flight this will help a lot.

Never ride a motorcycle at night in remote areas. There is too much wildlife, if you hit it while on a bike its all over. Also in poorer countries the road conditions can deteriorate very quickly, if you cant see the road your in for a world of hurt.

If you do get caught out at night pull over and wait for a truck to pass you. Then follow the truck, you can use it to clear your path of animals and people or any other hazards which may be on the road.

Spend a little time to learn the key phrases you'll need in the country your visiting. Being able to order food and place to stay will be invaluable.

Spread positive Karma. Do everything you can to be nice to the people you meet, it'll all come back.

Get a good rain jacket and pants, these are brilliant not just for the rain but keeping off the cold, you wont wear the pants much but the jacket will be seldom off.

Always take a crap before you leave in the morning. Have a couple of cups of coffee, normally a great way of getting things moving. There is nothing worse than being two hours from anywhere bursting to use the loo.

Always use ear plugs, riding a bike is very loud on your ears, and the effects are cumulative. Get in the habit of doing putting them in.

If you wear glasses, get prescription sun glasses that wrap around and fit comfortably in your helmet. You can protect your eyes not only from UV by doing this but every insect imaginable.

Bring a good moisturizer. It's not gay. The wind will play havoc with your face and most of the time you'll be walking around with a face redder than a baboons arse otherwise.

Upload your friends contact information online, if you need them for anything it can save time. Similarly if you want to burn an afternoon writing postcards its great to have the addresses handy.

Keep people at home apprised of where you are by using a blog or Facebook. If worst comes to worst, at least they'll know where to start searching.

Bring something that cures itch, you'll be eaten alive by mosquitos at various points, its inevitable.

Bring a Kindle and load it up before you leave. Great way to pass the time when you passing through the worlds crappy towns.

Bring a decent multivitamin. Your diet won't be great so its easy to get run down.

Make sure your set up with online banking so you can keep an eye on your credit cards and bank balance. This is especially important if you cards get stolen. Also make sure you tell your credit card company that your going traveling and to what countries and when so they don't put a stop on your card when they see a transaction coming in from Colombia.

Use your credit card to get money at ATM's, obviously this is only if you load up your card to a positive balance, this is the cheapest form of foreign exchange you can get. Key point to remember, don't put too much onto it because the banks only insure you stolen card for buys that put it in the red, so if you have money on the card and it gets used up fraudulently, they don't cover that.

Bring a light durable laptop. Lenovo are doing some very durable laptops which can withstand all manner of vibration. Its a great way to keep in touch with family and friends and plan your days ahead.

Bring a portable hard drive and back up your pictures and videos regularly.

Bring a spare key for the motorcycle.

Get all your teeth in great shape before you leave, you don't want to have to deal with that crap when your away. Bring an electronic toothbrush, they do a far better job of cleaning them

Never drink the water from a tap, only a bottle. Your arse is precious. Always order hot food in second and third world countries, absolutely no salads. What they are serving might not make the locals sick, but it will create a tornado in a lily livered westerner's colon.

Test yourself every day. Do the things you wouldn't normally do, this is your chance to be the person you always wanted to be. Don't let fear stop you.

ROUTE

DATE	DAY	COUNTRY	TOWN/CITY/ STATE	MILEAGE	CUM MILEAGE	COMMENTS
12-JUL-08	1	IRELAND	DUBLIN / TO-RONTO	0	0	FLEW DUBLIN TO TORONTO
13-JUL-08	2	CANADA	TORONTO	0	0	CN TOWER YONGE STREET - LONGEST STREET IN THE WORLD
14-JUL-08	3	CANADA	CORNWALL / ONTARIO	309	309	FIRST DAY ON THE ROAD
15-JUL-08	4	CANADA	RIVIERE DU LOUP - QBC	430	739	FOLLOWING THE ST LAW-ERENCE RIVER
16-JUL-08	5	CANADA	MONCTON / N. BRUNSWICK	409	1148	BAY OF FUNDY WORLDS LARGEST TIDES
17-JUL-08	6	CANADA	SYDNEY / N. SCOTIA	311	1459	
18-JUL-08	7	CANADA	BADDECK /N. SCOTIA	42	1501	
19-JUL-08	8	CANADA	NEW GLASGOW / N. SCOTIA	350	1851	COMPLETED THE CABOT TRAIL IN CAPE BRETON
20-JUL-08	9	CANADA	RIVIERE DU LOUP - QBC	525	2376	DAY MYSELF AND GEOFF SPLIT UP
21-JUL-08	10	CANADA	ARNPROIR / ONTARIO	485	2861	
22-JUL-08	11	CANADA	SAULT STE MA-RIE / ONTARIO	501	3362	HOME OF WORLD FAMOUS LOCKS - BUSIER THAN SUEZ AND PANAMA CANAL COM-BINED
23-JUL-08	12	CANADA	THUNDER BAY / ONTARIO	476	3838	ON THE BANKS OF LAKE SUPERIOR
24-JUL-08	13	CANADA	DRYDEN / ON-TARIO	237	4075	TOWN BASED ON PAPER INDUSTRY
25-JUL-08	14	CANADA	BRANDON / MANITOBA	399	4474	
26-JUL-08	15	CANADA	MOOSE JAW / SASKATCHE-WAN	296	4770	CANADIAN PRAIRIES
27-JUL-08	16	CANADA	CANMORE / ALBERTA	534	5304	ROCKIES
28-JUL-08	17	CANADA	HINTON / AL-BERTA	269	5573	THE ICEFIELDS PARKWAY, BANNF TO JASPER LAKE LOUISE
29-JUL-08	18	CANADA	GRANDE PRAI-RIE / ALBERTA	233	5806	MILE 0 OF ALASKA-CANA-DA HIGHWAY AT DAWSON CREEK
30-JUL-08	19	CANADA	FORT ST. JOHN / BC	161	5967	
31-JUL-08	20	CANADA	FORT NELSON / BC	266	6233	
1-AUG-08	21	CANADA	WHITEHORSE / YUKON	656	6889	TRAVEL THROUGH SIGN CITY AT WATSON LAKE

DATE	DAY	COUNTRY	TOWN/CITY/ STATE	MILEAGE	CUM MILEAGE	COMMENTS
2-AUG-08	22	USA	TOK / ALASKA	430	7319	GOOD TOWN TO SLEEP IN - EVERYONE GOING TO ALASKA COMES THROUGH HERE
3-AUG-08	23	USA	ANCHORAGE / ALASKA	359	7678	SEE ANCHORAGE.NET FOR INFORMATION - MOST THINGS TO DO CENTRE AROUND ECO TOURISM
4-AUG-08	24	USA	ANCHORAGE / ALASKA	0	7678	BIKE SERVICED
5-AUG-08	25	USA	ANCHORAGE / ALASKA	0	7678	BIKE SERVICED
6-AUG-08	26	USA	FAIRBANKS / ALASKA	445	8123	DENALI NATIONAL PARK
7-AUG-08	27	USA	DEADHORSE / ALASKA	543	8666	START / FINISH DALTON HIGHWAY ATIGUN PASS / BROOKES RANGE GET INTO THE ARCTIC OCEAN
8-AUG-08	28	USA	FAIRBANKS / ALASKA	541	9207	
9-AUG-08	29	USA	VALDEZ / ALAS-KA	406	9613	COLOMBIA GLACIER THOMPSON PASS
10-AUG-08	30	USA	VALDEZ / ALAS-KA	120	9733	WHALE WATCHING BOAT TRIPS WHERE YOU ALWAYS SEE WHALES
11-AUG-08	31	USA	VALDEZ / ALAS-KA	104	9837	TURNING SOUTH FOR USHUAIA
12-AUG-08	32	USA	TOK / ALASKA	311	10148	
13-AUG-08	33	CANADA	DAWSON CITY / YUKON	212	10360	RIDE THE TOP OF THE WORLD HIGHWAY VISIT TOWN OF CHICKEN OLD FRONTIER TOWN, HOME OF KLONDIKE GOLD RUSH
14-AUG-08	34	CANADA	WHITEHORSE / YUKON	306	10666	KAYAK ON THE YUKON RIVER
15-AUG-08	35	CANADA	COAL RIVER / B. COLOMBIA	411	11077	
16-AUG-08	36	CANADA	FORT ST. JOHN / B. COLOMBIA	526	11603	
17-AUG-08	37	CANADA	HINTON / AL-BERTA	376	11979	BACK INTO THE ROCKIES
18-AUG-08	38	CANADA	CANMORE / ALBERTA	269	12248	RIDE ICEFIELDS PARKWAY
19-AUG-08	39	CANADA	BLACK DIA-MOND / ALBER-TA	106	12248	ALBERTA PRAIRIES
20-AUG-08	40	USA	HUNGRY HORSE / MONTANA	263	12617	GLACIER NATIONAL PARK ROAD TO THE SUN HIGH-WAY

DATE	DAY	COUNTRY	TOWN/CITY/ STATE	MILEAGE	CUM MILEAGE	COMMENTS
21-AUG-08	41	USA	HELENA / MON-TANA	287	12904	PRAIRIE LANDS
22-AUG-08	42	USA	ENNIS / MON-TANA	129	13033	
23-AUG-08	43	USA	RED LODGE / MONTANA	226	13259	BEARTOOTH HIGHWAY (RED LODGE TO COOKE CITY) BIKERVILLE USA
24-AUG-08	44	USA	TREMONTON / UTAH	525	13784	
25-AUG-08	45	USA	WENDOVER / UTAH	214	13998	BONNEVILLE SPEEDWAY CON AIR PLANE PROP CASINOS WITH CHEAP RATES CLIMB THE HILL TO SEE THE ARC OF THE EARTH AT DUSK
26-AUG-08	46	USA	WENDOVER / UTAH	0	13998	BONNEVILLE SPEEDWAY
27-AUG-08	47	USA	PANGUITCH / UTAH	375	14373	BRYCE CANYON CAPITOL REEF NAT PARK
28-AUG-08	48	USA	PANGUITCH / UTAH	239	14612	CORAL PINK SAND DUNES NAT PARK /
29-AUG-08	49	USA	KANAB / UTAH	215	14827	ZION CANYON NAT PARK
30-AUG-08	50	USA	FLAGSTAFF / ARIZONA	216	15043	GRAND CANYON
31-AUG-08	51	USA	WILLIAMS / ARI-ZONA	323	15366	ROUTE 66
1-SEP-08	52	USA	PHOENIX / ARI-ZONA	453	15819	BIKE SERVICE / GET READY FOR MEXICO / CENTRAL AMERICA
2-SEP-08	53	USA	PHOENIX / ARI-ZONA	21	15840	
3-SEP-08	54	USA	PHOENIX / ARI-ZONA	0	15840	
4-SEP-08	55	USA	TUSCON / ARI-ZONA	166	16006	PIMA AIR AND SPACE MU-SEUM
5-SEP-08	56	MEXICO	HERMOSILLO / SONORA	376	16382	CROSSED BORDER AT DOUGLAS, SOUTH EAST OF TUSCON
6-SEP-08	57	MEXICO	GUAYMAS / SONORA	126	16508	SAN CARLOS BEACH AREA
7-SEP-08	58	MEXICO	NAVOJOA / SO-NORA	201	16709	
8-SEP-08	59	MEXICO	MAZATLAN / SINALOA	354	17063	BEACH / RESORT CITY
9-SEP-08	60	MEXICO	MANZANILLO / COLIMA	421	17484	FAMOUS FISHING CITY
10-SEP-08	61	MEXICO	GUADALAJARA / JALISCO	232	17716	BIG MODERN MEXICAN CITY
11-SEP-08	62	MEXICO	MORELIA / MICHOACÁN	217	17933	MORELIA CATHEDRAL

DATE	DAY	COUNTRY	TOWN/CITY/ STATE	MILEAGE	CUM MILEAGE	COMMENTS
12-SEP-08	63	MEXICO	TAXCO / GUER-RERO	224	18157	FAMOUS FOR SILVER MINES
13-SEP-08	64	MEXICO	TAXCO / GUER-RERO	21	18178	
14-SEP-08	65	MEXICO	TAXCO / GUER-RERO	30	18208	
15-SEP-08	66	MEXICO	TAXCO / GUER-RERO	11	18219	
16-SEP-08	67	MEXICO	TAXCO / GUER-RERO	99	18318	
17-SEP-08	68	MEXICO	OAXACA / OAX-ACA	250	18568	COLONIAL GEM
18-SEP-08	69	MEXICO	SAN CRISTOBAL DE LAS CASAS / CHAIPUS	290	18858	COLONIAL GEM
19-SEP-08	70	MEXICO	SAN CRISTOBAL DE LAS CASAS / CHAIPUS	16	18874	
20-SEP-08	71	GUATEMALA	QUET-ZALTENANGO	198	19072	SPANISH LESSONS DRAWS LOTS OF BACK PACKERS
21-SEP-08	72	GUATEMALA	QUET-ZALTENANGO	24	19096	
22-SEP-08	73	GUATEMALA	QUET-ZALTENANGO	28	19124	
23-SEP-08	74	GUATEMALA	QUET-ZALTENANGO	43	19167	
24-SEP-08	75	GUATEMALA	ANTIGUA GUA-TEMALA	139	19306	GORGEOUS COLONIAL TOWN WITH LOTS OF TOURISTS LAKE ATITLAN AND ITS VOLCANOS
25-SEP-08	76	EL SALVADOR	SANTA ANA	91	19397	SURFING IN LA LIBERTAD
26-SEP-08	77	HONDURAS	CHOLUTECA	216	19613	
27-SEP-08	78	NICARAGUA	GRANADA	190	19803	COLONIAL TOWN
28-SEP-08	79	NICARAGUA	GRANADA	0	19803	
29-SEP-08	80	COSTA RICA	LAKE ARENAL	311	20114	VOLCANO ARENAL AND LAKE ARENAL
30-SEP-08	81	COSTA RICA	SAN ISIDRO	159	20273	
1-OCT-08	82	PANAMA	PANAMA CITY	238	20511	PANAMA CANAL FLY BIKE TO COLOMBIA
2-OCT-08	83	PANAMA	PANAMA CITY	23	20534	
3-OCT-08	84	PANAMA	PANAMA CITY	23	20557	
4-OCT-08	85	PANAMA	PANAMA CITY	0	20557	

DATE	DAY	COUNTRY	TOWN/CITY/ STATE	MILEAGE	CUM MILEAGE	COMMENTS
12-SEP-08	63	MEXICO	TAXCO / GUER-RERO	224	18157	FAMOUS FOR SILVER MINES
13-SEP-08	64	MEXICO	TAXCO / GUER-RERO	21	18178	
14-SEP-08	65	MEXICO	TAXCO / GUER-RERO	30	18208	
15-SEP-08	66	MEXICO	TAXCO / GUER-RERO	11	18219	
16-SEP-08	67	MEXICO	TAXCO / GUER-RERO	99	18318	
17-SEP-08	68	MEXICO	OAXACA / OAX-ACA	250	18568	COLONIAL GEM
18-SEP-08	69	MEXICO	SAN CRISTOBAL DE LAS CASAS / CHAIPUS	290	18858	COLONIAL GEM
19-SEP-08	70	MEXICO	SAN CRISTOBAL DE LAS CASAS / CHAIPUS	16	18874	
20-SEP-08	71	GUATEMALA	QUET-ZALTENANGO	198	19072	SPANISH LESSONS DRAWS LOTS OF BACK PACKERS
21-SEP-08	72	GUATEMALA	QUET-ZALTENANGO	24	19096	
22-SEP-08	73	GUATEMALA	QUET-ZALTENANGO	28	19124	
23-SEP-08	74	GUATEMALA	QUET-ZALTENANGO	43	19167	
24-SEP-08	75	GUATEMALA	ANTIGUA GUA-TEMALA	139	19306	GORGEOUS COLONIAL TOWN WITH LOTS OF TOURISTS LAKE ATITLAN AND ITS VOLCANOS
25-SEP-08	76	EL SALVADOR	SANTA ANA	91	19397	SURFING IN LA LIBERTAD
26-SEP-08	77	HONDURAS	CHOLUTECA	216	19613	
27-SEP-08	78	NICARAGUA	GRANADA	190	19803	COLONIAL TOWN
28-SEP-08	79	NICARAGUA	GRANADA	0	19803	
29-SEP-08	80	COSTA RICA	LAKE ARENAL	311	20114	VOLCANO ARENAL AND LAKE ARENAL
30-SEP-08	81	COSTA RICA	SAN ISIDRO	159	20273	
1-OCT-08	82	PANAMA	PANAMA CITY	238	20511	PANAMA CANAL FLY BIKE TO COLOMBIA
2-OCT-08	83	PANAMA	PANAMA CITY	23	20534	
3-OCT-08	84	PANAMA	PANAMA CITY	23	20557	
4-OCT-08	85	PANAMA	PANAMA CITY	0	20557	

DATE	DAY	COUNTRY	TOWN/CITY/ STATE	MILEAGE	CUM MILEAGE	COMMENTS
5-OCT-08	86	COLOMBIA	BOGOTA	0	20557	GET BIKE BACK FROM CUS-TOMS
6-OCT-08	87	COLOMBIA	BOGOTA	21	20578	MONSERATTE - AMAZING VIEWS OF THE CITY
7-OCT-08	88	COLOMBIA	SAN GIL	231	20968	
8-OCT-08	89	COLOMBIA	AGUACHICA	159	20968	
9-OCT-08	90	COLOMBIA	CARTAGENA	270	21238	MASSIVE COLONIAL TOWN OLD CITY IS SURROUNDE WITH A FORT WHICH TOOK 200 YEARS TO BUILD
10-OCT-08	91	COLOMBIA	CARTAGENA	21	21259	EAT FOOD FROM THE STREET BAKERIES
11-OCT-08	92	COLOMBIA	CAUCASIA	279	21538	SIMON BOLIVAR STATUE
12-OCT-08	93	COLOMBIA	MANIZALES	379	21917	
13-OCT-08	94	COLOMBIA	POPAYAN	334	22251	AMAZING MOUNTAIN ROADS
14-OCT-08	95	COLOMBIA	PASTO	148	22399	MOUNTAINS
15-OCT-08	96	COLOMBIA	PASTO	30	22429	MOUNTAINS
16-OCT-08	97	ECUADOR	QUITO	208	22637	PASS THE EQUATOR BIKE SERVICED MASSIVE COLONIAL CITY
17-OCT-08	98	ECUADOR	QUITO	13	22650	
18-OCT-08	99	ECUADOR	BANOS	158	22808	COLONIAL TOWN SUR-ROUNDED BY MOUNTAINS WALL TO WALL TOURISTS
19-OCT-08	100	ECUADOR	BANOS	28	22836	CANYONING
20-OCT-08	101	ECUADOR	BANOS	26	22862	GET DRUNK!
21-OCT-08	102	ECUADOR	CUENCA	188	23050	COLONIAL CITY
22-OCT-08	103	PERU	MANCORA	276	23326	BEACH RESORT
23-OCT-08	104	PERU	PACASMAYO	343	23669	FISHING VILLAGE
24-OCT-08	105	PERU	PACASMAYO	18	23687	
25-OCT-08	106	PERU	HUANCHACO	111	23798	BEACH / SURFING RESORT FAMOUS FOR UNUSUAL FISHING CRAFTS
26-OCT-08	107	PERU	CHINCHA	506	24304	
27-OCT-08	108	PERU	NAZCA	187	24491	NAZCA LINES
28-OCT-08	109	PERU	CUZCO	444	24935	MACHU PICCHU
29-OCT-08	110	PERU	CUZCO	7	24942	
30-OCT-08	111	PERU	CUZCO	0	24942	
31-OCT-08	112	PERU	CUZCO	0	24942	
1-NOV-08	113	PERU	PUNO	243	25185	LAKE TITICACA
2-NOV-08	114	PERU	PUNO	4	25189	TAKE BOAT RIDE OUT TO SEE THE PEOPLE WHO LIVE ON THE LAKE

DATE	DAY	COUNTRY	TOWN/CITY/ STATE	MILEAGE	CUM MILEAGE	COMMENTS
5-OCT-08	86	COLOMBIA	BOGOTA	0	20557	GET BIKE BACK FROM CUS-TOMS
6-OCT-08	87	COLOMBIA	BOGOTA	21	20578	MONSERATTE - AMAZING VIEWS OF THE CITY
7-OCT-08	88	COLOMBIA	SAN GIL	231	20968	
8-OCT-08	89	COLOMBIA	AGUACHICA	159	20968	
9-OCT-08	90	COLOMBIA	CARTAGENA	270	21238	MASSIVE COLONIAL TOWN OLD CITY IS SURROUNDE-WITH A FORT WHICH TOOK 200 YEARS TO BUILD
10-OCT-08	91	COLOMBIA	CARTAGENA	21	21259	EAT FOOD FROM THE STREET BAKERIES
11-OCT-08	92	COLOMBIA	CAUCASIA	279	21538	SIMON BOLIVAR STATUE
12-OCT-08	93	COLOMBIA	MANIZALES	379	21917	
13-OCT-08	94	COLOMBIA	POPAYAN	334	22251	AMAZING MOUNTAIN ROADS
14-OCT-08	95	COLOMBIA	PASTO	148	22399	MOUNTAINS
15-OCT-08	96	COLOMBIA	PASTO	30	22429	MOUNTAINS
16-OCT-08	97	ECUADOR	QUITO	208	22637	PASS THE EQUATOR BIKE SERVICED MASSIVE COLONIAL CITY
17-OCT-08	98	ECUADOR	QUITO	13	22650	
18-OCT-08	99	ECUADOR	BANOS	158	22808	COLONIAL TOWN SUR-ROUNDED BY MOUNTAINS WALL TO WALL TOURISTS
19-OCT-08	100	ECUADOR	BANOS	28	22836	CANYONING
20-OCT-08	101	ECUADOR	BANOS	26	22862	GET DRUNK!
21-OCT-08	102	ECUADOR	CUENCA	188	23050	COLONIAL CITY
22-OCT-08	103	PERU	MANCORA	276	23326	BEACH RESORT
23-OCT-08	104	PERU	PACASMAYO	343	23669	FISHING VILLAGE
24-OCT-08	105	PERU	PACASMAYO	18	23687	
25-OCT-08	106	PERU	HUANCHACO	111	23798	BEACH / SURFING RESORT FAMOUS FOR UNUSUAL FISHING CRAFTS
26-OCT-08	107	PERU	CHINCHA	506	24304	
27-OCT-08	108	PERU	NAZCA	187	24491	NAZCA LINES
28-OCT-08	109	PERU	CUZCO	444	24935	MACHU PICCHU
29-OCT-08	110	PERU	CUZCO	7	24942	
30-OCT-08	111	PERU	CUZCO	0	24942	
31-OCT-08	112	PERU	CUZCO	0	24942	
1-NOV-08	113	PERU	PUNO	243	25185	LAKE TITICACA
2-NOV-08	114	PERU	PUNO	4	25189	TAKE BOAT RIDE OUT TO SEE THE PEOPLE WHO LIVE ON THE LAKE

DATE	DAY	COUNTRY	TOWN/CITY/ STATE	MILEAGE	CUM MILEAGE	COMMENTS
3-NOV-08	115	BOLIVIA	COPACABANA	91	25280	TOURISTY STOP OFF
4-NOV-08	116	BOLIVIA	ORURO	256	25536	
5-NOV-08	117	BOLIVIA	POTOSI	456	25992	HIGHEST CITY IN THE WORLD (4090M)
6-NOV-08	118	BOLIVIA	UYUNI	210	26202	SALAR DE UYUNI - INCRED-IBLE LOCATION IN THE MIDDLE OF THE DESERT
7-NOV-08	119	BOLIVIA	UYUNI	76	26278	TERRIBLE ROADS IN AND OUT OF THIS PLACE
8-NOV-08	120	CHILE	OLLAGÜE	179	26457	BORDER TOWN WITH CHILE - INCREDIBLE ROUTE THROUGH VOLCANOS AND SALT LAKES
9-NOV-08	121	CHILE	SAN PEDRO DE ATACAMA	368	26825	COLONIAL VILLAGE IN THE MIDDLE OF THE ATACAMA DESERT
10-NOV-08	122	CHILE	SAN PEDRO DE ATACAMA	149	26974	
11-NOV-08	123	CHILE	TAL TAL	467	27441	FISHING VILLAGE
12-NOV-08	124	CHILE	TAL TAL	15	27456	
13-NOV-08	125	CHILE	LA SERENA	422	27878	
14-NOV-08	126	CHILE	SANTIAGO	311	28189	SAN CRISTÓBAL HILL
15-NOV-08	127	CHILE	SANTIAGO	18	28207	MUSEUM OF MEMORY AND HUMAN RIGHTS
16-NOV-08	128	CHILE	SANTIAGO	0	28207	PLAZA DE ARMAS
17-NOV-08	129	CHILE	SANTIAGO	0	28207	
18-NOV-08	130	CHILE	SANTIAGO	0	28207	
19-NOV-08	131	CHILE	SANTIAGO	0	28207	
20-NOV-08	132	CHILE	SANTIAGO	0	28207	
21-NOV-08	133	CHILE	SANTIAGO	16	28223	BIKE SERVICED AND GET TIRES FOR THE RUTA 40
22-NOV-08	134	CHILE	VALPARAISO	41	28264	PASEO GERVASONI LUNCH AT THE FISH MAR-KET
23-NOV-08	135	CHILE	VALPARAISO	0	28264	
24-NOV-08	136	CHILE	CHILLÁN	339	28603	
25-NOV-08	137	CHILE	CASTRO / CHI-LOE	533	29136	UNIQUE FISHING VILLAGES
26-NOV-08	138	CHILE	CASTRO / CHI-LOE	0	29136	PENGUIN WATCHING
27-NOV-08	139	CHILE	PUERTO VARAS	221	29357	LOTS OF HILLS, LAKES, VOL-CANOS AND BEAUTIFUL LAKES
28-NOV-08	140	CHILE	PUERTO VARAS	0	29357	
29-NOV-08	141	CHILE	PUERTO VARAS	0	29357	

DATE	DAY	COUNTRY	TOWN/CITY/ STATE	MILEAGE	CUM MILEAGE	COMMENTS
30-NOV-08	142	ARGENTINA	BARILOCHE	320	29677	
1-DEC-08	143	ARGENTINA	SAN JOSE DE SAN MARTIN	326	30003	
2-DEC-08	144	ARGENTINA	PERITO MORE-NO	332	30335	
3-DEC-08	145	ARGENTINA	RIO GALLEGOS	652	30987	END/START OF THE RUTA 40
4-DEC-08	146	ARGENTINA	RIO GRANDE	256	31243	
5-DEC-08	147	ARGENTINA	USHUAIA	149	31392	FIN DEL MUNDO END OF THE WORLD
6-DEC-08	148	ARGENTINA	USHUAIA	0	31392	
7-DEC-08	149	ARGENTINA	USHUAIA	0	31392	
8-DEC-08	150	ARGENTINA	USHUAIA	0	31392	
9-DEC-08	151	ARGENTINA	PUERTO SAN JULIAN	617	32009	RUTA 3
10-DEC-08	152	ARGENTINA	PUERTO MADRYN	581	32590	RUTA 3
11-DEC-08	153	ARGENTINA	BAHIA BLANCA	481	33071	RUTA 3
12-DEC-08	154	ARGENTINA	BUENOS AIRES	434	33505	RUTA 3
13-DEC-08	155	ARGENTINA	BUENOS AIRES	0	33505	
14-DEC-08	156	ARGENTINA	BUENOS AIRES	0	33505	
15-DEC-08	157	ARGENTINA	BUENOS AIRES	0	33505	
16-DEC-08	159	ARGENTINA	BUENOS AIRES	0	33505	
17-DEC-08	160	ARGENTINA	BUENOS AIRES	0	33505	
18-DEC-08	162	ARGENTINA	BUENOS AIRES	29	33534	BRING BIKE TO AIRPORT FOR SHIPPING
19-DEC-08	162	ARGENTINA	BUENOS AIRES	0	33534	
20-DEC-08	163	USA	CHICAGO	0	33534	ENGINE FAILURE ON PLANE
21-DEC-08	164	USA	CHICAGO	0	33534	PLANE HIT ANOTHER PLANE DURING TAXI ON RUNWAY
22-DEC-08	165	USA	CHICAGO	0	33534	
23-DEC-08	166	IRELAND	DUBLIN / POR-TARLINGTON	0	33534	ARRIVE NEXT DAY IN IRE-LAND
28-DEC-08	167	IRELAND	PORTARLING-TON	48	33582	COLLECT BIKE FROM CUS-TOMS

20937120R00194

Printed in Great Britain
by Amazon